THE
ULTIMATE
HORSE
BOOK

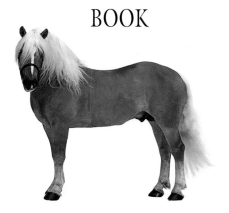

THE
ULTIMATE
HORSE
BOOK

ELWYN HARTLEY EDWARDS

INTRODUCED BY
• SHARON RALLS LEMON •

PHOTOGRAPHY BY
• BOB LANGRISH •

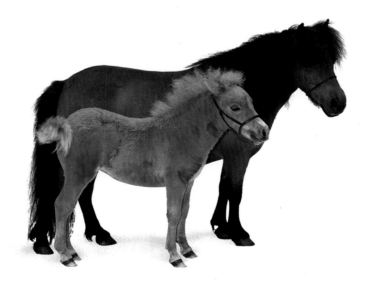

A DK PUBLISHING BOOK

Project Editor
Jo Weeks

Art Editor
Amanda Lunn

Editor
Susan Thompson

Editorial Assistant
Helen Townsend

Managing Editor
Jane Laing

Production Manager
Maryann Rogers

First American Edition, 1991
Published in the United States by DK Publishing, Inc.
95 Madison Avenue, New York, NY 10016

ISBN 1–879431–03–3

Library of Congress Catalog Card Number

91-060138

Typeset by The Cooling Brown Partnership in Great Britain
Reproduced by Colourscan in Singapore
Printed and bound by C&C Offset Printing Co., Ltd, Hong Kong

Contents

Introduction

*An addictive interest in the equine species compels us
to learn about breeds and styles.*

The hallmark of a true equestrian is a passionate interest in all things pertaining to horses. Perhaps this can be said of all enthusiasts regarding the focal point of their fancy, but there is a spark in the hearts of horse lovers that distinguishes us from mere hobbyists or sporting individuals. Those of us who make horses a part of our lives know from an early age that we are different. The thrill of being close to a member of the equine species is inherent to our nature. The enjoyment we feel in the presence of horses extends to stables, tack and, most of all, an in-depth knowledge of the subject.

Chasseurs à pied
The horse allowed man to wage war and win territories.

~ A COMMON HISTORY ~

I suspect that part of our fascination with horses is their tie with us throughout the ages. In truth, what civilization that has emerged in the past 20,000 years could have been built without the might of the horse? In so many ways, the story of the horse, both wild and domestic, parallels our own. This is the common bond that ties all equestrians. Possessing a true interest in horses does not mean enjoying only the breed of horse you own, or the riding style you prefer. For most of us, an addictive interest in the equine species compels us to learn about breeds and styles that differ from those that we come into contact with every day.

~ IN-DEPTH BREED GUIDE ~

The role that horses have played throughout history is one of my particular interests, especially as this history pertains to the variety of breeds that have developed. I am fascinated by the manner in which breeds have formed. Whether a breed is the result of a carefully guided, man-made breeding program with specific goals, or whether the breed has been forged by native conditions, and the laws of natural selection and survival of the fittest, it is enthralling to learn what factors played a role in modern horses' development. I know that I am not alone in my thirst for knowledge about horse breeds, as I am often asked for extensive information regarding the history and use of many breeds. Nowhere, however, could I find a book that held an adequate amount of information on the subject of horse breeds – until I was asked to look at

The mount of royalty
Frederick Wilhelm, the Great Elector of Brandenburg (1620–88).

Coal wagon
Horses were indispensable in transport.

The Ultimate Horse Book. In reading this remarkable work, my attention was held by its in-depth information. Horses, many that are largely unknown by Americans, and many that are old friends, are discussed at length, supported by details every horse person desires to know: history, physical statistics, temperament and the like. The superb photography and illustrations bring all the facts into sharp focus.

~ THE ULTIMATE REFERENCE ~

Modern British police mounts
Man still has need for the horse in many of his occupations.

A benchmark in the field of equestrian books, *The Ultimate Horse Book* goes beyond describing and explaining the breeds. It also contains excellent information on the development of the equine species, horse health and management, and the use and care of tack. It is, quite literally, an ultimate work on the subject of horses. A book for equestrians of all ages and interests, *The Ultimate Horse Book* should endure well, for it is not something that is read once and cast aside, but rather a book that should be savored and referred to frequently, even after a place of prominence has been found for it upon the shelf. Keep it within easy reach.

Sharon Ralls Lemon
1991

Devon pack horse
The horse has served man through the ages.

Horses running wild
Wild horses still roam free in the USA and Australia.

Fleeing from danger
Unusual objects that the horse sees as potential dangers, such as the windmill in this drawing, activate the finely tuned defense mechanism of this naturally highly strung animal whose instinctive reaction to danger is flight.

Equine extremes (below)
These two horses are at the opposite ends of the equine spectrum. The Avelignese on the left descends from heavy, cold-blooded ancestors, whilst the beautiful Arabian on the right is the original hotblood of the world's horses. Both, however, are capable of reposing trust and affection in those who take the trouble to understand them.

The Essential Horse

It is essential to understand both the mental and physical characteristics of horses if our association with them is to be rewarding and successful.

The horse's mental character governs its behavior, and its physical structure controls the activities it is capable of doing and the level of performance it can achieve in them. The horse's behavior is motivated by instincts acquired during the millions of years of its development. These are overlaid and supported by a set of very highly developed senses, giving the horse its particular character.

~ SELECTIVE BREEDING ~

The horse's physical structure is, of course, the result of evolution, controlled initially by environment. However, once man began to intervene with the process of nature, it was the human factor that increasingly influenced the subsequent development of the horse. By limiting breeding to selected, high-quality animals through cross-breeding between different types, in-breeding within families, as well as the safer line-breeding method to a common ancestor, a whole variety of distinctive horses and ponies gradually emerged. Some were encouraged to be very strong, others were bred for speed, while some animals, like the Arabian, developed a unique beauty that would not have been possible without man's direct intervention.

~ DEFENSE SYSTEM ~

In the course of evolution, horses have acquired senses far more developed than our own, which, although they are of some relevance to communication and sexual behavior, are largely part of a sensitive defense mechanism. Even the position of the eyes, allowing for lateral and almost 360-degree vision in a manner at variance with human sight, is concerned with the defense system.

Acute sense of smell
Horses rely on their sense of smell in all sorts of respects. They use it to identify members of their group and their home surroundings, and there is every reason to suppose they associate their human handlers with a specific scent.

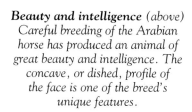

Beauty and intelligence (above)
Careful breeding of the Arabian horse has produced an animal of great beauty and intelligence. The concave, or dished, profile of the face is one of the breed's unique features.

Developed motion (left)
The grace and speed of a horse in motion is governed by the proportionate arrangement of its skeletal structure, which man has developed by over 5,000 years of selective breeding.

Origins

THE ORIGIN OF THE EQUINE SPECIES can be traced to the Eocene period, some 60 million years ago. In 1867, scientists excavating rock structures of that period in the American South discovered a remarkably complete skeleton of what became established as the first horse. The scientists called it *Eohippus*, the Dawn Horse, and from it could show a progression on the American continent that culminated in *Equus caballus*, the forebear of the modern horse.

Eohippus

Eohippus descends from the *Condylarth*, a group that was the distant ancestor of all hoofed creatures and lived on Earth about 75 million years ago. The *Condylarth* was no bigger than a dog and was five-toed, each toe having a horny nail.

Fifteen million years later, the feet of its descendant, *Eohippus*, had altered. On the forefeet there were four toes, while on the hind there were three. The creature is thought to have weighed about 12lb (5.4kg) on average, and stood about 14in (36cm) at the shoulder – about as big as a fox or a medium-sized dog. The color

THE EVOLUTION OF THE HOOF

The single hoof in the species Equus *developed over millions of years as a result of the changing environment. In the Eocene period the ancestors of the modern horse lived in forest conditions, and multitoed feet were necessary to prevent them sinking in the soft and marshy earth. These toes gradually disappeared as the jungle swamps gave way to open plains and savannah, which were much firmer underfoot.*

FOUR TOES
Eohippus *had four toes on the front feet.*

THREE TOES
In the Miocene period there were three toes, the central gradually bore most of the weight.

HOOF
The first single-hoofed horse was Pliohippus, with a longer leg and flexing ligaments, whose foot was almost identical to that of the modern horse.

FINAL FORM
The final metamorphosis to Equus. The cannon is longer and there is no sign of the vestigial toes.

NUMBER OF TOES
The progression from toes and a broad dog-like pad to a single hoof involved a gradual reduction in the number of toes. The third toe grew longer and stronger to form a hoof, while the cannon bone lengthened, contributing to greater speed.

and texture of the *Eohippus* coat is not known but it is not improbable that it was like that of a deer, the background dark but with lighter spots or blotches, which would provide camouflage in the dappled, forest surroundings that were the creature's habitat.

Environment is the deciding factor in evolution and as it changes, so the animals that are to survive adapt to the new circumstances. The toed feet, equipped with pads similar to those of a dog, and the horse's relationship with the tapir, indicate that *Eohippus* lived in an environment that included the sort of soft soil found on jungle floors and

around the edges of pools. The pads enabled the animal to cross wet and marshy ground without difficulty. These pads survive as the ergots of the modern horse, those superfluous horny growths on the back of the fetlocks. Neither the eyes nor the teeth bore much resemblance to those of the modern horse. The teeth were more like those of pigs or monkeys, but they were well suited to a diet of soft leaves growing on low shrubs.

Mesohippus and Miohippus

Eohippus was succeeded by two similar and probably overlapping types in the Oligocene period (25–40 million years ago). These were *Mesohippus* and the

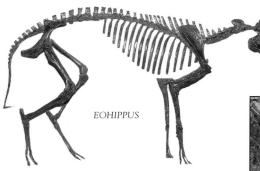

EOHIPPUS

🐎 **Skeletal reconstruction of Eohippus**
This skeleton of Eohippus *is unmistakably that of a horse, even allowing for its size, which is only 14in (36cm) at the shoulder, and for the formation of its feet. There were numerous variations within the* Eohippus *species. The smallest were probably no more than 10in (25cm) high, while the largest may have been 20in (50cm) and eight times heavier than their smaller contemporaries. During the later Miocene period, there was a mammoth variety of the species, Megahippus.*

🐎 **Artist's impression of Eohippus**
Eohippus *was a browsing animal that lived on soft leaves. It was well equipped to survive in jungle-type conditions, being camouflaged by a patterned coat, and its toed feet allowed easy movement over wet ground.*

🐎 **Artist's impression of Mesohippus**
By the Oligocene period, 25–40 million years ago, Eohippus *had been superseded by the three-toed* Mesohippus, *which had longer legs and much improved dentition, allowing for the consumption of a wider range of plant growth.*

somewhat more advanced *Miohippus*. Both were bigger with longer legs and equipped with teeth that enabled them to eat a variety of soft plant growth. Their toes had reduced to three on each foot, more weight supported by the central one.

The watershed in the development of the horse occurred between 10 and 25 million years ago in the Miocene period. This was the period when the jungle environment gave way to treeless plains and steppes, supporting a low growth of wiry grasses. Adapting to these changed conditions, the horse developed teeth that were suitable for grazing and a longer neck to make the grasses easier to reach. The position of its eyes altered to give it all-round vision against the approach of predators. Its legs became longer and were equipped with flexing ligaments and, eventually, a single toe or hoof; all of these changes increased the speed with which it could flee if attack was imminent.

Equus caballus

The first single-hoofed horse was *Pliohippus*, which evolved some six million years ago. *Pliohippus* was the prototype for the true horse, *Equus caballus*, which was established a million years ago (half a million years before man).

Equus spread from America over the existing land bridges to Europe and Asia.

🐎 *Artist's impression of* **Equus caballus**
Equus caballus, *the progenitor of the modern horse, evolved about one million years ago and was equipped for life on open, plain-type country, which supported wiry grasses. Unlike his predecessors, Equus was a grazing animal with a highly developed system of defense against carnivorous predators.*

When the glaciers retreated, perhaps 10,000 years ago, the land bridges had disappeared and, for reasons that can only be a matter for conjecture, the horse became extinct on the American continent. It was not re-established until the arrival of the Spanish conquistadores.

There were three, principal, primitive types of horse. These evolved according to the dictates of environment and may therefore be considered as the foundation for the world's breeds. They were the

Asiatic Wild Horse, which still exists in zoos; the lighter, more refined Tarpan of Eastern Europe and the Ukrainian Steppes, which is exemplified by the famous herd maintained at Popielno in Poland; and the heavy, slow-moving horse of the northern European marshlands known as *Equus silvaticus*, from which our heavy horse breeds derive.

Just prior to domestication, four sub-species had evolved – two pony-types and two horse-types:

Pony Type 1 was similar to today's Exmoor pony and became established in North West Europe. It was resistant to wet and thrived in harsh conditions. Pony Type 2 was bigger than Pony Type 1 (14–14.2hh). It was more heavily built, coarse and more heavy-headed. It inhabited northern Eurasia and was able to withstand the cold. The Highland pony most nearly resembles this type. Horse Type 3 was about 14.3hh. Long and narrow bodied, goose-rumped, long necked and with long ears, it inhabited central Asia. The nearest modern equivalent is the Akhal-Teke, a breed that is able to tolerate heat. Horse Type 4, while smaller than the others was nevertheless much more refined, with a concave profile and high-set tail. It came from western Asia and its present equivalent is the Caspian pony. It is postulated as the prototype Arabian.

🐎 *Tarpan* (above)
Equus przewalskii gmelini antonius, *the Tarpan, was a swift and lightly built, primitive horse that lived in Eastern Europe and the Ukrainian Steppes. Together with the Asiatic Wild Horse, it is the progenitor of the modern breeds of light horses.*

🐎 *Tarpan Przewalskii's horse* (right)
In 1881, Poliakov discovered the Asiatic Wild Horse, Equus przewalskii przewalskii poliakov, *in a wild Mongolian herd.*

Domestication

THE BULK OF EVIDENCE points to the horse being domesticated in Eurasia 5–6,000 years ago, at the end of the Neolithic period. The dog was domesticated perhaps 6,000 years earlier. Sheep and reindeer were domesticated around 11,000 years ago and goats, pigs and cattle some 2,000 years later.

Hunter and Hunted

Prior to domestication, the contact between man and horse was that of the hunter and the hunted. During the last stages of the Ice Age, there is much evidence to show that primitive man used the wild horse herds as a source of food. The favorite tactic was to kill the animals by driving a group of them over a cliff, a method with obvious advantages over individual pursuit.

The cave drawings at Lascaux in France and Santander in Spain vividly illustrate the pursuit of horses, as well as providing a remarkable record of primitive life. Huge depositories of horse bones – relics of horse herds driven to their destruction – have been found in many parts of France, particularly at Lascaux and Salutré but also at a number of other places.

Spanish cave painting (above) Found in Castillo Puente Viesgo, Spain, this painting is dated c.15,000B.C. The simple harness reveals the presence of a society accustomed to employing horses in its daily life.

French cave painting (below) This drawing of a running horse, in the caves at Lascaux, France, may be as much as 15,000 years old. Cave drawings were a form of communication, this one indicating the presence of horses.

First Domesticated Herds

The people responsible for domesticating the horse herds were probably nomadic Aryan tribes moving about the steppes bordering the Caspian and Black Seas. There is evidence of this happening, but it is probable that domestication was also taking place simultaneously elsewhere in Eurasia, in areas supporting a horse population.

These nomads possibly began as herders of semi-wild flocks of sheep, goats, and, more importantly, of the tractable reindeer. The switch to horses would have been made out of practical considerations. In the harsh steppe lands, horses were a better proposition than other animals, being better equipped to find food. Furthermore, horses are not migratory animals like the reindeer, whose movement is governed by the incidence of the "reindeer moss" on which they feed.

Initially, then, horses were herded. Their flesh provided food, their hides were used to make tents and clothes, and the dung could be dried to make fires. Mares supplied milk, which could be fermented into kummis, the fiery brew of the steppes. In time, the mobility of the tribes was increased by employing the quieter animals

Greek pottery (detail) (left) This piece of pottery is decorated with a stylized portrayal of a Greek ceremonial chariot. The Greek association with horses began around 2000B.C. but the earliest accounts of horses being used in battle occurs in Homer's Iliad (c.800B.C.), when the "heroes" fought from chariots.

Indian petroglyph (above) A hunter, armed with bow and arrow, surrounded by the beasts of the chase, is depicted in this Indian rock carving. The horse gave the Indian the ability to approach, hunt and kill such animals in numbers sufficient to provide food, clothing, and shelters for the whole tribe.

to transport the household effects. The natural consequence thereafter was for men and women to ride the horses, an accomplishment which made the task of herding that much easier. To this day, horse herds are kept in the same fashion throughout the eastern republics of the USSR, and still provide the very staff of life for the horse peoples of the twentieth century.

Riding and Driving

In rough, mountainous countries, men rode horses, even though these animals would have been of small stature. For the first time in history, in the flat, valley lands of the Middle East, horses provided the key to the establishment and maintenance of a succession of great empires. Their role was almost wholly confined to drawing the chariot. Two horses, however small, could pull a light chariot carrying two or even three men. The addition of two more horses, hitched abreast, reduced effort and increased speed potential. The solid wheel was being used in the Tigris-Euphrates valley around 3500B.C., and spoked chariot wheels were commonplace in Egypt by 1600B.C.

Valuable Animal

As methods of agriculture improved, horses could be hand-fed. This, combined

🐎 Viking tapestry
The great sea-faring Vikings brought horses with them on their raids to the coasts of Britain and the Scottish islands. This detailed tapestry, which is held at Baldishol, Hedmark, Norway, shows a Viking horseman (c.1180).

with selective breeding, produced bigger, stronger and faster horses suited to the particular requirements of the day. For the most part, those requirements were concerned with warfare and transport, as well as, of course, for the purposes of sport in the great circuses of the classical civilizations of Greece and Rome.

At no point in the early civilizations was the horse employed in cultivation or in menial tasks. The horse was considered altogether too valuable, and work of that sort was left to oxen. Indeed, in the pre-Christian era the horse had been an object of veneration, occupying an important place in mythology and religious ritual – often being regarded as the supreme sacrifice. In Ancient Greece, Ares, the god of war, traveled the firmament in a chariot drawn by white horses; the image of the goddess Demeter was the head of a black mare and her priests were known as "foals." White horses were occasionally drowned in honor of Poseidon, the god of the sea and the creator of horses, while horses belonging to kings and chieftains were frequently interred with their masters.

Possession of horses ensured mobility; it was the means of creating and extending civilizations, and sometimes it created new societies and a new concept of life. It did this for a short time with the American Indians. They formed the last of the world's true horse cultures, although they were not in the same class as the archetypal horse societies of the Mongols and Huns. Those nomadic horsemen of the steppes, under their greatest leader, Genghis Khan, built an empire on the backs of shaggy Mongolian ponies.

🐎 Greek mosaic (above)
This mosaic of a charioteer leading a horse clearly shows the small size of the horse in relation to the man. The mosaic dates from the second or third century A.D.

🐎 Bayeux Tapestry (right)
A detail in the eleventh-century Bayeux Tapestry shows a mounted hunt. Compare the size of the horses with that in the mosaic above.

Conformation

CONFORMATION IN THE EQUINE can be defined as the interest in the formation of the skeletal frame and its accompanying muscle structures, in terms of the symmetrical proportion of the individual parts to each other and the whole. The perfection of individual components and their proportionate relationships contribute to the perfection of the overall form. In the well-made horse, no one feature disturbs the overall symmetry.

Variation

Conformation varies according to the purpose for which the horse is required. At one extreme are the short, thick proportions and heavy musculature of the draft horse, which indicate strength and power. At the other extreme is the sleek Thoroughbred, based on a light frame and the length of proportions and muscles – conformation conducive to speed. Between, are horses that incline more or less to one than to the other.

Assessing Proportion

The key to assessing conformation is in the proportions. The diagram opposite, "The Proportionate Horse," provides

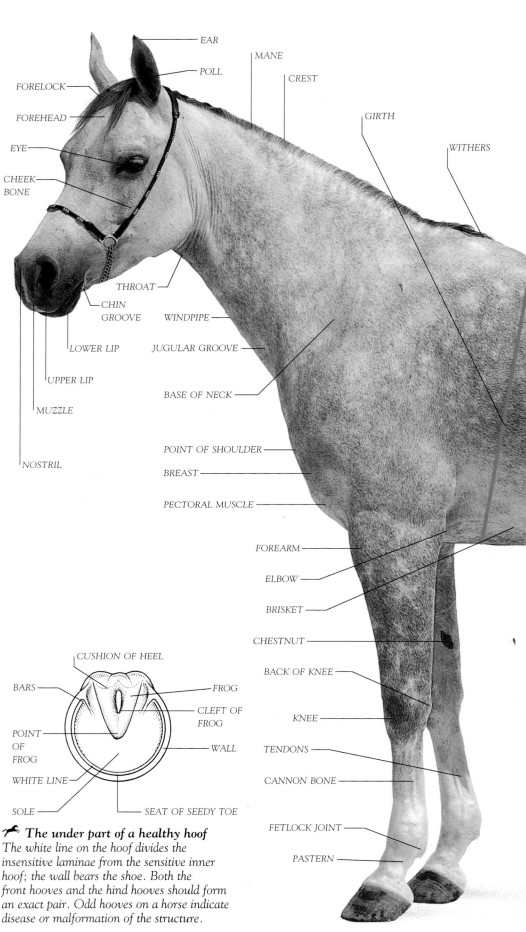

🐎 *Assessing conformation*
This Mogul miniature shows a horse being assessed for its conformation while standing against a neutral white background, a ploy that highlights the outline and clarifies the detail. In this instance, one wonders what was the verdict on this strangely shaped animal.

🐎 *The under part of a healthy hoof*
The white line on the hoof divides the insensitive laminae from the sensitive inner hoof; the wall bears the shoe. Both the front hooves and the hind hooves should form an exact pair. Odd hooves on a horse indicate disease or malformation of the structure.

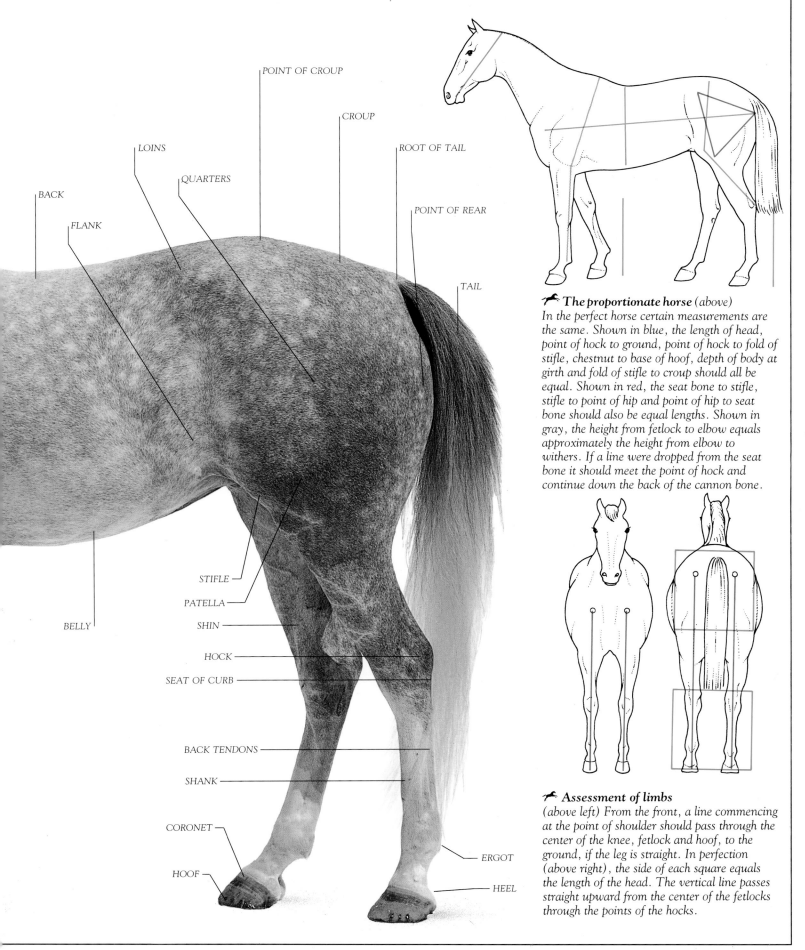

BACK

FLANK

LOINS

QUARTERS

POINT OF CROUP

CROUP

ROOT OF TAIL

POINT OF REAR

TAIL

BELLY

STIFLE

PATELLA

SHIN

HOCK

SEAT OF CURB

BACK TENDONS

SHANK

CORONET

HOOF

ERGOT

HEEL

The proportionate horse (above)
In the perfect horse certain measurements are
the same. Shown in blue, the length of head,
point of hock to ground, point of hock to fold of
stifle, chestnut to base of hoof, depth of body at
girth and fold of stifle to croup should all be
equal. Shown in red, the seat bone to stifle,
stifle to point of hip and point of hip to seat
bone should also be equal lengths. Shown in
gray, the height from fetlock to elbow equals
approximately the height from elbow to
withers. If a line were dropped from the seat
bone it should meet the point of hock and
continue down the back of the cannon bone.

Assessment of limbs
(above left) From the front, a line commencing
at the point of shoulder should pass through the
center of the knee, fetlock and hoof, to the
ground, if the leg is straight. In perfection
(above right), the side of each square equals
the length of the head. The vertical line passes
straight upward from the center of the fetlocks
through the points of the hocks.

a useful guide to help one assess the conformational perfection or imperfections of individual animals.

A most significant proportion to observe is the depth of girth. The length from the top of the withers to below the elbow should equal or exceed the measurement from that point to the ground if there is to be sufficient room for the lungs to expand without restriction. The depth of girth should give the horse the appearance of being short in the leg.

There are other rule-of-thumb measurements for horses. For speed, the neck needs to be reasonably long. Its length should equal approximately one and a half times the measurement from the poll, down the front of the face, to the lower lip; a shorter, thick neck is associated with strength and power, but not speed. The back, from the rear of the withers to the croup, should be short in comparison with the measurement from the point of shoulder to the last of the "false" ribs. Ideally the last should be twice the length of the former. (There are eight "true" sternal ribs, attached to both vertebrae and sternum bone, and ten

🐎 *Ewe neck*
A horse is termed ewe-necked when the topline is concave and the heavily muscled lower line bulges outward. It is a weak formation that makes bridling difficult and causes the saddle to shift forward.

"false," asternal ribs attached only to vertebrae. If the horse is to be sufficiently deep, the true ribs must be long and, for the rider's comfort, flat. The false ribs must be "well sprung" or rounded and also of sufficient length if the horse is not to run up light when in work. These false ribs lie over and protect the kidneys and other vital organs.)

Value of Conformation
A correctly proportioned horse will be naturally well balanced, moving freely and economically. Its performance level should, therefore, exceed that of less well-made animals. Because it is more mechanically efficient, it will be less prone to unsoundness and strain, and will have a longer working life. Physical limitations, imposed by poor conformation, may have an adverse effect upon the temperament when the horse is compelled to carry out movements that cause him discomfort as a result of faults that are not of his making.

Head and Neck
The head reveals the horse's nature. Large, generous eyes are desirable and nostrils should be big and wide, to permit the maximum inhalation of air. In the well-bred horse, the head is both lean and chiseled, with no signs of fleshiness, and the ears are fine and mobile.

The size of the head in relation to the body is important. If the head is too heavy for the neck, it will overweigh the forehand and upset the balance; too

THE SKELETON
The framework of the body is comprised of bones, which combine to form the skeleton. The bones support the body mass and their movement, when activated by joints and in concert with the muscles, results in the body's subsequent locomotion.
A joint is formed at the juncture of two bones. The joint is held together by ligaments, tough, fibrous and flexible tissues attached to each bone, which govern the degree to which the joints can move. Inelastic tendons run through the muscle and are attached to the bone. They are a form of support and prevent the muscles from being torn.

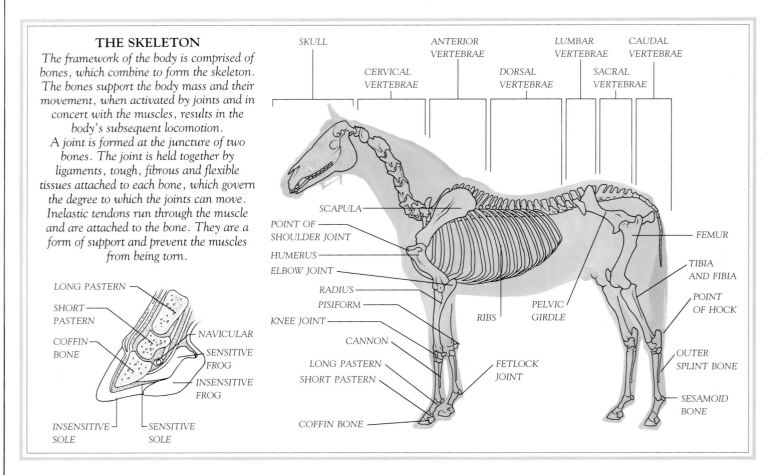

small a head (certainly less usual) also disturbs the balance. Necks should be curved and graceful; ewe necks are a serious fault. A fleshy throat prohibits flexion to the bit.

Shoulders and Withers

The ideal riding shoulder is well sloped: long in the scapula, short in the humerus, and positioned well forward. The ideal slope, which produces a long, low stride, is about 43 degrees from the highest point of the withers to the point of the shoulder. Withers need to be well laid back and prominent if the shoulder is to be sufficiently oblique. Upright shoulders produce a shortened action.

Chest and Trunk

The chest is neither too broad nor too narrow. If the chest is too broad, the horse rolls in movement; if too narrow, the legs are so close that they brush against each other. The observations regarding girth and ribs apply to the trunk.

Back

The back rises slightly to the croup and is well muscled on either side of the spine. If too long, it weakens the structure. If too short or broad, it restricts the action. Between the saddle and the croup lie the loins on which the propulsive power of

🐎 Dishing
Dishing is a fault in the action due to the leg's conformation. It causes the toe to turn out and the foot to move in an outward circle. It is uneconomical and imposes strain but can be corrected, in part, by careful shoeing.

the quarters depend. They must be short, thick and powerful. The croup in the mature horse is in alignment with the withers, if the horse is in balance. A pronouncedly sloping croup with a low-set tail indicates weak quarters.

Quarters

The quarters of a horse must give the impression of great strength. The second diagram on page 15 provides a useful method to assess the quarters. If the hock is placed correctly, it is in line with the chestnut on the foreleg. Viewed from the side, a line dropped from the point of the buttock to the ground should touch the hock and continue down the vertical line formed by the rear of the cannon bone.

Forelegs

The straightness of the forelegs is judged from the front as in the same diagram. In addition, the elbow must be free from the body and not lie hard up against the ribs. In other words, it should not be tied-in. Forearms should be long and muscular, knees large and flat, cannons short for strength and the measurement round the bone should be constant down its length. There must be no puffiness in fetlock joints, and the pasterns – the shock absorbers – should be of medium length.

🐎 Unusual ears
These unusual, curved ears meeting in the middle and capable of full rotation, are a unique feature of the Kathiawari Horse, an indigenous species of India.

TEETH
The incisor teeth provide a fairly accurate guide to the age of the horse in its first 10 years, but experience is required to estimate the age thereafter. At birth the foal has no teeth. Then, when it is 10 days old, the central incisors cut through the gums. By the time it is 6 to 9 months old, the foal has acquired a full set of milk teeth. His full set of permanent teeth are in place when he is between 5 and 6 years old.

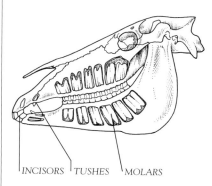

INCISORS TUSHES MOLARS

MATURE HORSE
The two jaws of the mature horse each have 12 molar (grinding) teeth as well as 6 incisor (biting) teeth.

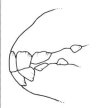

FLAT, OVAL TABLES
LONG, SMALL CUPS

FIVE YEARS
Central, lateral and corner incisors are permanent; cup marks appear on "tables."

ROUND TABLES
OVAL CUPS

TWELVE YEARS
At 12 years, the slope of the teeth has increased and cup marks are less distinct.

TRIANGULAR TABLES
ROUNDED CUPS

OLD AGE
In old age, the slope of the teeth is very pronounced and the groove on the corner teeth has almost disappeared.

The Gaits

THE HORSE HAS FOUR natural gaits and a number of specialized ones, which are based largely on the old ambling, or pacing, gait. This peculiar gait occurs naturally in some American breeds, notably the Tennessee Walking Horse, the Saddlebred, the Fox Trotter and Standardbred, as well as in the Icelandic Horse.

The Natural Gaits

The natural gaits are simply walk, trot, canter and gallop. The sequence of footfalls at walk, when it is begun with the left hind leg, is: 1. left hind; 2. left fore; 3. right hind; 4. right fore – four distinct and regular beats.

The trot is a two-beat gait in which the horse puts one pair of diagonal legs to the ground simultaneously, and, after a moment of suspension, springs on the other diagonal. Two beats can be heard, the first when the left hind and right fore touch the ground, and the second when the opposite diagonal pair of legs touches down, following a brief interval.

The canter is a three-beat gait. If it begins on the left hind, the sequence is: 1. left hind; 2. left diagonal, the left fore and right hind touching the ground simultaneously; 3. right fore, which is then termed the "leading leg." On a circle to the right, the horse "leads" with

Lope

The lope is a characteristic gait of the western horse. In fact, it is an easy, uncollected canter with the conventional three beats. The speed is reckoned to be 6–8 mph (9.5–13kph) and can be sustained over long distances.

the inside foreleg, i.e. the right fore. On a circle to the left, when the sequence is reversed, the horse leads with its left foreleg. A horse cantering a right-handed circle on the left lead, or vice versa, is said to be on the "wrong lead" or moving with a "false lead." However, in the advanced school balancing exercise of counter-canter, the horse is required to canter on just such a false lead.

The gallop is usually a gait of four beats, but the sequence varies according to the speed. As a four-beat gait, when the right fore leads, the sequence is: 1. left hind; 2. right hind; 3. left fore; 4. right fore, followed by full suspension when all four hooves are off the ground.

Development of the Natural Gaits

The requirements of modern dressage further subdivide the gaits, apart from the gallop. The walk and trot are both divided into four subdivisions.

In the medium walk, there is moderate extension, with the hind hooves touching the ground in front of the prints of the fore hooves. The collected walk is shorter, more energetic and more elevated, and the hind hooves touch the ground behind the prints of the fore hooves. In the extended walk, when head and neck are stretched, the horse is expected to cover as much ground as possible while maintaining the four, distinct footfalls. The hind hooves touch the ground in front of the prints of the fore hooves. In free walk, the horse moves again in extended outline, but while the four beats remain distinct, this is a pace of rest.

The working trot is between the medium and collected trots and inclines more toward the latter. Medium trot lies between extended and collected, inclining more to the former, and the hind hooves touch down in the prints of the fore hooves. The canter is similarly divided and the same criteria apply as in the trot.

Specialized Gaits

The gaits based on the pace and the specialized variations of the natural gaits are found mostly on the American continent. The Icelandic Horse is an exception and a number of the Russian breeds still pace naturally. The pacing gait is uncommon in Europe, outside of harness racing, although it was highly regarded up to the sixteenth century.

Trot

A medium trot with a good, swinging, hacking pace. The head carriage is pleasing and there is particularly good engagement of the hind leg under the body.

Canter

A pleasant, smooth, three-beat canter on the left lead is shown here, with the horse going freely in good contact with the bit and well balanced.

Gallop

The gallop is the fastest and most exhilarating gait, in which there is a period of suspension when all four hooves are off the ground.

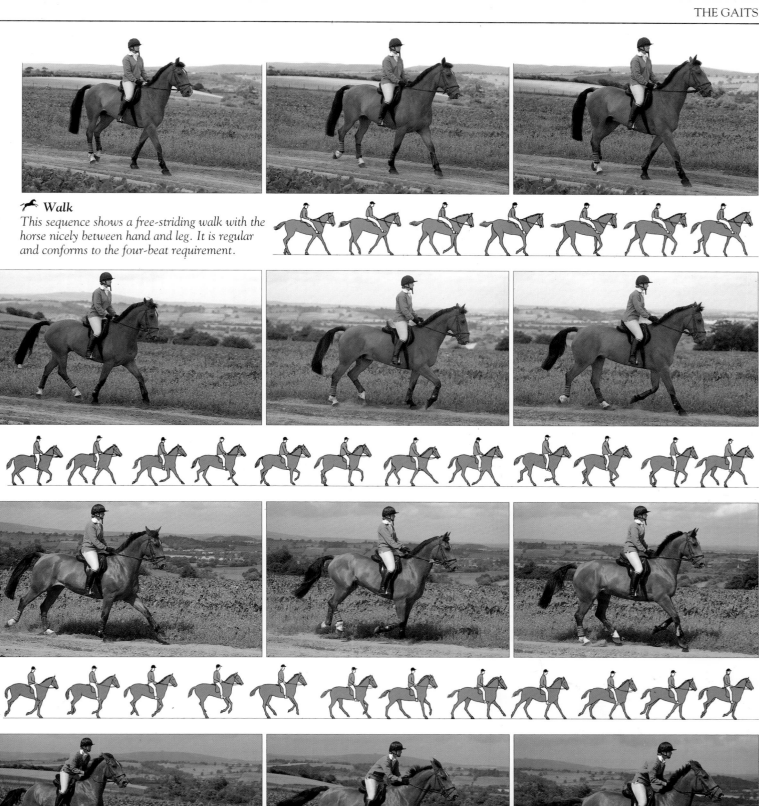

Walk

This sequence shows a free-striding walk with the horse nicely between hand and leg. It is regular and conforms to the four-beat requirement.

Markings and Coat Colors

THE COAT COLORS originate in the genes of the breeding stock. A total of 39 genes can appear in many combinations, and these are responsible for the characteristics, including the coat color. In horses, gray dominates black, bay and chestnut; bay dominates black; and chestnut is recessive to all colors.

Color Possibilities

If one parent is gray and the other is bay then the foal will be gray, since gray is dominant. A bay gene and a chestnut gene will result in a bay foal because the chestnut gene is recessive to bay. The foal of that union will produce sex cells, half of which contain bay genes and half chestnut. If two such animals were mated, it is possible that the two chestnut genes would be united and the progeny would be chestnut. Chestnut horses must have two chestnut genes in each cell, therefore, the mating of two chestnuts always produces a chestnut foal. The color of foals is not necessarily constant—Lipizzaners are born black and mature to white. Doubtful cases are decided by the color of the hair on the muzzle.

Horses are described by their coat color, with further identification being made by the white markings on the body.

Part-colors

Part-colored horses – called Pintos in America (also known as Paints) – are distinguished by having two coat colors. Odd-colored horses have patches of more than two colors, which may merge. The Tobiano (basic color white) of Southwest America is believed to possess the more dominant gene. Eyes may be dark or blue in either type.

COAT COLORS

GRAY
Black skin, with a mixture of white and black hairs.

PALOMINO
Gold coat, white mane and tail, with a minimum of black.

BAY
Reddish coat with black mane, tail and points.

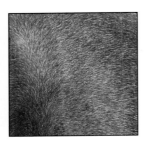

STRAWBERRY-ROAN
Chestnut body color with white hairs interspersed.

SPOTTED
This coat is often referred to as Appaloosa coloring.

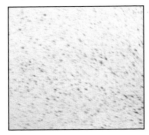

FLEABITTEN
Brown specks of hair fleck an otherwise gray coat.

CHESTNUT
Various shades of gold, from pale gold to a rich, red gold.

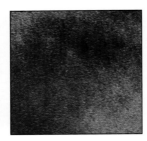

BROWN
Mixed black and brown in coat, black limbs, mane, tail.

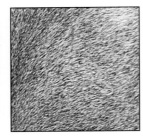

BLUE-ROAN
Black or brown body with a percentage of white hair.

SKEWBALD
Large patches of white on another base color.

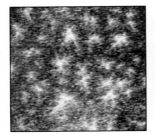

DAPPLE-GRAY
Dark gray hairs form distinct rings on a gray base.

LIVER-CHESTNUT
This is the darkest of the permissible chestnut shades.

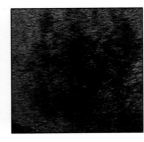

BLACK
Black pigment throughout, with occasional white marks.

DUN
Yellow, blue or mouse, depends on diffusion of pigment.

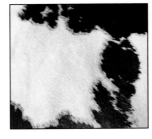

PIEBALD
Usually irregular, large patches of white and black.

STAR

STRIPE

BLAZE

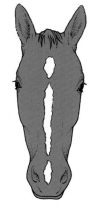

INTERRUPTED STRIPE

BALD FACE
A bald face is defined as the horse having white hairs covering the forehead and the front of the face and extending laterally towards the mouth, and possibly also encompassing the muzzle and lower ear.

WHITE MUZZLE

WHITE LIPS

🐎 **Natural markings**
The common forms of natural markings occur in areas of white hair on the face and the legs, although "flesh marks" occur on the underside of the belly, flanks and so on.

SNIP

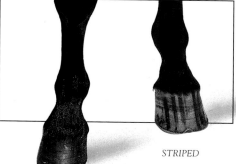
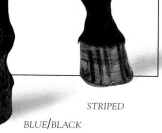

STRIPED

BLUE/BLACK

🐎 **Hoof coloring**
Variations in hoof coloring are incorporated in identifying the horse. On the left, the hooves are blue or black, those on the right are vertically striped. Hooves can also be light or white.

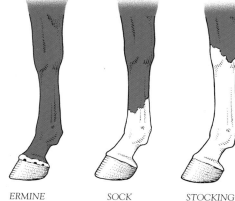
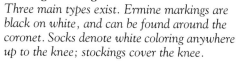

ERMINE   SOCK   STOCKING

🐎 **Leg markings**
Three main types exist. Ermine markings are black on white, and can be found around the coronet. Socks denote white coloring anywhere up to the knee; stockings cover the knee.

"ACQUIRED MARKINGS"
"Acquired markings" are also included in identifications, such as brand marks and also saddle and girth marks that appear as white hair.

BRAND MARKS
Brand marks constitute positive identification of animals. They comprise the herd or stud mark and often the number of the animal within the herd.

FREEZE MARK
A freeze mark is another form of positive identification used as a precaution against theft. The animal can be immediately identified by the number.

🐎 **Dorsal eel-stripe**
The dorsal eel-stripe occurs most usually in conjunction with a dun coat color. It is a primitive marking found on animals like the Tarpan and Mongolian Wild Horse.

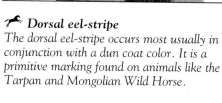
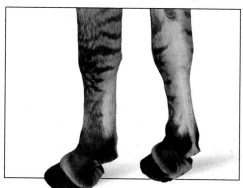

🐎 **Zebra bar markings**
Zebra bar markings on the leg are a primitive camouflage. They are seen on ancient breeds like the Norwegian Fjord (see pp.132–3) and on the Highland Pony (see pp.154–5).

The Senses

THE HORSE PERSONALITY is made up of a number of deeply ingrained instincts that were acquired in the process of evolution. The horse, like humans, possesses the five senses: taste, touch, hearing, smell and sight. In the horse, however, these five senses are far more developed than in ourselves. Furthermore, the horse has an enigmatic sixth sense, a heightened perception, which is apparent in their species but rare in ours.

Taste

Little is known about the horse's sense of taste, although we know that it is associated with touch and that it plays an important role in mutual grooming. We presume that horses like sweet things, and feed manufacturers add sweeteners to their products to make them more palatable, but there is no proof to support this assumption. Many horses, indeed, appear to relish the bitter herbs found in old pasture. Chicory, for instance, is a favorite with horses and so is comfrey.

Touch

The sense of touch is more relevant to our understanding of the horse. It is used as a means of communication between horses, and between humans and horses. The act of grooming is one example, and in riding the horse much of the language of the aids is concerned with touch. The leg, for instance, exerts small pressures on the receptor cells on the horse's sides and the hand communicates by touching the mouth through the rein and the bit.

The whiskers on the muzzle evaluate by touch objects that the horse cannot see, such as the contents of a feed bucket. Inexplicably, it is the practice to trim off these whiskers for fashion's sake, thus depriving the animal of a natural faculty.

LISTENING AHEAD

LISTENING BEHIND

ALERT TO
SOUNDS FROM
ALL DIRECTIONS

🐎 Hearing

Hearing is acutely developed in the horse, whose head is almost perfectly designed to receive sound. Large, mobile ears, capable of full rotation, can pick up sounds from all directions. They operate with the eyes. When one ear is pricked forward, the appropriate eye looks to the front to focus on the object of interest. The closer the ears are placed together, the better the corresponding forward vision.

🐎 Flehmen (right)

Flehmen, the curling back of the lip, can be caused by a stallion licking, or touching, a mare in season, but it can also occur in response to strong and/or unusual tastes and smells, such as garlic, lemon or vinegar.

🐎 Smell and touch
Relationships are established by touching and smelling, as when horses blow into each other's nostrils. Foals instinctively recognize the smell of their dam, just as the dam knows her foal. It is likely that members of a group are further identified by a corporate smell.

Hearing

A horse's hearing is far more sensitive than our own. Indeed, its head may be likened to a receiver served by the large, enormously mobile ears that can be rotated to pick up sounds from any direction. The horse is particularly responsive to the human voice, probably the most valuable training aid. Combined with a firm, soothing hand (touch), the voice is effective in reassuring and calming the horse. Used sharply but not loudly, it can encourage the sluggard or the faint-hearted.

Smell

Smell is similarly acute and, like hearing, plays an obvious part in the defense system, enabling horses to recognize each other and probably their home surroundings too. It is suggested that the sense of smell may be related to the horse's pronounced homing instinct, its ability to find its way home. Horses can smell human odor and by this detect any nervousness in the handler. They are particularly sensitive to the smell of blood, often showing disquiet and nervousness when near an abattoir, for instance. Smell also plays a large part in sexual behavior (see Behavior and Communication pp.24–5).

Sight

Equine sight is unusual in many respects. The horse's eye is large in comparison with that of other animals, such as pigs and elephants, suggesting a heavy reliance upon sight. Unlike humans and other animals, the horse focuses on objects by raising and lowering its head, rather than altering the shape of the eye's lens. Much of its ability to focus on objects in front depends upon the position of the eyes. Placed on the side of the head, as in many heavy breeds, there is wide lateral vision but much poorer frontal vision. In the riding horse such a conformation would be an obvious disadvantage. All horses, as part of the defensive mechanism, have a degree of lateral vision, and are able to move the eyes independently. Indeed, when grazing, the horse has all-around vision without needing to raise or turn its head, and it is quite possible that it can see something of its rider. Although not nocturnal, the horse can see quite well in the dark due to the size of its eyes.

The Sixth Sense

There are numerous examples of horses demonstrating an almost inexplicable perception. The reluctance of horses to pass reputedly haunted places is well-documented. They also have an uncanny ability to sense impending danger and they can be hyper-sensitive in detecting the moods of their handlers and riders.

🐎 Touch
Horses gain confidence by touching strange objects with their nose and also with the foot, involving both the senses of touch and smell. They will often touch or paw at a ground pole in training before crossing over it.

Behavior and Communication

HORSES HAVE A SOPHISTICATED language of communication, which involves physical and tactile signals, or body-language, such as the laying back of ears and mutual grooming. Smell is also an important form of communication: the animals produce and receive pheromones, smell messages, which are produced by the skin glands.

🐎 **Ears and eyes** (above)
The ears reveal very clearly the horse's state of mind and its possible intentions. Should they be laid back in intense irritation and aggression, the action is usually accompanied by the animal showing the whites of the eyes.

The Importance of Smell

Foals instinctively recognize the smell of their dams. Furthermore, members of a group are identified by what may be a corporate odor. Smell also plays a significant part in sexual behavior. The pheromone sent by a mare in estrus is a clear message to the stallion that she is ready to mate. She also sends physical messages, the flashing of the vulva, for example, and the adoption of the mating posture when she holds the tail to one side. She communicates just as clearly if she is not ready to accept the stallion's attentions, by baring her teeth and attempting to bite or kick him. Indeed, she may further indicate her displeasure vocally by squealing.

Though horses are not as territorial as other animals, stallions do scent-mark their territory with urine and feces piles. The stallion will also urinate over the urine or feces of mares within his group, sending a clear message to outsiders that the mares are part of his harem.

Flehmen

Stallions check the reproduction cycle of mares by sniffing their vulva and urine. As the mare approaches estrus, the stallion becomes excited and indulges in a form of foreplay. He licks the mare and engages in tactile stimulation, which may be accompanied by flehmen, the peculiar curling back of the lip. Flehmen is not always associated with sexual excitement and it is not the sole prerogative of the male horse. It can be provoked in both sexes by strong and unusual smells and tastes, such as garlic, lemon or vinegar.

Vocal Communication

Horses communicate vocally, although in a limited way. Squeals and grunts are usually signs of aggression or excitement. Snorts are made when horses see or smell something that interests them particularly or something that is potentially dangerous. Horses whinny for separated companions, and may whinny out of excitement. A mare will whicker softly to reassure her foal, and both sexes make the same noise in anticipation of being fed or receiving a tidbit. Some horses even learn to attract human attention by whinnying loudly if their feed is delayed.

Communication with Humans

It seems certain that humans do communicate unconsciously with horses by the smells they exude. Frightened people and, perhaps, aggressive ones too, give off odors that reveal their state of mind to the hypersensitive equine, either causing it to become apprehensive

🐎 **Mutual grooming** (above)
Mutual grooming cements a relationship between the two participants. Mares groom their foals in this way and stallions use it to stimulate mares sexually.

🐎 **Herd instinct** (left)
In the wild, the horse lives in herds composed of a number of groups. In part, it is possible that members of a group recognize each other by a corporate smell.

🐎 **Play fighting**

Young horses fight in play in the process of growing up, but they are also engaged in establishing a pecking order within the group. These encounters rarely result in either of the protagonists coming to any harm.

or aggressive, depending on whether the animal is of a recessive or dominant nature. Old-time horsemen smeared their hands in aromatic fluid when dealing with young or difficult horses. The saying "a bold man makes a bold horse" is revealing of the horse's hypersensitivity and another example of communication between the species. Horses sense their rider's moods and react accordingly.

Taste and Touch

Horses also communicate through the closely related senses of taste and touch. They do so when they groom each other, thus creating a friendly relationship. Humans seek to communicate or introduce themselves by touching and patting horses. In fact, it might be more effective to do as horses do and blow into the nostrils. Grooming is another way to communicate with horses and it builds up a relationship between the two.

Understanding Signals

It is not difficult to understand that a horse standing with a hind hoof rested, head down, ears held slightly back, lower lip hanging and eyes partially closed, is in a relaxed state. The posture of tension is equally easy to interpret. Horses that turn their quarters to humans who enter their stalls are sending an unmistakable message. Stamping a hind leg, shaking the head and/or swishing the tail are signals of irritation.

The Ears

Horses' ears give crystal clear messages. Enormously mobile, they can be rotated at will, controlled as they are by 13 pairs of muscles. Their positions reveal the horse's state of mind. Pricked firmly forward, they indicate a strong interest in some object and a corresponding lack of attention to the rider. When relaxed or dozing, the horse lowers the ears and allows them to become flaccid. When laid hard back, they indicate displeasure, temper or aggression. When one is stuck sideways, its owner has probably heard a wasp or fly. Twitching, mobile ears are comforting to a rider for they assure him that the horse is attentive.

🐎 **Rearing**

Horses may rear if startled. They also rear in play and as a way of displaying their dominant qualities. They may also rear out of excitement or sheer joie de vivre, particularly if they are being restrained. Stallions are prone to rearing for many of those reasons, but only a very few horses indulge in rearing as a vice.

Mountain ponies
Ponies bred in mountainous regions developed natural skills to suit their environment with little assistance from man. They are innately sure-footed and sensible, strong and hardy.

Equine jigsaw
There are, perhaps, as many as 160 distinctive breeds and types of horse throughout the world. However, it is possible to trace a relationship between them all. The only pure breed is the Arab, which is unique. For the rest, predominant influences can be discerned, like those of the Barb, the Spanish Horse, and, within the past two centuries, the Thoroughbred.

The Breeds

Within the equine jigsaw puzzle, you can trace a relationship between all the world's breeds.

Initially, horse breeds and types developed gradually by adapting to their environment, and through the natural kinship that existed between groups of horses occupying particular regions. Once the horse was domesticated, however, human intervention accelerated and altered the development of specific breeds and types. The practice of gelding male horses, allowing breeding to be carried on by a selective process from only the best stock, increased the quality and accentuated the characteristics most suited to the purposes for which the animals were used. Better methods of agriculture and husbandry produced more nutritious feedstuffs and, from the earliest times, the chariot people of the Middle East were feeding grain to their horses. As a result, horses became bigger, stronger and/or faster, according to the purposes for which they were required.

~ PREPOTENT BREEDS ~

It is abundantly clear that the world's light horse population is founded on a trio of prepotent breeds of eastern origin. Foremost among them is the hot-blooded Arabian, acknowledged as the fountainhead. Then there is the Barb of North Africa, also an eastern horse, which originally may have owed little or nothing to the Arabian. From the Barb was derived the "third man", the Andalusian, otherwise known as the Spanish Horse. The Arabian, possibly with a little assistance from the Barb and the Spanish Horse, is responsible for the Thoroughbred, whose influence now exceeds all others in the world's horse breeds.

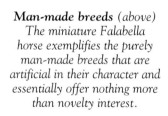

Man-made breeds (*above*)
The miniature Falabella horse exemplifies the purely man-made breeds that are artificial in their character and essentially offer nothing more than novelty interest.

Arabian and Thoroughbred influence
(*left*) *Without doubt, the principal influence in the development of the world's horse population was the Arabian Horse, the first progenitor. From it was later developed the bigger and faster Thoroughbred Horse, which is now the essential element in the modern competition horse.*

An adaptable animal (*left*)
Most horse breeds are remarkably adaptable, particularly, perhaps, those with a coaching background. These Lipizzaners are employed at hay-making, while their cousins at Vienna's Spanish Riding School can demonstatrate to perfection the intricate movements of classical dressage.

Arabian

T HE ARABIAN HORSE is arguably the most beautiful of all; it is unmistakable in character and appearance. It is also the purest and oldest of all breeds, having been carefully bred for thousands of years.

INFLUENCE

The Arabian's influence is apparent in the greater part of the world's equine population. It is acknowledged as the foundation of the Thoroughbred, which exceeds its progenitor in size and speed but cannot compare in terms of soundness and stamina.

ORIGINS

While the exact origin of the Arabian is unclear, the evidence from art shows that a race of horses of fixed Arabian type was in existence on the Arabian Peninsula at least 2,500 years before the Christian era. The Bedouin, the people who were most intimately concerned with this "desert horse," trace their association, albeit tenuously, from around 3000B.C. to the mare, Baz, and the stallion, Hoshaba. The mare, Baz, is claimed to have been captured in the Yemen by Bax, the great-great grandson of Noah, tamer of the wild horses. The spread of the all-pervasive Arabian blood throughout the world was made possible by the Muslim conquests, which were initiated by the Prophet Mohammed in the seventh century when the green banners of Islam, and the desert horses, swept through Iberia into Christian Europe.

WITHERS
The neck curves gracefully into rounded withers, and shoulders that are distinctly set.

NECK
A distinctive feature of the Arabian is the *mitbah*, a word applied to the angle at which the head meets the neck. This results in a particular arched curve that allows the head to turn freely in all directions.

MANE
The mane and also the tail are uniquely fine and silky.

MUZZLE
The skin of the small, tapered muzzle is very soft.

🐎 Head

The head is unmistakable and unforgettable. It is short and of great refinement, the face being pronouncedly concave or dished. The nostrils are exceptionally large and so are the eyes, which are widely spaced and lower than in other breeds. The ears are small, fine and sometimes curve inwards. A feature of the head is the jibbah, the shield-shaped bulge between the eyes, which extends from the ears to the nasal bone. It is unique among equines.

HEIGHT
The ideal height for an Arabian is between 14.2 and 15hh.

🐎 Endurance
The modern Arabian excels naturally at endurance riding although it is outclassed in the other competitive disciplines. Nonetheless, it is bred in great numbers throughout the world with rare dedication, and is still a major upgrading influence on other breeds.

🐎 Skeleton
The Arabian outline is governed by the unique skeletal formation. The Arabian has 17 ribs, 5 lumbar bones and 16 tail vertebrae in comparison with the 18–6–18 arrangement of other breeds. This difference in formation contributes to the high carriage of the tail.

🐎 Marengo
This etching is of the Emperor Napoleon mounted on his favorite charger, Marengo, whom he rode in his last battle at Waterloo in 1815. Napoleon made a point of riding gray horses and had his personal stud of gray Arabian chargers. He greatly encouraged the use of Arabians at the French national studs.

• BODY
The Arabian back is short and slightly concave, the loin is strong and the croup is long and level.

• COLOR
Chestnut, gray, bay, as here, and black are the Arabian coat colors.

• TAIL
The root of the tail is set noticeably high in the croup. In movement, it is carried arched and well up.

🐎 Stamina
Arabian stamina is legendary and there are numerous records of the breed's remarkable powers of endurance. In the nineteenth century, races were often held over long distances in the desert and could last for three days.

LIMBS •
Arabian limbs are hard and clean, but without excessive bone measurement under the knee of the forelimbs. The tendons are clearly defined and the hooves are near perfect in shape and size. Hind legs in the Arabian were, for many years, a failing, but for all that the breed is inherently sound and the movement is remarkably free.

🐎 Action
The action is described as "floating," the horse moving as though on springs. The Arabian is fiery and courageous but also possesses an exceptionally gentle nature.

Barb

THE BARB IS SECOND ONLY to the Arabian as one of the foundation breeds of the world's equines. Like the Arabian it is a desert horse, but it is unrelated in appearance and character. Its habitat is Morocco, in North Africa. There is a theory that the Barb may have constituted a pocket of wild horses that escaped the Ice Age. If that is so, then it is a breed as old as or older than the Arabian.

Present to Queen Victoria
(left) This etching from the Illustrated London News *of April 1850 shows some Barbs that the Sultan of Morocco presented to Queen Victoria.*

ORIGINS
Crossings with Arabian horses have occurred throughout history, and the modern Barb must have a percentage of Arabian blood. Some authorities hold that it belongs to a desert (Arabian) racing strain that resembled a horse very like the Akhal-Teke in the period just prior to domestication. Whatever the origin, the breed is possessed of a massively dominant gene, for there is no sign of the Arabian prepotency in the long, convex profile of the Barb, nor in its sloping quarter and low-set tail.

INFLUENCE
The Barb played a major part in the development of the Andalusian (see pp.32–3), and thus exerted a worldwide influence. It was just as influential in the evolution of the Thoroughbred, and a dozen or more European breeds. Perhaps because it is less numerous and less visually attractive than the fashionable Arabian, the Barb has never received due recognition.

TAIL
Unlike the Arabian, the Barb tail is usually low-set in sloping quarters that are also quite different to that of the Arabian in their proportions.

QUARTERS
The hind legs and quarters are by no means exemplary, but the Barb can go very fast over short distances and has unplumbed depths of stamina and endurance.

LIMBS
The limbs are slender and certainly not perfect and the hooves are often narrow – but no horse is tougher and more frugal than the Barb.

Spahi cavalry
Overall, a lightly built horse, unimpressive in size and general proportion but possessed of an extraordinary primitive vigor, the Barb was the traditional mount of France's famous Spahi cavalry, which was mounted on stallions.

Moroccan festival
Moroccan horsemen, descendants of the Berbers who led the Muslim conquest, display their riding skill in the wild, rifle-firing charge that is a feature of the North African festival.

• HEAD
Arabian blood has improved
the head but the Roman nose is
often evident and is indicative
of primitive genes.

• SKULL
The Barb's skull verges
on the primitive,
its shaping being
pronouncedly narrow.

• WITHERS
The withers are reasonably well
defined but the shoulder is flat
and often surprisingly upright
for a horse of such agility.

• BODY
The back is short and
very strong and runs up
to an often pronounced
croup. Usually, there is
depth through the girth.

• COLOR
Originally, the Barb colors seem to
have been bay, dark bay and black
but the addition of Arabian blood
has produced a large proportion of
gray horses. This Barb is black.

🐎 **North African fighters**
*For centuries the Barb was the mount of
the fierce, North African horsemen who
penetrated Spain and were eventually repulsed
by Charles Martel and his Frankish knights
at Poitiers in A.D.732.*

🐎 **Action**
*The Barb is renowned for its speed
over short distances. It does not have
the ethereal, floating action of the
Arabian but it is just as enduring,
just as sound and just as tough.*

HEIGHT
The Barb is between
14.2 and 15.2hh.

Andalusian

I N THE DEVELOPMENT of the modern
horse breeds, the most significant
influences are the Arabian and then
the Barb. Discounting the Thoroughbred,
and its history goes back only about
200 years, there is a third presence, the
veritable *éminence grise* of the equine
race. This is the Andalusian, for
centuries known as the Spanish Horse.

ORIGINS

The center of Andalusian breeding is
in old Spain, in sunscorched Jerez de la
Frontera, Cordoba and Seville. In these
areas, Carthusian monks preserved the
purity of the breed with dedication.
However, the precise origins of so old a
breed are difficult to establish. Before
the Ice Age a land bridge, now the
Straits of Gibraltar, existed between
Spain and North Africa. Barb horses
could have crossed over it into Spain.
At the time of the Muslim occupation
of the Iberian Peninsula, between
A.D.711 and 1492, the indigenous stock
was exemplified by the Sorraia Pony, a
primitive type with a Barb connection.
It seems highly likely that the Spanish
Horse evolved from crossbreeding
between this native stock and that of
the largely Berber invaders – the
North African Barbs.

HEAD •
The handsome head is often hawk-like in
profile and it owes much to the Barb (see
pp.30–31). The appearance is always arresting.

COLOR •
The usual colors are bay and shades of gray, as
here, and a characteristic mulberry shade that is
very striking. There were strains in the old
Spanish Horses that were spotted and parti-
colored. The coat patterns of the American
Appaloosas and Pintos are inherited from
Spanish stock imported by the conquistadores
in the sixteenth century.

🐴 *Carthusian influence*
*In the seventeenth and eighteenth
centuries outcrossing to heavy
stallions, in a mistaken effort to
breed bigger horses, nearly ruined
the Andalusian, but the
Carthusian monks of Jerez
selectively bred the Andalusian,
and the best lines today trace to
those original Carthusian horses.*

🐴 *Bullfighters and herders*
*The Andalusian, the mount of the
rejoneadore (Spanish bullfighter), is also
the riders' favorite at the colorful ferias.*

🐎 Influence

The Lipizzaner is an almost direct descendant of the Andalusian. Other breeds that owe much to this noble horse include the Friesian, Frederiksborg, Kladruber, Connemara, Cleveland Bay and Welsh Cob. The Alter-Real and Lusitano are its blood brothers. Also, most American breeds descend from Spanish Horses.

🐎 Babieca

Babieca, for over 20 years the mount of Spain's national hero Ruy Diaz, El Cid (c.1040–1099), died at the age of 40 and was buried at the monastery of San Pedro de Cardena. A memorial stands there in his honor.

● QUARTERS
The strength of the quarters and the possible degree of articulation in the hind joints makes the Andalusian particularly suitable for the advanced movements of the *manège*.

🐎 Sorraia Ponies

The Iberian Peninsula was the first European area in which the horse was domesticated. The ancient base stock, primitive in character, is represented by the Sorraia Pony and the more refined Garrano of Portugal. The Sorraia is probably a descendant of both the Asian Wild Horse and the Tarpan, bearing an extraordinary resemblance to the latter. In height, the ponies vary between 12 and 13hh and in appearance they are less than attractive. Their heads are large, with a typical, primitive, convex profile, the shoulders are straight and the tails low-set. There are grays, and yellow duns with black points and, in particular, the dun coloring accompanied by a dorsal eel-stripe and barred, zebra legs – the hallmarks of the primitive equine. Like their primitive forebears, Sorraias are incredibly tough and hardy, resistant to both cold and heat, and able to thrive on poor soils and forage.

🐎 Action

The action is proud and lofty. The walk is showy and rhythmical, the trot high-stepping and full of impulsion, the rocking canter smooth and spectacular. The natural balance, agility and fire of the Andalusian, together with its spectacular paces and docile temperament, make the breed well-suited to the Haute Ecole.

🐎 Strong and enduring

The short-coupled Andalusian, sometimes having a sloped croup and low-set tail, is not fast, but is enormously strong and enduring.

● TAIL
A feature of the Andalusian is the long, luxuriant and frequently wavy tail and mane, which enhances the natural presence.

HEIGHT
Generally, the Andalusian stands at 15.2hh.

Thoroughbred

THE THOROUGHBRED is the fastest and most valuable of the world's breeds, and around it has grown a huge racing and breeding industry. It evolved in England in the seventeenth and eighteenth centuries as a result of the crossing of imported Arabian stallions with a native stock of "running horses."

ORIGINS

Successive monarchs from Henry VIII onward founded Royal studs where the "running horses" were created by mixing Spanish and Italian imports with the Irish Hobby and the Scottish Galloway, subsequently reinforcing with oriental blood. Further impetus was given by Charles II following his restoration in 1660, after which the town of Newmarket became the headquarters of racing.

The breed has three foundation stallions – the Byerley Turk, the Darley Arabian and the Godolphin Arabian. The Byerley Turk was captured by Robert Byerley at the Battle of Buda and ridden by him at the Battle of the Boyne in 1690. He is responsible for the first of the four great Thoroughbred lines: Herod, Eclipse, Matchem and Highflyer, who was Herod's son. The Darley Arabian came from Aleppo in 1704 and stood in Yorkshire. He was the sire of the first great racehorse, Flying Childers, and the founder of the Eclipse line. The Matchem line is the responsibility of the Godolphin Arabian brought to England in 1728.

GIRTH
Depth through the girth allows for maximum expansion of the lungs, essential in a racehorse.

FOREHAND
A long, graceful neck running into well-defined withers and a long, sloping shoulder is typical of the Thoroughbred.

EYES
The eyes are big and alert.

NOSTRILS
The nostrils are large.

HEIGHT
The average Thoroughbred racehorse is 16–16.2hh but horses above and below that height are frequently found.

🐎 Head

The head of the Thoroughbred is clean-cut, lean and very fine with a covering of skin thin enough for the veins to be seen beneath. The profile, unlike that of the breed's Arabian ancestors, is straight. The eyes are big and alert and the nostrils are large. There is no thickness through the jowl, and the ears are alert and mobile.

• COAT
The Thoroughbred refinement extends to the body and the coat. They are both fine, and the coat is thin and silky.

• BODY
Length of proportion characterizes the Thoroughbred and is indicative of speed. However, there must be strength in the back, loins and quarters.

Iroquois (left)
This engraving is of Iroquois, American-bred winner of the Epsom Derby in 1881 when he was ridden by the legendary figure of the Turf, Fred Archer. Archer, who started racing at 13 years old, was champion jockey for 13 seasons, winning a total of 2,748 races. In 1886 when he was 29 years old, he committed suicide at Newmarket, where he is buried.

• COLOR
Principal Thoroughbred colors are brown, bay, as here, chestnut, black and gray, the last a color attributed to the seventeenth-century Alcock Arabian.

Temperament
The Thoroughbred possesses both physical and mental stamina and is very courageous, battling on when less well-bred horses have given up. Not surprisingly, it is highly strung, nervous and sensitive and can be difficult temperamentally.

Maturing young
The modern Thoroughbred is bred to mature at an early age, and horses are raced at two years old. This practice is wasteful and many youngsters break down under the strains imposed. It continues largely on account of the economics involved.

Action
The action of the Thoroughbred is long, low and economical. The length of the hind leg from the hip to the hock is long so that the hind legs attain the maximum possible thrust when galloping.

Second
Second was bred by the Duke of Devonshire in 1732. He was by the great Flying Childers out of an unnamed mare by Basto, a son of the Byerley Turk. He was not a remarkable racehorse but he won two King's Plates, ran in heats of two and four miles (3.2 and 6.4km) and he carried 12stone (168lb/76kg)! The portrait is by James Seymour (1702–52).

Anglo-Arab

THE ANGLO-ARAB originated in Britain but is bred elsewhere, especially in France, where great attention has been paid to the production of a specialist all-around horse for more than 150 years. Both in Britain and France this horse is recognized as a composite breed, but as yet no standard has been laid down.

ORIGINS

In Britain, an Anglo-Arab is a cross between a Thoroughbred stallion and Arabian mare or vice-versa, with their subsequent re-crossing. These are the only two strains in the pedigree.

In France a number of permutations are possible, though to be entered in the stud book there must be a minimum of 25 percent Arabian blood, and ancestors must be Arabian, Thoroughbred or Anglo-Arab. The Anglo-Arab's place in earlier days was largely filled by native mares carrying eastern blood.

In theory, the Anglo should combine the best of Arabian and Thoroughbred. It should retain the Arabian's qualities of soundness, endurance and stamina while incorporating the scope and some of the speed of the Thoroughbred, but without its excitable temperament.

• WITHERS
Anglo withers are more prominent than those of the Arabian, and the well-set neck is longer.

🐎 Breeding for size
In Britain, the popular practice is to use an Arabian stallion on a Thoroughbred mare, when the progeny are likely to exceed either of the parents in size. Crossing the Thoroughbred stallion with an Arabian mare is considered to produce smaller offspring of less monetary value than the purebred.

MANE
The mane is fine and silky, as are the tail and coat.

🐎 Breeding the Anglo-Arab in France
In France, the principal breeding centers are the studs of Pau (shown here), Pompadour, Tarbes and Gelos. The systematic breeding of Anglo-Arabs in France began in 1836 when E. Gayot was director at Pompadour. It was based on two Arabian stallions, Massoud and Aslan (a Turk), and three Thoroughbred mares, Dair, Common Mare and Selim Mare.

🐎 Head
The head is more Thoroughbred than Arabian. The profile is straight, ears mobile and eyes expressive. Although there is no breed standard, the Anglo also tends toward the Thoroughbred, rather than the Arabian, in overall appearance. French Anglos from the southwest are lighter in type and have specific races reserved for them.

Tough horses

The Anglo-Arab from Pompadour is a larger, more muscular specimen, noted particularly as being an excellent jumper. The overall object is to produce tough horses of the best riding type that will race, jump, go cross-country and compete at dressage.

BODY
The back of the Anglo is usually short, the chest is deep and the shoulder very oblique and powerful.

QUARTERS
The quarters have a tendency toward being long and horizontal. The frame is well up to weight and is more solid than the Thoroughbred.

George IV driving on the Brighton road
This etching of George IV driving "Mrs Q" in his elegant, private carriage on the road to Brighton (c.1800) shows a pair of horses that were probably Thoroughbred. At that time, however, they would have displayed a pronounced, oriental influence.

COLOR
Colors vary in this excellent saddle horse. Chestnut, as here, and bay are usual but brown also occurs.

LIMBS
The limbs are sound and uniformly good. Any lightness of bone is compensated for by its density and good quality.

Action
The speed of the Anglo is not as great as that of the Thoroughbred (see pp.34–5), but the best are enormously agile and athletic and are distinguished by the correctness of their action.

HEIGHT
The height of the Anglo-Arab is between 16 and 16.3hh.

Shagya Arabian

U NTIL ITS COLLAPSE in the early part of the twentieth century, the vast Austro-Hungarian Empire dominated horse breeding in Europe. At the end of the nineteenth century it had a horse population in excess of two million and some of the greatest studs in the world. Hungary's oldest stud farm, Mezöhegyes, was founded in 1785, and in 1789 the stud at Babolna was established. Hungary is famous for its superb Arabian horses and Babolna became the center for their breeding.

ORIGINS

After 1816, the Babolna stud concentrated on the production of purebred "desert" Arabians and on part-breds, which were called Arabian Race. Arabian Race were the progeny of purebred stallions crossed with mares of very oriental appearance that carried strains of Spanish, Hungarian and Thoroughbred blood. This last policy produced the Shagya Arabian, which is now bred throughout Central and Eastern Europe as well as in Hungary.

The race was founded on the Arabian stallion, Shagya, a horse of the Kehil/Siglavi strain, born in Syria in 1830 and imported to Babolna in 1836. He was a cream-colored horse and big for an Arabian, for he was 15.2$\frac{1}{2}$hh. He was the sire of many successful stallions and his direct descendants are at Babolna and at studs throughout Europe.

The Shagya typifies the Arabian horse in every respect but possibly displays more bone and substance than the modern "straight" Egyptian type, for example. It is, above all, a practical horse used for every sort of purpose under saddle and in harness.

HEIGHT
Height is usually around 15hh.

COLOR
The predominant color is gray, as here, but all Arabian colors occur. The superb O'Bajan XIII, the "Black Pearl of Hungary" and his son, both stallions at Babolna following the Second World War, were black, the rarest of Arabian colors.

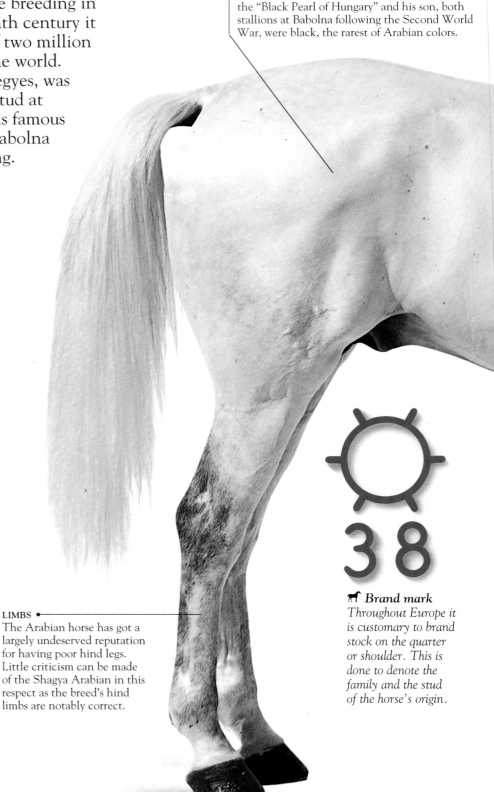

🐎 **Brand mark**
Throughout Europe it is customary to brand stock on the quarter or shoulder. This is done to denote the family and the stud of the horse's origin.

LIMBS
The Arabian horse has got a largely undeserved reputation for having poor hind legs. Little criticism can be made of the Shagya Arabian in this respect as the breed's hind limbs are notably correct.

OUTLINE
The outline of the Shagya Arabian is identical to that of the purebred Arabian and is quite unmistakable. In general, however, the Shagya is bigger and more substantially framed.

HEAD
The foundation stallion, Shagya, was noted for the beauty of his head, and his descendants inherit his great quality. The profile is pronouncedly dished, the muzzle tapered and small and the skin especially fine, while the very large eyes dominate the head.

BODY
Like purebred Arabians, the Shagya has 17 ribs, 5 lumbar bones and 16 tail vertebrae in comparison with the 18–6–18 formation of other horses. This largely accounts for the high-set carriage of the tail and the distinctive line of the back.

SHOULDERS
Bred as a saddle horse, the Shagya has the necessary oblique shoulder that contributes to the freedom of movement and the length of the stride. If anything, the withers are more prominent than in many Arabian strains.

BONE
In the Shagya Arabian, a practical riding horse, the measurement of bone taken around the cannon below the knee will rarely be less than 7¹/₂in (19cm).

🐎 **Action**
The action of the Shagya, like that of all Arabians, is unique. Free and elastic, it is as though the horse moves on springs.

HOOVES
Shagya hooves, as with the great majority of Arabian horses, should be, and usually are, near perfect in both shape and size.

🐎 **At liberty**
At the home of the Shagya at the Babolna state stud farm, it is customary for small herds of mares, often accompanied by a stallion, to run out at liberty for much of the year, although under supervision.

Lusitano

THE LUSITANO is the Portuguese version of its illustrious neighbor, the Spanish Andalusian (see pp.32–3). While there is no doubting the Andalusian base, the Lusitano has developed a little differently from it, probably because of an Arabian outcross. It is, for instance, notably more "on the leg" than the Andalusian – in other words, the horse shows a lot of daylight between its body and the ground.

HISTORY

The Lusitano was once the mount of the Portuguese cavalry. It was used for light agricultural work as well as for general riding and as a showy carriage horse. The breed's principal claim to fame is on account of its choice as the partner for the Portuguese bullfighter – called the *rejoneadore*.

In Portugal, the bull is not killed and it would be a disgrace for the horse to suffer injury. In consequence, the very valuable horses of the *rejoneadores* are highly schooled in the most advanced movements. To face the charging bull and to work the enraged animal calls for great courage and exceptional agility – qualities that the Lusitano possesses in full measure.

CHARACTERISTICS

The Lusitano is a very cooperative, intelligent and responsive breed and, consequently, it is well suited to the discipline of the *Haute Ecole*. As a result, it is also in growing demand for use as a dressage horse. Although the Lusitano must be quick and balanced, the action tends to be elevated which, of course, is not detrimental to its use in the bullring, nor as a carriage or dressage horse.

HEIGHT
The Lusitano is 15–16hh on average.

NECK
The neck is placed well into the strong shoulders, which contributes to the balance and agility, but it is somewhat thick and short.

SHOULDERS
The Lusitano is not perfect in respect of its conformation, but it has the compensatory asset of a pair of powerful shoulders.

LIMBS
Despite the length of the forearm, the Lusitano has a conformational failing in the length of the cannons. These are overly long and contribute to the appearance of the horse being "on the leg."

🐎 *Rear view*
Despite a probable infusion of Arabian blood, the full, wavy tail, derived from the Andalusian, is set rather lower than might be expected. It is certainly not carried in the Arabian fashion.

• GIRTH
In many specimens of the breed, the depth of girth is less than might be expected in what is otherwise a compact and athletic horse.

 Personality
While the Lusitano is perhaps no more than an Andalusian with a different accent and, indeed, has much of the Andalusian's more noticeable characteristics, it lacks the latter's "noble" presence. Nonetheless, it has all the courage of the Spanish Horse and is remarkably agile.

• BODY
The short back, good loin and powerful, sloping quarters complement the excellence of the shoulder, and make up for any other failings.

• COLOR
The Lusitano comes in every sort of solid color but it is predominantly gray. This striking dun coloring, inherited from the Andalusian, is less usually seen.

Head
The head should be fine and small with small ears and jaws. Its shape inclines more toward the Andalusian and the profile is more likely to be straight than dipped after the Arabian fashion.

Alter-Real
In 1784 the Royal House of Braganza founded a stud farm at Vila de Portel in Portugal's Alentejo province. Later the stud was moved to Alter, which gave its name to a breed of horses founded on 300 Andalusian mares. Its purpose was to produce horses for the Royal manège for the pursuit of classical riding, and those Alter-Real horses exist to this day.

Hispano-Arabian
The Hispano-Arabian is basically a Spanish-style Anglo-Arab (see pp.36–7) that shows more of its Arabian antecedents than the average Anglo. It derives from crosses between Spanish Arabians and English Thoroughbreds and sometimes the subsequent progeny are interbred. A spirited, courageous and athletic horse it is, nonetheless, tractable and intelligent. It is used for all equestrian sports as well as for the herding and testing of young fighting bulls.

Akhal-Teke

THE AKHAL-TEKE is one of the most distinctive and unusual horses in the world, and also one of the oldest. It is bred around the oases of the Turkmenistan Desert, north of Iran, and centered in Ashkabad. Horses were bred and raced here 3,000 years ago, and the present day Akhal-Teke is almost exactly like the Horse Type 3 (see Origins pp.10–11). There is also some resemblance to the Arabian racing strain, the *Munaghi*.

Kuban Cossack (left)
The Kuban Cossacks, incredibly skillful riders, as enduring as their horses, were often mounted on Akhal-Tekes. Well adapted to climatic extremes, the Akhal-Teke's legendary stamina was well suited to these indomitable horsemen.

HISTORY

There is nothing quite like this mystery horse. Its endurance and its resistance to heat are phenomenal. In 1935, Akhal-Tekes completed a ride from Ashkabad to Moscow, a distance of 2,580 (4,152km) miles, in 84 days. The ride included some 600 (966km) miles of desert, much of it crossed virtually without water. This extraordinary feat has never been equaled.

Racing is endemic to the Turkoman people. They used to feed their charges a high-protein diet of dry lucerne, when available, pellets of mutton fat, eggs, barley and *quatlame*, a fried dough cake. The horses were wrapped in heavy felt to protect them from the cold, desert nights and from the heat of the midday sun. Today, the Akhal-Teke is a racehorse, a long-distance performer, and the Russian sports horse in the dressage and jumping disciplines.

QUARTERS •
The quarters are narrow and mean and would be a nightmare in a show class, but they are spare and sinewy and the thighs are long and muscular.

COAT •
The coat is exceptionally fine and the skin thin, in character with a horse of desert origin.

TAIL •
A feature of the breed is a short, silky tail and a sparse, short forelock and mane, here roached.

HIND LEGS •
The long hind legs are usually sickle-shaped and cow-hocked, the hocks being carried high off the ground.

Color
Colors found in the Akhal-Teke include chestnut (main picture), black and gray but the most striking is the dun with its golden-metallic bloom (above), which is amazingly beautiful in the sunlight. A silvery color also occurs.

• NECK
The long, thin neck is set very high and almost vertically to the body, the head joining it at an angle of 45 degrees. Because of the long neck and the angle of the head, the line from the mouth is often higher than the withers, a feature peculiar to the breed.

• HEAD
The head is fine, and the big eyes give an impression of boldness. The nostrils are wide, the profile straight and there is width between the large, beautifully shaped ears.

🐎 Character
The Akhal-Teke can be rather obstinate and bad-tempered and cannot be said to have an easy temperament.

🐎 Conformation
The Akhal-Teke incorporates almost every conventional conformational failing, even though the high withers run into a sloped shoulder. The body is tube-like, the back too long, the ribcage shallow and the loin poor.

🐎 Action
The action, like the horse, is unique: the horse "slides" over the ground in a flowing movement without swinging its body.

🐎 Mares at pasture
Akhal-Teke mares are now kept at pasture during the day and they are stabled at night, in contrast to the old ways. The traditional practices of weaning foals at two months old and racing yearlings has also been discontinued, along with the outcrossing to the Thoroughbred, a practice that diluted the essential character of the breed.

• FORELEGS
The forelegs are usually set too close together but they are otherwise straight, and the forearm long.

HEIGHT
The average height is 15.2hh. Mares may be smaller.

• HOOVES
The hooves are small but regular although the heels are set low.

Lipizzaner

ALTHOUGH THE WHITE LIPIZZANER is usually associated with the famous Spanish Riding School in Vienna, it is bred all over what was once the Austro-Hungarian Empire. The School horses are raised at Austria's Piber Stud near Graz, but the state studs of Hungary, Romania and Czechoslovakia also specialize in the breed. Naturally, variations in type occur and the smaller Piber Lipizzaner is by no means predominant. Hungary, for example, breeds a bigger, very free-moving horse, which, like so many Lipizzaners, excels as a carriage horse.

ORIGINS

The breed takes its name from Lipizza (Lipica), now in Yugoslavia, where it originated and is still bred. The stud and the breed were founded in 1580 when nine Spanish stallions and 24 mares were imported from the Iberian Peninsula at the command of Archduke Charles II.

The Archduke's object was to ensure the supply of a suitably grand horse to the ducal stables at Graz and the court stable in Vienna. The Spanish School (so called because, from the outset, it used Spanish Horses) was established in 1572 to instruct noblemen in classical equitation in a wooden arena next to the Imperial Palace. The present school, the Winter Riding Hall, was built on orders of Charles VI and completed in 1735.

🐎 *Kladruber*
The Kladruber, a carriage horse, was based on Spanish stock and has had considerable influence on the development of the Lipizzaner. The stud at Kladrub in Czechoslovakia was founded in 1572, and is the oldest in Europe.

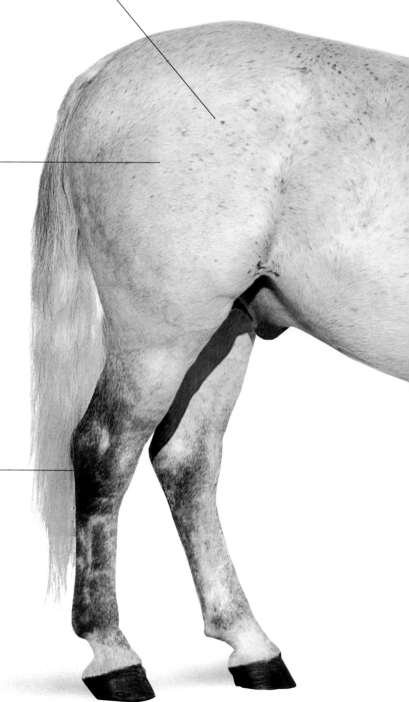

• COLOR
The color is uniformly white, although foals are born black or brown. Occasionally, bay occurs. By tradition, a bay horse is always kept at the Spanish School.

QUARTERS •
Although not built for speed, the Lipizzaner is ideally suited to the school disciplines because of its powerful quarters. The fine, silky tail is set high.

LIMBS •
Short, powerful limbs, with flat joints, good bone and hard hooves are characteristic of the Lipizzaner, and a legacy of the rocky, limestone country around Lipizza.

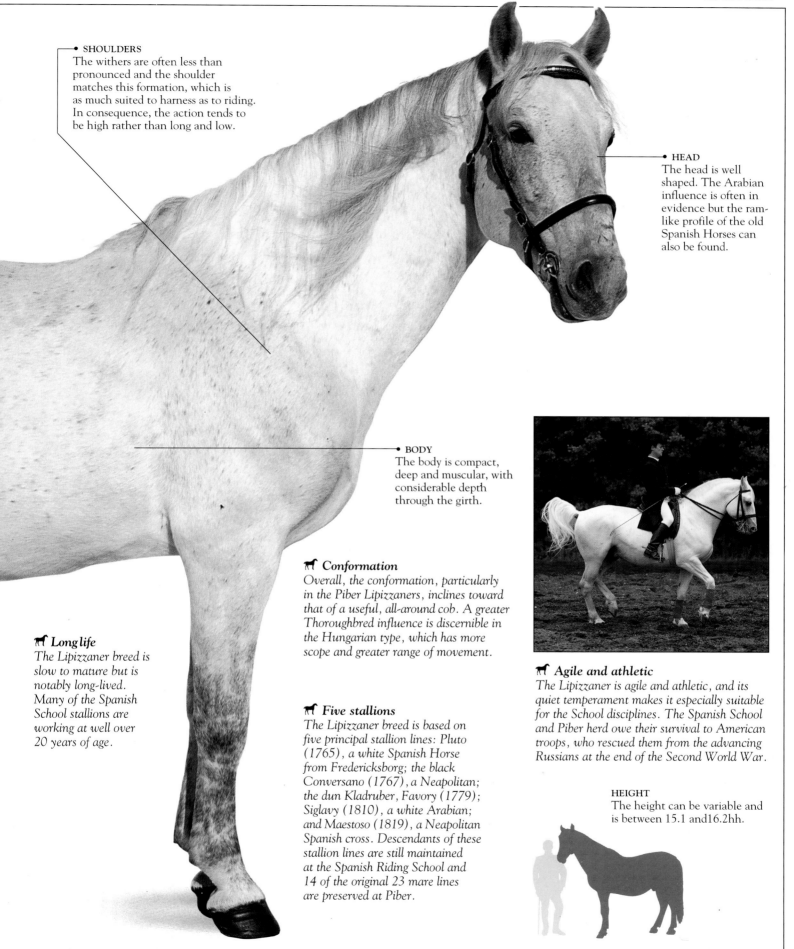

SHOULDERS
The withers are often less than pronounced and the shoulder matches this formation, which is as much suited to harness as to riding. In consequence, the action tends to be high rather than long and low.

HEAD
The head is well shaped. The Arabian influence is often in evidence but the ram-like profile of the old Spanish Horses can also be found.

BODY
The body is compact, deep and muscular, with considerable depth through the girth.

🐎 **Conformation**
Overall, the conformation, particularly in the Piber Lipizzaners, inclines toward that of a useful, all-around cob. A greater Thoroughbred influence is discernible in the Hungarian type, which has more scope and greater range of movement.

🐎 **Long life**
The Lipizzaner breed is slow to mature but is notably long-lived. Many of the Spanish School stallions are working at well over 20 years of age.

🐎 **Five stallions**
The Lipizzaner breed is based on five principal stallion lines: Pluto (1765), a white Spanish Horse from Fredericksborg; the black Conversano (1767), a Neapolitan; the dun Kladruber, Favory (1779); Siglavy (1810), a white Arabian; and Maestoso (1819), a Neapolitan Spanish cross. Descendants of these stallion lines are still maintained at the Spanish Riding School and 14 of the original 23 mare lines are preserved at Piber.

🐎 **Agile and athletic**
The Lipizzaner is agile and athletic, and its quiet temperament makes it especially suitable for the School disciplines. The Spanish School and Piber herd owe their survival to American troops, who rescued them from the advancing Russians at the end of the Second World War.

HEIGHT
The height can be variable and is between 15.1 and 16.2hh.

Budonny

THE BUDONNY IS TYPICAL of the move begun in the USSR during the 1920s to create new breeds – a process that involved complex experiments in crossbreeding. Originally intended as a cavalry horse of endurance, today it is a specialized riding horse that is good enough to compete internationally at show jumping and dressage, as well as race over fences.

BREEDING
The Budonny breed is based on Chernomor (similar to the Don but lighter and smaller) and Don mares crossed with Thoroughbred stallions. Kazakh and Kirgiz crosses were also involved, though less successfully. The progeny was reared carefully on a generous diet, and performance tested at 2 and 4 years of age.

Of the 657 mares used in the original experiment to produce the Budonny, 359 were Anglo-Don (a Thoroughbred cross), 261 Anglo-Don x Chernomor and 37 Anglo-Chernomor. These mares were put to Anglo-Don stallions, halfbreds that are regarded as the breed's foundation. When Thoroughbred characteristics were insufficiently pronounced in mares, they were re-crossed with Thoroughbred stallions.

NECK AND SHOULDERS
The long, straight neck runs into high withers and is joined to a reasonably sloped shoulder. The shoulder, however, lacks the length of that of the Thoroughbred.

SKIN
The head is "dry," veins show clearly through the fine, supple skin.

Head
Overall, the neck and head are of good proportion, with the head having a straight or slightly concave profile. It is a handsome, quality head that shows the Thoroughbred influence.

LIMBS
The limbs are fine and light, though there are some failings in the size and quality of joints.

FORELEG
An original fault in the breed was splayed forelegs, resulting in clumsy action. Don/Kazakh crosses suffered from this failing.

BONE
Pasterns are usually properly sloped. Bone is inclined to be light in comparison with the body, but the medium-size hooves are quite well formed.

The Tersk (right)
Another Russian creation, the Tersk, was developed between 1921 and 1950 at the Tersk and Stavropol Studs in the Northern Caucasus. The Tersk is founded on the Strelets Arabian – a part-bred produced by crossing Arabian stallions with Orlov and Orlov-Rastopchin mares. Thoroughbreds were also involved in the Strelets make-up to a lesser degree. By the early 1920s, the Strelets had nearly died out. What stock remained was transferred to Tersk, where the new breed was created. The Tersk, a beautiful horse, retains the Arabian appearance and movement.

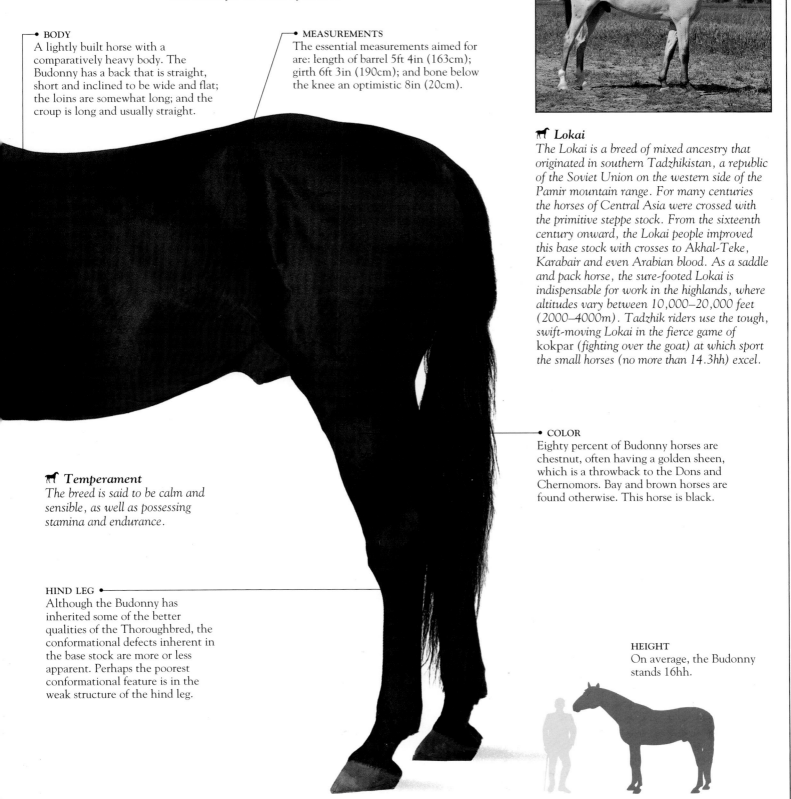

🐎 Endurance
The Budonny is rigorously tested on the racetrack and over long distances. A Budonny has won the Czechoslovakian Pardubice Chase. Another Budonny stallion, Zanos, covered 192 miles (309km) under saddle in 24 hours; he was ridden for 20 hours of the 24.

BODY
A lightly built horse with a comparatively heavy body. The Budonny has a back that is straight, short and inclined to be wide and flat; the loins are somewhat long; and the croup is long and usually straight.

MEASUREMENTS
The essential measurements aimed for are: length of barrel 5ft 4in (163cm); girth 6ft 3in (190cm); and bone below the knee an optimistic 8in (20cm).

🐎 Lokai
The Lokai is a breed of mixed ancestry that originated in southern Tadzhikistan, a republic of the Soviet Union on the western side of the Pamir mountain range. For many centuries the horses of Central Asia were crossed with the primitive steppe stock. From the sixteenth century onward, the Lokai people improved this base stock with crosses to Akhal-Teke, Karabair and even Arabian blood. As a saddle and pack horse, the sure-footed Lokai is indispensable for work in the highlands, where altitudes vary between 10,000–20,000 feet (2000–4000m). Tadzhik riders use the tough, swift-moving Lokai in the fierce game of kokpar (fighting over the goat) at which sport the small horses (no more than 14.3hh) excel.

🐎 Temperament
The breed is said to be calm and sensible, as well as possessing stamina and endurance.

COLOR
Eighty percent of Budonny horses are chestnut, often having a golden sheen, which is a throwback to the Dons and Chernomors. Bay and brown horses are found otherwise. This horse is black.

HIND LEG
Although the Budonny has inherited some of the better qualities of the Thoroughbred, the conformational defects inherent in the base stock are more or less apparent. Perhaps the poorest conformational feature is in the weak structure of the hind leg.

HEIGHT
On average, the Budonny stands 16hh.

Kabardin

THE KABARDIN, the breed of the Northern Caucasus, is derived from the horses of the steppe people crossed with Karabakh, Persian and Turkmen strains. This mountain horse, well-known since the sixteenth century, is capable of working in difficult terrain and is undeterred by snow and fast rivers. Temperamentally, it is a tractable and obedient animal, being both hardy and infinitely enduring.

🐎 **Work horse** (left)
Although the Kabardin is considered primarily to be a saddle horse, it can also be used for every sort of work in harness, as shown in this seventeenth-century etching.

MODERN TYPE

Following the Russian Revolution, the breed was much improved by the Kabardin-Balkar and Karachaev-Cherkess Studs. These studs created a stronger type for riding and agricultural work. The Kabardin is the principal breed of the Kabardin-Balkar Republic, and is used to improve native stock in Armenia, Azerbaijan, Dagestan, Georgia and Osetia.

The best Kabardins are raised at the Malo-Karachaev and Malkin studs. They are kept out but are given extra feed in the winter and they are performance-tested on the racetrack – the breed is noted for its endurance over distance.

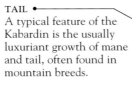

TAIL
A typical feature of the Kabardin is the usually luxuriant growth of mane and tail, often found in mountain breeds.

COLOR
Predominant colors found in the breed are bay, dark bay and black, as here, without other distinguishing marks.

HIND LEGS
Mountain horses, as a rule, do not have hind legs that are perfect. The Kabardin is no exception, the hind legs usually being sickle-shaped.

HOOVES
Strong hooves are usual in the breed. They can be worked without shoes on the roughest ground.

🐎 **Mountain home**
The Kabardin is at home in the mountains and has developed characteristics that are suited to the terrain and the rigors of the climate. It is sure-footed and agile and has an uncanny ability to find its way in mist and darkness.

• BACK
The back is short and straight and the quarters slope away from the croup. The loins, though very strong, are often slightly concave.

• NECK
The neck is of medium length and well muscled. It runs into somewhat flat withers that give the shoulders a lumpy appearance.

• POLL
Between the ears, the poll is curiously narrow and the occipital crest is ill-defined.

• SHOULDERS
By western standards, the shoulders are loaded and even straight, which accounts for the high action – not a disadvantage in the mountain horse but not, of course, conducive to speed.

EARS
The ears are very sharp, alert and mobile.

🐎 Action
The paces are good and the Kabardin is especially sure-footed. The walk is even and rhythmical, the trot and canter light and smooth. Some Kabardins are natural pacers.

🐎 Head
The thick-set Kabardin has a long head to match its general proportions, although the skin is fine. The profile is Roman nosed and the impression is that of a typical steppe horse, whose roots extend to the primitive Asian Wild Horse and the Tarpan.

• FORELEGS
The forelegs are a good feature. They are strong and clean, with clearly defined tendons, good joints and short, strong cannons. The bone measurement, which is 7–8in (17–20cm), is more than sufficient in relation to the build.

HEIGHT
On average, stallions are 15.2hh and mares 15hh.

🐎 Anglo-Kabardin
The Anglo-Kabardin was created by crossing Kabardins and Thoroughbreds. Anglo-Kabardins are bigger, faster and nearer to the Thoroughbred in conformation but are well suited to the climate of the Caucasus.

Don

T HE DON is traditionally associated with the Don Cossacks, and evolved in the eighteenth and nineteenth centuries. Its foundations were the steppe horses of the nomadic tribes. Early influences were the Mongolian Nagai and breeds like the Karabakh, the Persian Arabian and the Turkmen.

HISTORY

Don horses were hardly pampered. They lived in herds on the steppe pastures and fended for themselves, scraping away the snow in winter to get at the frozen grass beneath. The Don is not a prepossessing specimen but it is incredibly tough and adapts easily to every sort of climatic hardship.

The breed and its riders became famous in 1812–14 when 60,000 Cossacks, mounted on Dons, helped to repel Napoleon's forces from Russia. Dons were then improved using Orlovs (see pp.60–61), Thoroughbreds and Strelets Arabians, high-class part-breds from the Strelets Stud. No other blood has been introduced since the early twentieth century, when the breed emerged as a solid army remount that could be put in harness, requiring minimum attention.

NECK
The neck is of medium length and usually straight.

HEAD
The head is of medium size with a straight profile. The short, constricted poll makes flexion difficult.

COLOR
This Don is light bay although the predominant colors are chestnut and brown, often with a golden sheen.

FORELEGS
The forelegs are usually well muscled but there is a tendency toward calf knees, that is, an inward curve below the knee.

 Karabakh (left)
The Karabakh, a principal influence on the Don, was established as long ago as the fourth century, and originates in the mountains of Karabakh in Azerbaijan. The best are bred at the Akdam Stud where they are crossed with Arabian stallions. The Karabakh stands at about 14hh, has a calm temperament and good action. Like many of the eastern Russian breeds, it usually has the metallic, golden dun coloring. It is performance-tested on the racetrack and is used in games like chavgan – a form of polo – and surpanakh – a type of mounted basketball.

BODY
The modern Don is a comparatively, massively framed horse with a strong constitution to match. Its faults include short, straight shoulders that limit the length of stride but the chest is well developed and the ribs long and well sprung.

BACK
The back is straight and wide, the withers low and the loin straight.

Budonny Stud
The Don is raced, mainly in long-distance events, and the present-day horse is larger and of better conformation than formerly. Some of the best are bred at the Budonny Stud, where the Budonny Horse was developed as the result of crossing Don mares with Thoroughbred stallions.

QUARTERS
The croup is rounded and the quarters tend to slope away, the tail being occasionally low-set.

Bringing in the harvest (above)
Don horses are good-natured, calm and easily managed and quite able to work in harness and in light, agricultural draft. Energetic workers, with a high level of endurance, they do not demand any special attention. The early Don was inclined to be wiry, but later developments have produced a heavier horse.

HIND LEGS
The hind legs have a tendency to be sickle-hocked and, in the old types, the pelvic corner was so placed that it restricted the freedom of movement.

Action
Because of the conformational deficiencies that, in addition to the straight shoulder and faulty forelegs, include somewhat upright pasterns, the action of the Don is sometimes restricted and rough. It is regular but neither elegant, elastic nor very comfortable.

HEIGHT
The Don stands at about 15.3hh but is sometimes larger.

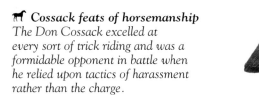

Cossack feats of horsemanship
The Don Cossack excelled at every sort of trick riding and was a formidable opponent in battle when he relied upon tactics of harassment rather than the charge.

Morgan

THE MORGAN is used for hunting, jumping, in dressage and for competing in the more artificial Park classes, either under saddle or between the shafts. It is also used for western and pleasure riding, driving and trail riding. It owes its existence to a phenomenal stallion of unprecedented prepotency, Justin Morgan, the undisputed sire of the first American breed.

⚘ Morgan colt
This stylized depiction of a Morgan colt would meet the Morgan Horse Association's breed standards in some respects, but not in others!

HISTORY

Justin Morgan, a dark bay, was a horse of no more than 14hh. He was born in either 1789 or 1793 at West Springfield, Massachussetts and was originally called Figure. He came into the possession of the schoolmaster Justin Morgan, after whom he was named, in 1795 and he died in 1821. He worked incredibly hard plowing, hauling and clearing woodland, but through all his lifetime of hard work and exploitation, he was never beaten in hauling matches or in races, either under saddle or in harness.

All Morgans trace to Justin Morgan through his most famous sons: Sherman, Woodbury and Bullrush. The breed played a large part in the evolution of the Standardbred, the Saddlebred and the Tennessee Walking Horse, and it was the chosen remount for the US Army until mechanization.

TAIL •
The show Morgan is always exhibited with a long, flowing tail that reaches to the ground when the horse is not in movement.

QUARTERS •
The official standard of the American Morgan Horse Association stipulates, at length, perfect quarters and hind legs – and they usually are very good.

⚘ Origin of Justin Morgan
The breeding of Justin Morgan, the foundation stallion, has never been established. There are suggestions that an early Thoroughbred, True Briton, was the sire. Others attribute the horse to a Friesian import, and the Welsh claim him as the progeny of a Welsh Cob, which is not probable.

• LIMBS
The Morgan's cannon bones are short and, though the limbs are slender, there is plenty of bone and the joints are particularly well formed. The pasterns are strong, of medium length and not too sloping.

⚘ Show horse
The modern Morgan, shod to produce an elevated action, is a popular show horse in America. Although tractable and versatile, the Morgan moves with great fire and spirit.

• NECK
The neck must be well crested, of medium length and very clean through the throat. The withers are clearly defined but slightly higher than the point of the hip.

• MANE
The mane and forelock are full and the hair is soft and silky, never harsh.

• SHOULDERS
Sloped well from the withers, the shoulders are of particular strength. The neck joins low at the point of the shoulder.

EARS
The ears are pointed and set wide apart.

BODY •
The body is distinctive. The back is short, broad and muscled, the barrel large and round, the chest wide and deep and the whole close-coupled.

• COLOR
Morgan colors are bay, as here, black, brown and chestnut. There are no grays or part-colors.

Head
The Morgan has a medium-sized head that is clean-cut and tapers from jaw to muzzle. The profile is straight or just slightly dished, but never Roman-nosed. The muzzle is fine, of medium size and with small, firm lips and large nostrils. The eyes are large and bright.

Action
The walk is long, straight and elastic; the trot very free, straight, well balanced and collected; the canter is smooth and easy, straight and in balance.

HEIGHT
The height is from 14.1–15.2hh. Some may be a little over or under.

Temperament
The Morgan is a spirited and courageous horse but easily handled and intelligent. It is also a hard, versatile horse, very powerful, well proportioned in all respects, and possesses great stamina.

• HOOVES
All hooves are round, of medium size and of smooth, dense horn.

Quarter Horse

THE AMERICAN QUARTER HORSE is the first all-American breed. A distinctive type, it was bred in Virginia and the Seaboard Settlements very early in the seventeenth century. Its supporters claim that it is "the most popular horse in the world." To support that claim, there are more than 2½ million entries in the American Quarter Horse Association's register.

🐎 *Old "Bulldog"* (above)
The old "Bulldog" stamp of Quarter Horse was the equivalent of a strongly built, human 100-yard sprinter – muscular and fast.

HISTORY

The first significant import of English horses to Virginia was in 1611, well before the establishment of the Thoroughbred in England. Therefore, they would have had a background of native, eastern and Spanish blood. Crossed with the stock of Spanish origin already in America, these horses became the foundation for the Quarter Horse, which quickly evolved into a compact horse with massively muscled quarters.

The settlers used them for farm work, herding cattle, hauling lumber, in light harness and under saddle. The sport-loving, English settlers also raced them on quarter-mile stretches – hence the name Quarter Horse. This also explains why the breed developed an explosive ability to sprint over short distances.

In the West, the Quarter Horse made another name for itself as the perfect cow pony. Today, it excels as a trail mount, cutting horse, hunter and pleasure horse.

QUARTERS
Heavy, muscular quarters of depth and width are characteristic of this chunky horse.

HIND LEGS
The hind legs are heavily muscled through the thighs and gaskins down to the strong hock joint.

WIDTH
The stifle is very deep. When viewed from behind, it extends out below the hip and above the gaskin and is the widest part of the horse.

JOINTS
The cannons are short with the hock set low to the ground. There is no play in the joint other than directly forward.

UNDERLINE
The underline, or belly, is longer than the back and must never cut high into the flank to disturb the compact symmetry of the outline.

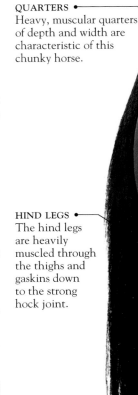

🐎 *Action*
The Quarter Horse became the perfect cow pony because of its speed, inherent balance and agility, and it developed an uncanny instinct for working cattle virtually independently of its rider. It was said that "he could turn on a dime and toss you back nine cents change."

• WITHERS
The excellent saddle back of the Quarter Horse is due to the well-defined withers that extend back beyond the top of the shoulder to hold the saddle firmly in place.

• NECK
The neck needs to be fairly long and flexible as the Quarter Horse works with its neck extended and its head down. An arched or crested neck would be undesirable.

• COLOR
The usual Quarter Horse color is chestnut but any solid color is acceptable. This horse is bay.

SETTING •
The head joins the neck at an angle of 45 degrees. There should not be too much thickness through the jowl, but the jawbones are wide apart at the top so as not to restrict the breathing.

HEAD •
The Quarter Horse does not have or need the Thoroughbred's length of head. Instead, it is relatively short and wide, with a small muzzle and a shallow, firm mouth.

🐎 Conformation
The photographic convention is to take the horse from a three-quarter, rear view to accentuate the massive quarters. In front, this chunky horse has powerful forelegs set wide, blending smoothly into the shoulder and deep, broad chest. It is essential for the pastern to be sloped (about 45 degrees). A straight pastern would not stand up to the powerful movement of the breed.

HEIGHT
The Quarter Horse stands between 15 and 16hh.

Hackney

THERE IS NO DISPUTING that the brilliant, high-stepping Hackney is the world's most spectacular harness horse. Today, it is largely confined to the show ring but it also has all the courage and ability to compete with equal distinction in competitive driving events. The early Trotters, on which the breed was founded, were noted for their speed and endurance under saddle and in harness. One Trotter, Bellfounder, trotted 2 miles (3.2km) in 6 minutes, and 9 miles (14.5km) in 30 minutes.

🐎 **Omnibus** (above)
Hackney Horses are commonly associated with the Hackney cab. Here, a horse is drawing one of the early omnibuses, a vehicle that originated in Paris.

ORIGINS

The origin of the word Hackney is doubtful but probably derives from the French *haquenée*. In Old French *haque*, a word related to the Spanish *haca*, means a "nag" or gelding.

The Hackney, both horse and pony, has its base in the tradition of English trotting horses of the eighteenth and nineteenth centuries. The pony also has a Fell influence through the Wilson ponies, bred by Christopher Wilson of Kirkby Lonsdale in Cumbria. There were two recognized English Trotters or Roadsters, those of Norfolk and those of Yorkshire. Both shared a common ancestor in the Original Shales, a horse born in 1755 out of a "hackney" trotting mare by Blaze. (Blaze was related to Messenger, founder of the American Standardbred harness racer.)

TAIL •
The tail is set and carried high.

COLOR •
Colors in both Hackney Horses and Ponies are usually dark brown, black, bay, as here, and chestnut.

LIMBS •
Limbs must be short with the hocks strong and "well let-down," i.e. not standing high from the ground. At rest, the Hackney stands firm and four-square with forelegs straight and the hind legs back to cover the maximum ground.

BODY •
Without undue length in the back, the body of the Hackney is compact but has great depth through the chest.

🐎 **Action**
Brilliance of action is always paramount in the judging of the Hackney. It has to be straight and true, with no cheating or throwing of the hooves from side to side.

🐎 **In harness**
A hackney cart is frequently one of the most exciting sights in the show ring. The vehicle that is used is very light, single-seated and fitted with four pneumatic wheels.

• HEAD
The head is small and the profile is convex with small, neat ears and a fine, quality muzzle. The eye is large and very bold.

Stamina
The high courage and stamina of the modern Hackney is largely due to the selective breeding of its ancestors, which was based, unconsciously, on a form of performance-testing, in the way of matches.

• SHOULDERS
The shoulders are powerful and the withers are low – not like those of a riding horse.

NECK •
The neck is fairly long and well formed. It rises almost vertically out of the shoulders.

• HEAD CARRIAGE
The Hackney head carriage is always high, and the expression is one of great alertness and spirit.

• COAT
The coat of both horse and pony is particularly fine and silky.

Hackney Pony (above)
The Hackney Pony combines the brilliance of Hackney action with real pony character. It was largely the creation of Christopher Wilson, who perfected a distinctive type based mainly on Fell Ponies crossed with selected Trotters and Roadsters.

HEIGHT
The Hackney Horse is 15–15.3hh on average, and the Hackney Pony does not exceed 14hh.

French Trotter

T HE SPORT OF TROTTING, both in harness
and under saddle, was established in
France in the early nineteenth century
and the first purpose-built raceway was
constructed at Cherbourg in 1836. The
development of the French Trotter
from the horses already in existence in
Normandy was a result of this interest.

ORIGINS
Supported by the Administration of
the National Studs, the astute and
forward-looking Normandy breeders
imported English Thoroughbred and
half-bred stallions, as well as the
incomparable Norfolk Roadsters, to
produce lighter, more active progeny
from their native mares. Chief among
the imports were The Norfolk
Phenomenon, a Roadster, and the
half-bred son of Rattler, Young Rattler,
both of whom exerted a profound
influence. The Thoroughbred, the
Heir of Linne, was also used. These and
other imported stallions resulted in five
important bloodlines to which most
modern French Trotters trace back.

STANDARDBRED BLOOD
In due course, infusions of American
Standardbred blood were made. This
was in order to give the Trotter more
speed, but it has had no effect upon the
unique character of the tough French
Trotter, which is now capable of taking
on, and beating, the best harness racers
in the world. In trotting races under
saddle, and 10 percent of all French
races are for ridden Trotters, the
French product has no equal. Ridden
races encourage the bigger, more
powerful horse, which is invaluable at
stud for a variety of purposes.

Apart from its contribution to harness
races, the Trotter has been instrumental
in the development of the Selle Français
(see pp.88–9) and is noted as a sire of
jumpers. The French Trotter was
recognized as a breed in 1922 and the
stud book closed to non-French entries
in 1937. Recently, however, it has been
opened just a little to permit the entry
of selected Standardbred crosses.

SHOULDERS •
Formerly the French Trotter
tended to have straight shoulders.
The modern Trotter has more
quality with good shoulders.

JOWL
*There is no thickness
through the jowl.*

🐎 Head
*As a fixed breed, the French Trotter has a
unique, characteristic appearance. The head of
the modern Trotter inclines more to the English
Thoroughbred than to the old Anglo-Norman
type of horse from which it descends. Though it
is less refined than that of the Thoroughbred, it
gives the impression of intelligence and spirit.*

🐎 Races

France's leading harness race is the Prix d'Amérique. The all-age championship of Europe, it is run at Vincennes over 1 mile 5 furlongs (2,650m). The premier ridden race is the Prix de Cornulier over the same distance. Ourasi, the leading French Trotter, completed a hat trick of successes in the top Prix d'Amérique in 1988, and broke a new kilometer record of 1 minute 15.6 seconds.

• QUARTERS
Immensely powerful quarters are characteristic of the modern French Trotter, which has replaced the somewhat coarse and rawboned animal of former times. The modern Trotter also has much more quality about it.

🐎 Racing rigs

In the 1890s, the original large wheels were replaced by smaller, bicycle-type, ball-bearing wheels fitted with pneumatic tires. They contributed to a notable increase in speed. The modern, modified rig, racing sulky, perfected by Joe King – an American aeronautical engineer – came into use in the 1970s and immediately produced record-breaking performances.

• COLOR
This French Trotter is chestnut. Predominant coat colors for the breed are chestnut, bay and brown. There are some roans but it is rare to find grays.

🐎 Vincennes

The Hippodrome de Vincennes is the leading French raceway. This 1¼ mile (2km) track is recognized as the supreme test for both the harness and saddle trotter. It begins downhill, then levels out until the last 1,000 yards (900m), which have a severe uphill gradient. Unique in the trotting world, it has helped to produce a similarly unique breed of trotting horse.

🐎 Speed

In 1989, the qualification time permitting entry in races for horses of four years and over was 1 minute 22 seconds over ³/₅ mile (1km).

🐎 Fuchsia

The most prepotent trotting line is that of Fuchsia, an English half-bred foaled in 1883. He sired some 400 Trotters, and over 100 of his sons were the sires of winners.

HEIGHT
Average height is 16.2hh. The bigger horses make the best ridden Trotters.

Orlov Trotter

T HE ORLOV TROTTER is one of the oldest and
most popular breeds in Russia. At the end of
the eighteenth century, the white Arabian stallion,
Smetanka, was used at the Orlov Stud with Dutch,
Mecklenburg and Danish mares. He left only five
progeny but among them was Polkan I, out of a
Danish mare that carried much Spanish blood.

🐎 Droshky (above)
*A Russian Droshky, presented to Queen
Victoria's husband, Prince Albert. It is drawn
by an Orlov wearing a typical Russian harness
that includes the arch, or douga.*

FOUNDATION STALLION
Polkan I was the sire of the Orlov
breed's foundation stallion, a gray
called Bars I out of a substantial, free-
moving Dutch mare. Bars I was foaled
in 1784 and was used extensively at the
new stud of Khrenov. It was at Khrenov
that from 1788 Count Orlov and his
stud manager, V.I. Shishkin, continued
to work on the evolution of the Orlov.

Bars I was mated with Arabian,
Danish and Dutch mares as well as
English half-breds and Arabian/
Mecklenburg crosses. Thereafter, the
policy was to in-breed to Bars and
his sons to establish the desired type.
The pedigrees of all purebred Orlov
Trotters show a strong connection
with the foundation stallion.

Training and a regular program
of trotting races were carried out in
Moscow from 1834 onward. Orlov
and Shishkin did a great deal to
encourage improvement in the breed
and to increase the performance levels.

🐎 Conformation
*The ideal Orlov combines
height with a light, powerful
build and an overall elegance
of conformation based on
good proportions throughout
the skeletal frame. The legs
are fine and set square, and
there should be pronounced
muscular development.*

COLOR •
The predominant
color, derived
largely from the
Arabian influence,
is gray. This Orlov
is a dapple-gray.
Black and bay are
also common but
chestnut is only
rarely found.

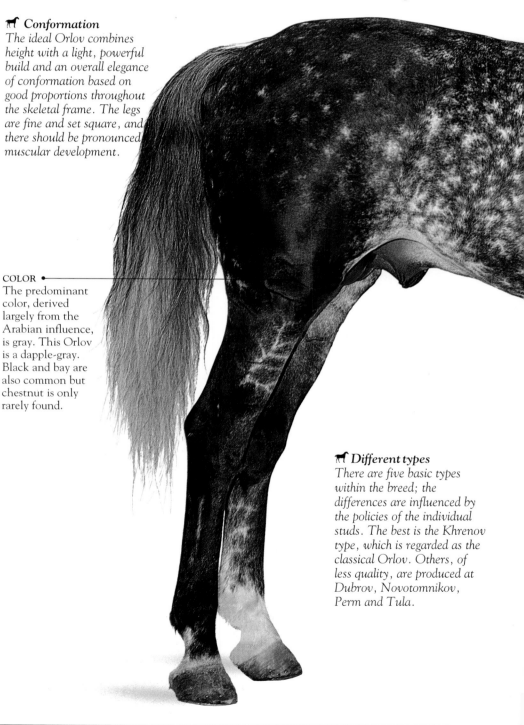

🐎 Different types
*There are five basic types
within the breed; the
differences are influenced by
the policies of the individual
studs. The best is the Khrenov
type, which is regarded as the
classical Orlov. Others, of
less quality, are produced at
Dubrov, Novotomnikov,
Perm and Tula.*

🐎 Troika
*The troika is a Russian method of harnessing
three horses side-by-side. The center horse
works at a fast trot. The out-spanners are bent
outward by tight side reins. They must canter
or gallop to keep up with the center horse.*

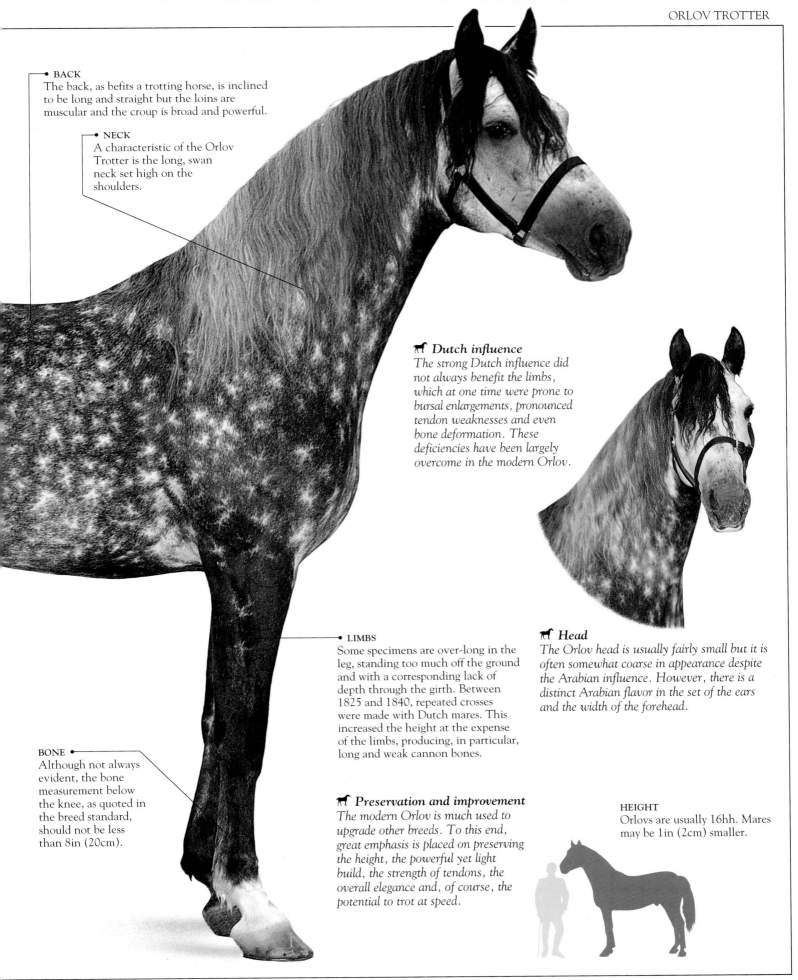

• BACK
The back, as befits a trotting horse, is inclined to be long and straight but the loins are muscular and the croup is broad and powerful.

• NECK
A characteristic of the Orlov Trotter is the long, swan neck set high on the shoulders.

🐎 Dutch influence
The strong Dutch influence did not always benefit the limbs, which at one time were prone to bursal enlargements, pronounced tendon weaknesses and even bone deformation. These deficiencies have been largely overcome in the modern Orlov.

• LIMBS
Some specimens are over-long in the leg, standing too much off the ground and with a corresponding lack of depth through the girth. Between 1825 and 1840, repeated crosses were made with Dutch mares. This increased the height at the expense of the limbs, producing, in particular, long and weak cannon bones.

🐎 Head
The Orlov head is usually fairly small but it is often somewhat coarse in appearance despite the Arabian influence. However, there is a distinct Arabian flavor in the set of the ears and the width of the forehead.

BONE •
Although not always evident, the bone measurement below the knee, as quoted in the breed standard, should not be less than 8in (20cm).

🐎 Preservation and improvement
The modern Orlov is much used to upgrade other breeds. To this end, great emphasis is placed on preserving the height, the powerful yet light build, the strength of tendons, the overall elegance and, of course, the potential to trot at speed.

HEIGHT
Orlovs are usually 16hh. Mares may be 1in (2cm) smaller.

Standardbred

I N AMERICA, HARNESS RACING attracts a following of over 30 million people. In many European countries, and in Scandinavia and Russia, it is more popular than Thoroughbred racing. The supreme harness racer is, without doubt, the American Standardbred, many of which can go one mile (1.6km) in around 1.55 minutes. A few are even faster.

🐎 **Ancestor** (above)
The incomparable Norfolk Roadster was a far-off ancestor of the Standardbred. In its day, it regularly carried 170lb (77kg) riders at average speeds of 15–16mph (24–27kph).

HISTORY

The term Standardbred was first used in 1879, and refers to the speed standard required for entry into the breed register. Separate harness races are held for conventional, diagonal trotters, and for pacers that employ the lateral gait. The pacer, faster and less likely to break gait, is vastly preferred in the USA. In Europe, trotters are more numerous.

The Standardbred was founded on Messenger, a Throughbred imported from England in 1788. He did not race in harness but, like all early Thoroughbreds, had trotting connections with the old Norfolk Roadster. The foundation sire of the breed is Messenger's inbred descendant, Hambletonian 10, foaled in 1849. He, too, never raced in harness but he had a peculiarity of conformation that contributed to his success as a sire of harness racers. He measured 15.3$\frac{1}{4}$hh at the croup, and 15.1$\frac{1}{4}$hh at the withers, a structure that gives enormous propulsive thrust to the quarters.

BODY •
The Standardbred is longer and lower than the Thoroughbred and without its quality and refinement. The croup in this powerfully built horse is always high.

QUARTERS •
Quarters are exceptionally powerful so as to deliver the maximum possible, forward thrust at the trot or pace.

HOCKS •
The hocks and the hind leg have to be very correct in their structure if the horse is to stand up to the demands of racing.

🐎 **Red Mile Raceway**
The popular sport of harness racing is featured at the famous Red Mile Raceway at Lexington, Kentucky. There are over 70 major tracks in America, which hold at least 50 meetings a year. All tracks are left-handed and evening racing under floodlights is the rule.

Increased speed
The greatest contribution to faster racing speeds was the introduction in 1892 of the light, bicycle-wheel sulky with pneumatic tires – an English invention. Star Pointer paced the first sub-2 minute mile five years later.

WITHERS
Withers are fairly well defined but may be lower than the croup.

SHOULDERS
The breed is notable for the strength of the shoulders and their perfect relationship to the neck.

COLOR
Colors are predominantly bay, as here, brown, black and chestnut.

STRENGTH
Iron-hard legs, very good hooves and the straightest of actions are essential for the Standardbred to race at high speed without risk of injury.

Head
Robust is a good description of the muscular, courageous Standardbred and the head can be described in similar fashion for, in comparison to the Thoroughbred, it is coarse and rather plain, though honest enough in its outlook.

HEIGHT
The Standardbred is, on average, 15.2hh.

Friesian

T HE COLD-BLOODED FRIESIAN, a descendant of the primitive Forest Horse of Europe, is bred on sea-girt Friesland in the north of the Netherlands. In Holland, it is an object of fervent admiration today, as in the past. Indeed, it occupies an important place in human history and among the equine races.

HISTORY

The Romans acknowledged the Friesian as a powerful working horse despite it being ugly, in their eyes. A thousand years later, it had become better looking, and it proved itself as an animal of strength, docility and endurance when it carried the Friesian and German knights to the Crusades. Contact with eastern horses improved the breed still more, as did the infusion of Andalusian blood (see pp.32–3) when Spain occupied the Netherlands during the Eighty Years' War.

Because the Friesian excelled in harness, under saddle and as a farm horse, it was much used to improve neighboring breeds. The famous Oldenburg (see pp.102–03) was founded largely on Friesian blood. England's Dales and Fell Ponies (see pp.150–53) were also influenced by it when the Frieslanders and their black horses formed the flank-guard for the Roman legions. Through its derivative, the Old English Black, the Friesian also influenced England's Great Horse, now the Shire (see pp.164–5), and also the Norwegian Døle Gudbrandsdal.

HEIGHT
The Friesian stands 15hh and upward.

TOPLINE
The relatively small Friesian has an impressive topline, accentuated by the arched and proudly carried neck.

HEAD
The head is long with short ears, but alert, finely drawn and very expressive of the breed's cheerful willingness and lovable character.

🐴 *A superb harness horse*
Because of its agility and temperament, the Friesian makes a good riding horse. However, it is as a harness horse that the breed excels, for it is beautifully balanced and moves impressively at an energetic, active trot. In its own land it is driven, to popular acclaim, to the traditional Friesian gig.

🐎 **Funerals** (left)
An engraving of the Duke of Wellington's funeral car drawn by black horses through London's streets. Because of their black coats, their presence and their notable action, Friesians were much in demand for the "funeral business." These same attributes meant that many also found their way to the circus ring.

🐎 **Døle Gudbrandsdal** (above)
The Døle Gudbrandsdal originates in Norway's Gudbrandsdal valley, yet it is very like the English Fell and Dales Pony, probably sharing similar ancestors, such as the Friesian. The close contact between Norway and England resulted in the Fresian being exported to both countries.

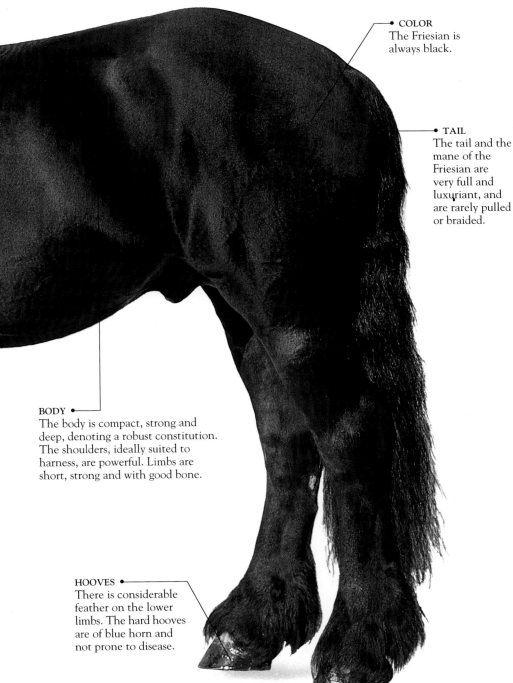

COLOR
The Friesian is always black.

TAIL
The tail and the mane of the Friesian are very full and luxuriant, and are rarely pulled or braided.

BODY
The body is compact, strong and deep, denoting a robust constitution. The shoulders, ideally suited to harness, are powerful. Limbs are short, strong and with good bone.

HOOVES
There is considerable feather on the lower limbs. The hard hooves are of blue horn and not prone to disease.

🐎 **Rear view**
The quarters of the Friesian are sloping and somewhat low-set, like those of the Dales Pony, which shows Friesian influence. They are strong, but not massive, as in the heavy draft breeds.

American Saddlebred

THE AMERICAN SADDLEBRED, originally called the Kentucky Saddler, evolved in the southern states of America in the nineteenth century. It was a practical horse, as well as one of great elegance. It could perform a variety of farm tasks; it could carry a man in great comfort over rough terrain throughout a long, working day; and it could also serve as a smart carriage horse.

ORIGINS

The American Saddlebred developed from the Canadian Pacer and the Narragansett Pacer (the work horse of plantation owners of Rhode Island), two naturally gaited breeds. Morgan and Thoroughbred blood was also introduced to produce a distinctive, impressive horse.

The modern Saddlebred, either three- or five-gaited, is generally regarded as a brilliant, if artificial, show horse, rather like the English Hackney (see pp.56–7). It is still shown in harness and, with its hooves trimmed normally, is used as a pleasure and trail-riding horse. It can also work cattle, jump and compete in dressage tests. Despite its versatility, however, the American Saddlebred Association still describes it as "America's most misunderstood breed" because of the artificial way in which it is produced and its show ring image of a cropped, high-set tail, over-long hooves and the use of somewhat dubious training aids.

🐎 Fire, speed and beauty
The specialized action is a legacy of the old, Spanish-based pacers and amblers. The American Saddlebred's fire, speed and beauty of form derive from the Thoroughbred.

🐎 Three-gaiters and five-gaiters
A three-gaited American Saddlebred performs at walk, trot and canter. Each gait is performed with high action and in a slow, collected manner. The five-gaiter has two additional paces, the "slow gait," a four-beat prancing movement, and the full-speed, brilliant "rack," a high, four-beat gait free from any pacing movement.

QUARTERS
The quarters are well muscled to the hocks, giving the necessary brilliance of action. The croup should be level and the tail set high.

TAIL
Three-gaited horses are shown with the mane roached and the tail trimmed. The supreme, five-gaited American Saddlebred is shown with full mane and tail. It is customary for the tail to be set high by nicking.

LIMBS
The strength of limb, without a heavy appearance, is a feature of the breed.

OUTLINE
The trunk is reminiscent of the English Hackney but conforms more to the riding requirement. The ribs are particularly well sprung and the outline, even when stood out in the show fashion, as here, is elegant.

• NECK
The neck is long and arched with no fleshiness in the jowl. It is set in the prominent withers, which give a high head carriage, one of the breed's signature features.

• HEAD
The head is full of quality – the eyes set well apart, the ears small and alert, the muzzle well shaped and the nostrils wide and open.

• WITHERS
The withers are clean, sharp and much higher than those of the pure harness horse. The back is notably short and strong.

• SHOULDERS
The Saddlebred has a particularly good, sloped shoulder. The scapula blades at the withers are placed fairly close together to give a wonderfully free action.

• COLOR
The range of permitted coat colors is surprisingly wide. Bay, as here, and chestnut are the most common colors, but blacks, grays and palominos occur, as well as the occasional roan. The coat hair is noticeably silky and fine.

🐎 *Elegance at large*
A champion Saddlebred at liberty, moving with great, natural elegance and freedom. The high carriage of head and tail is typical, adding to the stately presence of this uniquely attractive horse.

🐎 **Hooves**
To enhance the action, the hooves are grown unnaturally long and shod with heavy shoes. The pasterns are long and sloping to provide a comfortable, springy ride, which is exceptionally smooth.

🐎 **Harness performer**
The Saddlebred is a brilliant performer in harness. Show classes are judged on the quality of the walk and the arresting, controlled, park trot.

HEIGHT
The height is between 15 and 16hh, although sometimes it is a little more.

Missouri Fox Trotter

THE MISSOURI FOX TROTTER is one of the trio of North American, gaited horses. It was established in about 1820, although a stud book for the breed was not published until 1948. The breed evolved in the Ozark Mountains of Missouri and Arkansas, as the early settlers interbred Morgans, Thoroughbreds and horses of predominantly Spanish Barb ancestry.

Modern Fox Trotter
The modern Missouri Fox Trotter is an all-round pleasure and show horse. Although the stud book for the breed did not open until 1948, today there are well over 15,000 registered Fox Trotters. The breed is usually ridden in western tack.

HISTORY
The objective of the early settlers was to produce a fixed type of enduring, utility horse that would carry a rider comfortably and at a steady, mile-devouring speed over long distances and rough terrain. Following later infusions of Saddlebred and Tennessee Walking Horse blood, they created a compact, plain horse of amiable disposition that moved sure-footedly in a very smooth, peculiarly broken gait. The horse actually walks actively from the shoulder in front and trots behind, the hind hooves stepping on to the track of the fore hooves and then sliding forward. This sliding action minimizes the concussive effect and the rider is carried along while scarcely being aware of the movement. The horse can maintain this gait for long distances at a regular 5–8mph (8–13kph) and over short distances will reach 10mph (16kph). This is the famous Fox Trot gait. In it the horse is expected to move with style and animation, in perfect rhythm and with a degree of collection.

TAIL AND QUARTERS
The tail is inclined to be low set but the hind leg and quarter are, nonetheless, muscular and powerful.

LIMBS
The body is well muscled throughout, deep and relatively compact. The limbs are muscular, and the hind legs appear to be more heavily built.

Cayuse Indian Pony (left)
The Cayuse Indian Pony developed as a strain from the Spanish Mustang stock, although the name is sometimes used loosely to indicate the Indian pony of the American West. Many of the Indian ponies were poor specimens, but the Cayuse was noted for its qualities of speed, strength and hardiness. There is a possible connection to the Fox Trotter.

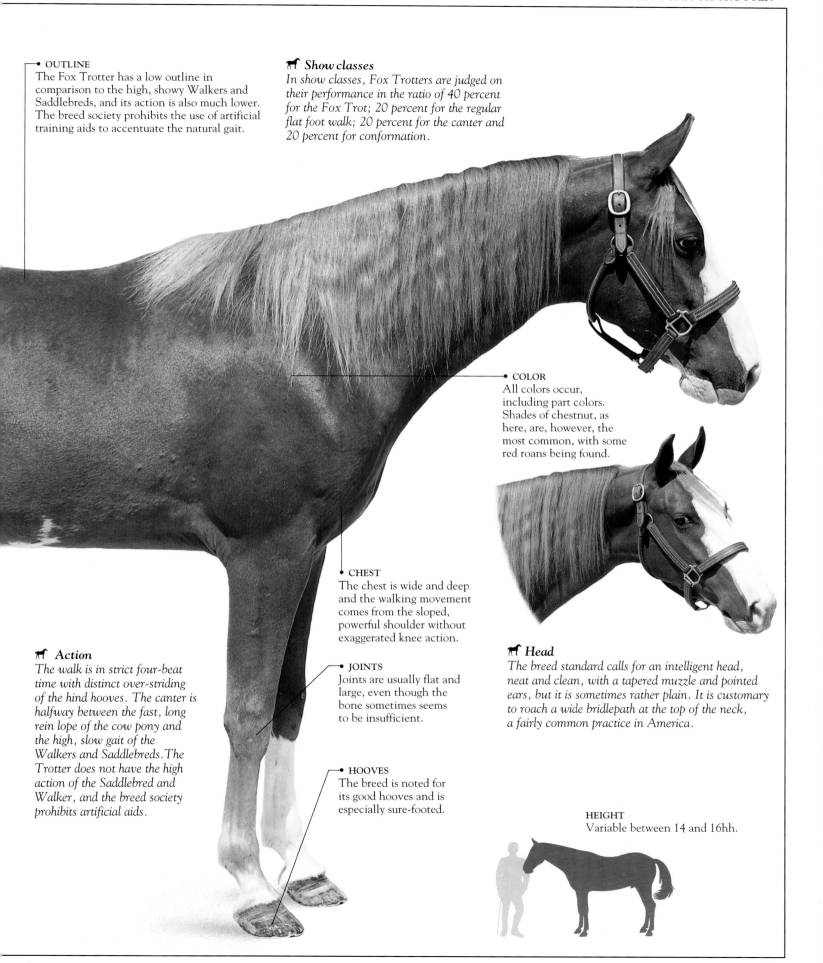

OUTLINE
The Fox Trotter has a low outline in comparison to the high, showy Walkers and Saddlebreds, and its action is also much lower. The breed society prohibits the use of artificial training aids to accentuate the natural gait.

Show classes
In show classes, Fox Trotters are judged on their performance in the ratio of 40 percent for the Fox Trot; 20 percent for the regular flat foot walk; 20 percent for the canter and 20 percent for conformation.

COLOR
All colors occur, including part colors. Shades of chestnut, as here, are, however, the most common, with some red roans being found.

CHEST
The chest is wide and deep and the walking movement comes from the sloped, powerful shoulder without exaggerated knee action.

Action
The walk is in strict four-beat time with distinct over-striding of the hind hooves. The canter is halfway between the fast, long rein lope of the cow pony and the high, slow gait of the Walkers and Saddlebreds. The Trotter does not have the high action of the Saddlebred and Walker, and the breed society prohibits artificial aids.

JOINTS
Joints are usually flat and large, even though the bone sometimes seems to be insufficient.

HOOVES
The breed is noted for its good hooves and is especially sure-footed.

Head
The breed standard calls for an intelligent head, neat and clean, with a tapered muzzle and pointed ears, but it is sometimes rather plain. It is customary to roach a wide bridlepath at the top of the neck, a fairly common practice in America.

HEIGHT
Variable between 14 and 16hh.

Tennessee Walking Horse

THE TENNESSEE WALKING HORSE is one of the unique, American groups of gaited horses. Its origins, like those of the American Saddlebred and the Missouri Fox Trotter (see pp.66–9), are in the southern states, all of which have their roots in early Spanish stock. The Walker evolved in nineteenth century Tennessee as a practical horse that could carry its owner in comfort for hours while inspecting crops on the plantations.

HISTORY

The breed traces back to the old Narragansett Pacer of Rhode Island. It evolved as a mix of Standardbred, Thoroughbred, Morgan and American Saddlebred blood. The foundation sire is recognized as the Standardbred Black Allan, who came from a line of trotters (not pacers) out of a Morgan mare. As a harness racer, Black Allan was a failure because of his peculiar walking pace, a characteristic that has now won his descendants wide acclaim.

The Walker is noted for three exceptional gaits: the flat walk, the famous running walk (the predominant feature) and the high, smooth, rocking-chair canter. All are said to be "bounce-free." In addition, the breed has a most amiable disposition and has the reputation of being the most reassuring horse for a novice or a nervous rider.

🐎 Ready for the ring
The Tennessee Walking Horse turned out for showing. Very long hooves assist the action, which is largely inbred and cannot be taught successfully to other horses. Boots are fitted for protection. Walkers that are not shod specially are called Plantation Walkers.

🐎 Temperament
The outstanding feature of the Tennessee Walking Horse is its temperament. Steady and reliable, it can be ridden by a beginner with absolute confidence. This, as well as the easy comfort of the movement, makes it a popular family mount. It is claimed to be the most naturally good-tempered of all horses and the most comfortable in the world.

QUARTERS ●
The horse's tail is grown long and is usually nicked and high-set. The quarters are strong and, in movement, the hind legs are brought well under the body.

🐎 Promotion
The Tennessee Walking Horse Breeders and Exhibitors' Association was formed at Lewisburg, Tennessee, in 1935. It promotes its breed by promising that if you "ride one today, you'll own one tomorrow."

LIMBS ●
The limbs are powerful, though not outstanding in terms of conformational correctness.

● HIND HOOVES
The hind shoes have elongated heels to accentuate the gliding movement.

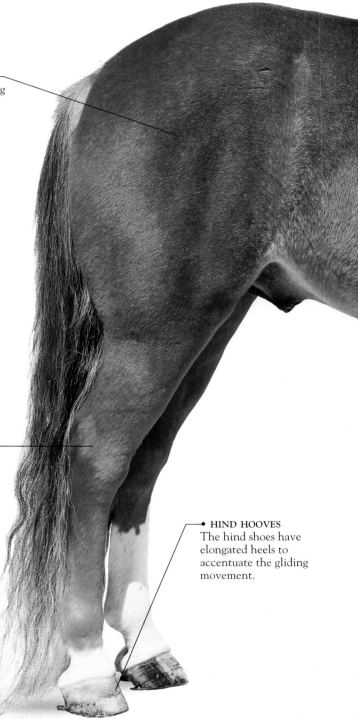

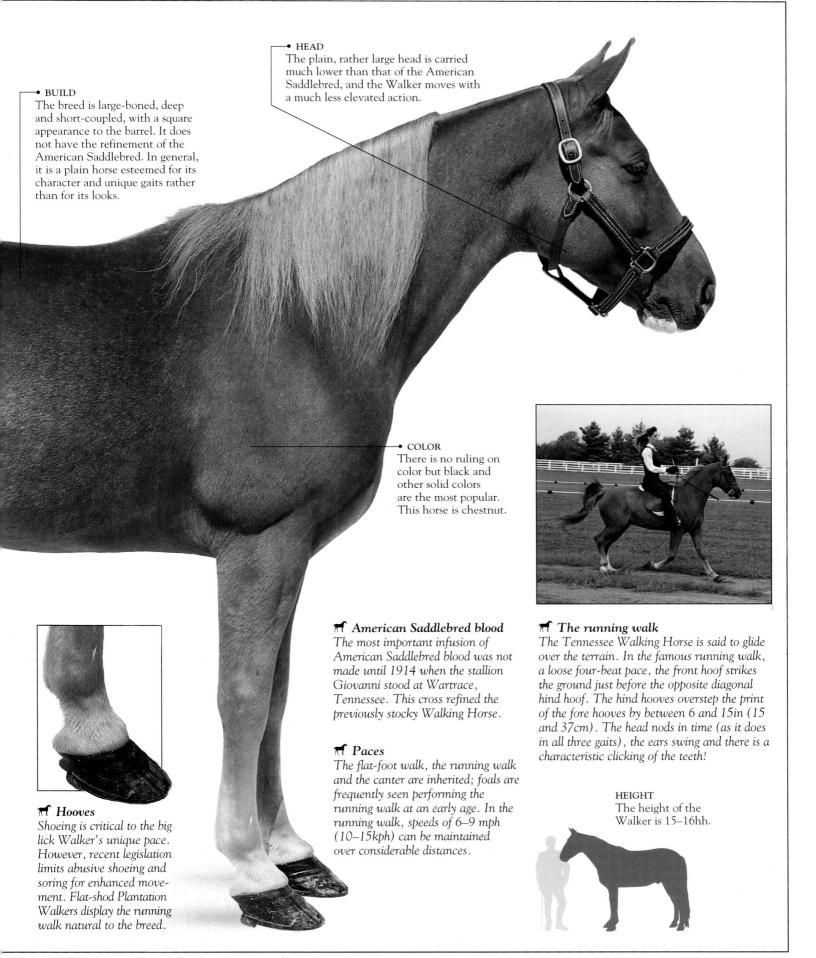

• BUILD
The breed is large-boned, deep and short-coupled, with a square appearance to the barrel. It does not have the refinement of the American Saddlebred. In general, it is a plain horse esteemed for its character and unique gaits rather than for its looks.

• HEAD
The plain, rather large head is carried much lower than that of the American Saddlebred, and the Walker moves with a much less elevated action.

• COLOR
There is no ruling on color but black and other solid colors are the most popular. This horse is chestnut.

☛ Hooves
Shoeing is critical to the big lick Walker's unique pace. However, recent legislation limits abusive shoeing and soring for enhanced movement. Flat-shod Plantation Walkers display the running walk natural to the breed.

☛ American Saddlebred blood
The most important infusion of American Saddlebred blood was not made until 1914 when the stallion Giovanni stood at Wartrace, Tennessee. This cross refined the previously stocky Walking Horse.

☛ Paces
The flat-foot walk, the running walk and the canter are inherited; foals are frequently seen performing the running walk at an early age. In the running walk, speeds of 6–9 mph (10–15kph) can be maintained over considerable distances.

☛ The running walk
The Tennessee Walking Horse is said to glide over the terrain. In the famous running walk, a loose four-beat pace, the front hoof strikes the ground just before the opposite diagonal hind hoof. The hind hooves overstep the print of the fore hooves by between 6 and 15in (15 and 37cm). The head nods in time (as it does in all three gaits), the ears swing and there is a characteristic clicking of the teeth!

HEIGHT
The height of the Walker is 15–16hh.

Peruvian Paso

THE PASO, meaning "step," of South America originates in Peru, with which country it is particularly associated. It is also bred in Colombia and in the United States, where it has achieved considerable popularity.

HISTORY

Horses were first brought to Peru in 1532 by the Spanish adventurer Francisco Pizarro (c.1478–1541), and over the centuries they have retained the lateral gait associated with the ambling, Spanish Jennet. Indeed, the gaits have been developed and perfected to such a degree that they are now regarded as a breed characteristic that distinguishes the Paso (thought to be 75 percent Barb and 25 percent Spanish, or Andalusian, blood) from the other Criollos of South America. These gaits allow the Paso to cover long distances over mountain passes and plains at a remarkable speed, while affording great comfort to the rider.

Highly selective breeding of this small, very specialized riding horse over hundreds of years has produced a most distinctive animal of great endurance. The Paso represents "the triumph of Peruvian horse breeding."

🐎 The Paso's gaits
The Paso Corto *is the normal, easy, traveling gait;* Paso Fino, *the slow, collected and elevated display gait; and the* Paso Largo, *an extended, fast gait. The Paso can reputedly reach speeds of 16mph (26kph) without discomfort to the rider.*

🐎 Conformation
The Paso is not a big horse nor does it have the characteristics of a galloper. It is a compact, muscular animal, broad and deep through the body and standing on short, strong limbs.

TAIL
A long, abundant tail of fine hair is well placed in rounded quarters. The skin is covered with fine, shiny hair.

HOCK JOINTS
To perform any of the three gaits, particularly over long periods of time, the hock joints must be large and particularly well constructed.

HIND LEG
There is exceptional strength in the construction of the hind leg, which is carried well under the body when the animal is in movement.

LIMBS
Sound limbs are essential in any riding horse, and those of the Paso are excellent, with exceptionally strong pasterns to meet the requirements of its unique gait.

HOOVES
Hooves of the Paso are strong and hard, and the horse is naturally sure-footed and agile.

• NECK
The arched, muscular neck is fairly short and in proportion to the frame. It sits well into the withers and the broad, deep chest.

• COLOR
Bay and chestnut, as here, are possibly the most common colors but every other coat coloring occurs, including part-colored coats.

SHOULDERS •
The shoulders are obviously strong and just sufficiently sloped to produce the required elevation in the forelegs. The Paso is able to canter, but rarely does so, preferring its natural gait.

🐎 The paso
Essentially, the paso is a four-beat, lateral gait in which the forelegs arc out to the side, rather like a swimmer's arms. The hind legs take very long, straight strides, the quarters held low with the hocks well under the body. There are three carefully preserved divisions to the gait, which is quite unlike the lateral movements of other gaited breeds. The combination of the loose, flowing foreleg movement with the powerful drive of the hind legs results in a ride of exceptional smoothness, which the horse can maintain over long periods of time.

🐎 Head
The flat and broad face complements the overall conformation of the Paso. The eyes are bright and very expressive; the muzzle and jaw are fine, although there is a natural thickness through the throat; and the Paso is intelligent, kindly and easily managed.

HEIGHT
The Paso stands between 14 and 15hh.

73

Mustang

THE TERM "MUSTANG" derives from the Spanish *mesteña*, which means a group or a herd of horses, and is applied to the "wild" horses of western America. The Mustangs were the mounts of Indian and white man alike. The Mustang was also the foundation for a large number of the American breeds. It retained many of the Spanish characteristics, especially in respect of color.

⚘ On the plains (above)
Both Indian, as shown here, and white settler made use of the Mustang, which is agile, tough and surprisingly fast.

ORIGINS

When the Spanish conquistadores landed on the American continent, the horse had been extinct on that continent for some 10,000 years. The Spanish introduced both horses and cattle to the New World. These cattle were the foundation stock for the great cattle industry that was to develop extensively during the nineteenth century.

Once the Spanish had become established, after the destruction of the Aztecs and other Indian peoples, numbers of Spanish Horses escaped or were turned loose and became feral. The Spanish Horses, which we now describe as Andalusians (see pp.32–3), were from the finest strains of Europe and were regarded as the foremost breed in Europe. They formed the nucleus of the great herds of wild horses that spread upward from Mexico into the United States and the western plains country.

At the beginning of the twentieth century, an estimated one million wild horses roamed the western states. By 1970, their numbers had been drastically reduced as a result of wholesale massacre to supply pet food and meat for human consumption. The Mustang is now protected by law and preserved by bodies like the Wild Horse Research Center at Porterville, California.

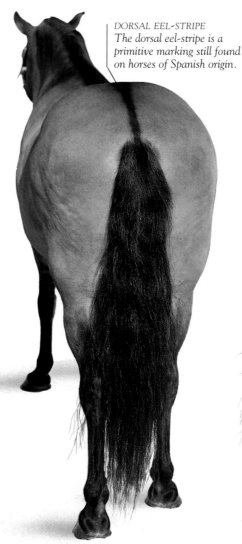

DORSAL EEL-STRIPE
The dorsal eel-stripe is a primitive marking still found on horses of Spanish origin.

HEIGHT
The height varies between 13.2 and 15hh.

⚘ Rear view
This Mustang, which in America might be called Spanish/Barb or Authenticated Barb, is an excellent specimen far removed from the degenerate, scrub "Mustang" of the past. The coloring and the luxurious tail confirm his Spanish ancestry. From horses like this came the Chickasaw Indian Pony, which influenced the evolution of the Quarter Horse (see pp.54–5).

COLOR
J. Frank Dobie, author of *The Mustangs* (1952) gives the colors as being: "bay and sorrel, brown and grullo (dark gray), roan, dun and gray, with here and there black, white and paint." All the equine colors, in fact. This Mustang is bright bay.

OUTLINE
The outline of this horse and his whole appearance is entirely Spanish. The impression is of strength combined with balance and athleticism.

PROFILE
This horse has the classic Spanish profile, the thick, crested neck and the luxurious growth of mane that is typical of the modern Andalusian. The old sort of Mustang was often much less attractive and many were heavy in the head.

FOREHAND
This is a good, strong foreleg and a powerful shoulder. The withers are not prominent but are typical of the old Spanish stock.

Hardness
Few wild Mustangs would compare in conformation to this well-made horse. Nonetheless, the wild horses retained the hardness of constitution that characterized their Spanish forebears.

LIMBS
The Mustang's legs and hooves, unprotected by shoeing, are hard and enduring and the horses are able to travel over the roughest terrain without the hooves becoming unsound.

New strains
Determined efforts are now being made to preserve what is left of the wild horses of America and, as a result, some very attractive strains are emerging. The Cayuse Indian Pony, which may have had the influence of Norman blood, is one, along with the Rocky Mountain Pony (see pp.106–07) and those whose Spanish/Barb ancestry is particularly evident.

Irish Draft

THERE IS NOT MUCH DOUBT that the Irish hunter is the best cross-country horse in the world. It is produced as the result of a Thoroughbred cross with what has been called "the horse of the countryside" – the Irish Draft, a versatile horse that can turn its hand to every sort of work.

ORIGINS
Very early in the breed's development, the indigenous stock of Ireland was upgraded by the ubiquitous Spanish Horse. The size and character came from the heavy European horses, mostly French and Flemish, which were imported into Ireland from the time of the Anglo-Norman invasion of 1172.

Subsequently, these strong mares were improved by more eastern and Spanish, or Andalusian, blood. The progeny were used for every sort of farming purpose, in harness and under saddle, on the small Irish farms.

The rich limestone pastures and the mild climate produced bone, substance and size, while the Irishman's innate love of hunting resulted in the Irish Draft developing an uncanny ability to get across country over the most fearsome of obstacles.

The cross with the English Thoroughbred gives quality, added scope and speed to the progeny without detracting in any way from the breed's inherited hunting sagacity.

COLOR
This Irish Draft is dapple-gray. All solid coat colors occur in the breed.

SHOULDERS
The shoulders of the older type of Irish Draft tended to be upright and the neck was short. These failings have been eradicated in the modern horse.

FOREHAND
The breed is naturally deep chested and, because of the improvement in the shoulder, the forelegs of the modern Irish Draft are well placed to give a longer stride.

HEIGHT
The height is about 16hh. Stallions often reach 17hh.

 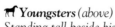 *Youngsters* (above)
Standing tall beside his mother, this foal has wonderful substance, bone and limb, and an arresting outlook. Progeny of the Irish Draft, usually the result of a Thoroughbred cross, are strong, well-grown animals that are increasingly making their mark in show-ring classes.

• BACK
Above all, the Irish Draft combines great substance with quality. Sometimes, the back may be a little long and the quarters too sloping, but in most cases the overall structure is one of splendid strength.

🐴 *Temperament and character*
The modern Irish Draft is a natural jumper, agile, very athletic and bold. The majority of the Irish Draft stallions that are registered with the Irish Draft Horse Society of Great Britain are regularly hunted and take part in jumping competitions. The breed is temperamentally equable, cooperative and economical to keep.

🐴 *Head*
The head of the Irish Draft, in relation to the size of the horse, is small and intelligent with a decidedly knowing look about it. The eye is generous and the expression honest – altogether a thoroughly workman-like sort.

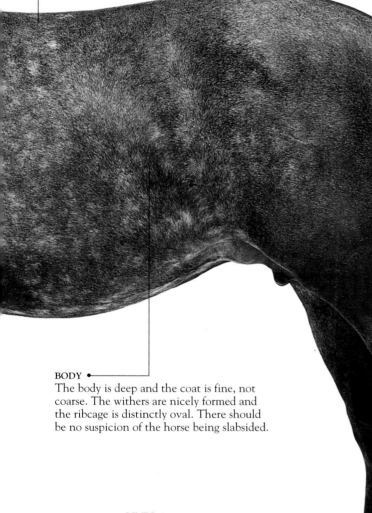

BODY •
The body is deep and the coat is fine, not coarse. The withers are nicely formed and the ribcage is distinctly oval. There should be no suspicion of the horse being slabsided.

LIMBS •
Irish Draft limbs are massive with good flat bone and no feather at the extremities. The old fault of being tied-in below the knee on the forelimbs has disappeared.

🐴 *Rear view*
Great strength in the jumping quarters is one of the great hallmarks of the Irish Draft. The action is straight, level and balanced. It is not exaggerated, but it is athletic and covers the ground.

Norman Cob

NORMANDY IS ONE of the world's greatest horse-breeding areas. For centuries, the studs of Le Pin and Sainte Lô in Normandy have produced a variety of horses, each one bred to fulfill a specific need. French Trotters, Percherons, Thoroughbreds, Boulonnais and Anglo-Normans are all kept, but also resident at both of these prestigious studs is a lesser-known but, nonetheless, very popular horse, the Norman Cob.

ORIGINS

Le Pin was founded as a Royal stud by Louis XIV in 1665. The first stallions were installed in 1730. Sainte Lô was founded by imperial decree in 1806 and by 1912 it housed 422 stallions.

At the beginning of the twentieth century, half-bred breeders were making the distinction between horses suitable as cavalry remounts and the heavier type that could be used in light draft. The tails of those heavier horses were docked, and soon the animals were termed cob after the English cobs they resembled. No stud book is kept, even though many cob stallions are kept at the national studs, but there is performance testing for young stock and the breeding is, of course, documented.

The La Manche region is the cob country of Normandy, and cobs are still regularly worked there. They perform various light draft jobs on the land and work in general farm transport. Over the years, the Norman Cob has become progressively heavier to meet the demands of the work it is expected to do but it has never lost its energetic paces nor its appealing character.

• NECK
A crested neck and a sensible head are typical of the Norman Cob.

BUILD •
The Norman Cob is stockily built throughout and is obviously strong and powerful, but it is not a true heavy breed and lacks the massive frame and proportions of the heavy horses. On the other hand, it is more active and energetic.

🐎 *Pack horses*
Normandy has always been a land of horses, and its people have used them for every sort of purpose. They supported this rich agricultural area, working the land, carrying produce to market and providing a means of transport. These pack animals carry wood in carefully designed panniers, and one carries the woodcutter's wife.

BODY
Just like the lighter English riding cobs, the Norman is compact through the body with a short, strong back running into powerful quarters. The barrel of the horse is characteristically deep and round and the strong shoulder is nicely sloped.

COLOR
The traditional coat colors of the Norman Cob are chestnut, bay or bay-brown, as here. Occasionally red-roan or gray occurs but rarely any other color.

🐎 *Mail coach*
Ancestors of the Norman Cob were the obvious choice to draw the mail coaches of the mid-nineteenth century. They were strong enough to cope with the poor roads and could trot steadily at a fair speed for long distances.

TAIL
The tails of the Norman Cob began to be docked early in the twentieth century, a practice still carried out in France although it is illegal in Britain.

🐎 *Action*
The modern Norman Cob is heavier than the sort bred earlier in the breed's history, which was closer to the riding type of horse and was bred in vast quantities for military purposes. It still retains, however, much of the activity and freedom of action, particularly at the trot – the working gait of the light draft horse.

LIMBS
The limbs of the Norman Cob are short and very muscular but they are lighter than those of the heavy breeds and do not carry the same profuse feather. Nonetheless, in the forelimbs the bone measurement is more than ample.

HEIGHT
The Norman Cob is bigger than its British counterpart, standing between 15.3 and 16.3hh.

Cleveland Bay

A S LONG AGO as the Middle Ages, a bay-colored pack-horse was bred in the northeast quarter of Yorkshire's North Riding, an area that includes Cleveland. It was known as the Chapman Horse because it carried the wares of the chapmen, who were the merchants, traveling salesmen and carriers of the day.

ORIGINS

The Chapman Horse was the foundation for the modern Cleveland Bay, later influenced by infusions of Spanish blood. There were numerous Andalusians in Northeast England in the latter part of the seventeenth century and there was also the Barb, for there was much trafficking between the Barbary Coast of North Africa and the northeast sea ports.

From this amalgam was bred, without recourse to either cart or, in later times, Thoroughbred blood, a powerful, clean-legged horse able, as none other, to work heavy clay lands and to haul considerable loads; a horse that could carry heavy men out hunting and was a notable jumper. Above all, of course, it was a coach horse unsurpassed by any other up to the reign of George II.

With the arrival of the paved roads, the Cleveland Bay was judged too slow for coaches able to travel at an average speed of 8–10mph (12–16kph). As a result, the Yorkshire Coach Horse, a Thoroughbred/Cleveland cross, came into being. The Yorkshire Coach Horse's stud book was only closed in 1936 when it was, to all intents, extinct.

NECK
The modern Cleveland Bay, though lighter than its predecessors, is especially powerful in its neck and through the shoulder.

COLOR
The Cleveland Bay is always bay with black points.

HEIGHT
Most Cleveland Bays stand between 16 and 16.2hh.

🐎 *Head*
The head of the Cleveland Bay still displays some characteristics that are reminiscent of the Andalusian (see pp.32–3), from which it is thought in part to descend, although these features are not so notable in the modern Andalusian as they were in his Renaissance ancestors. The sometimes convex profile, which in former days was termed "ram-like" or "hawk-like," is a typical characteristic of Spanish stock.

Mulgrave Supreme
By 1962 there were only four Cleveland Bay stallions in Britain. The breed survived largely because Queen Elizabeth II made available the stallion Mulgrave Supreme, originally destined to be sold to America. He was so successful that by 1977 there were 15 stallions, most of them being his progeny.

Constitution
The Cleveland remains an important cross with the Thoroughbred to produce jumpers, hunters, and, of course, superb carriage horses. It transmits to all of these size, bone, a hardy constitution, stamina and strength. Clevelands are among the longest-lived breeds and they are particularly fertile.

Royal favorites
Cleveland Bays have always featured at the Royal Mews, and great encouragement was given to the breed by the Duke of Edinburgh's successes with teams of Cleveland Bays and part-bred Cleveland Bays in international competition driving.

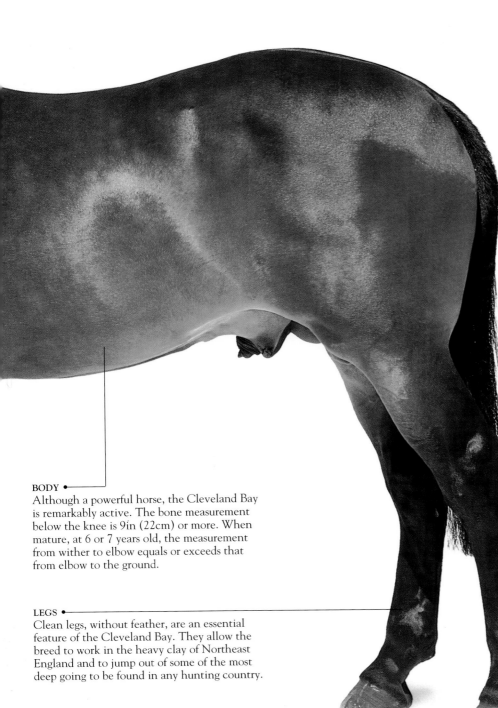

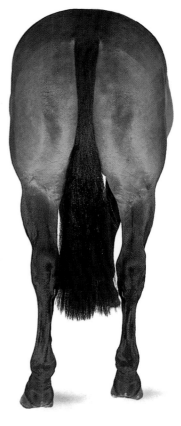

BODY
Although a powerful horse, the Cleveland Bay is remarkably active. The bone measurement below the knee is 9in (22cm) or more. When mature, at 6 or 7 years old, the measurement from wither to elbow equals or exceeds that from elbow to the ground.

LEGS
Clean legs, without feather, are an essential feature of the Cleveland Bay. They allow the breed to work in the heavy clay of Northeast England and to jump out of some of the most deep going to be found in any hunting country.

Rear view
Quarters big enough to carry a heavyweight "over a house," with second thighs, hocks and fetlock joints to match are common attributes to what is probably as good a heavyweight hunter as any in the world.

Gelderlander

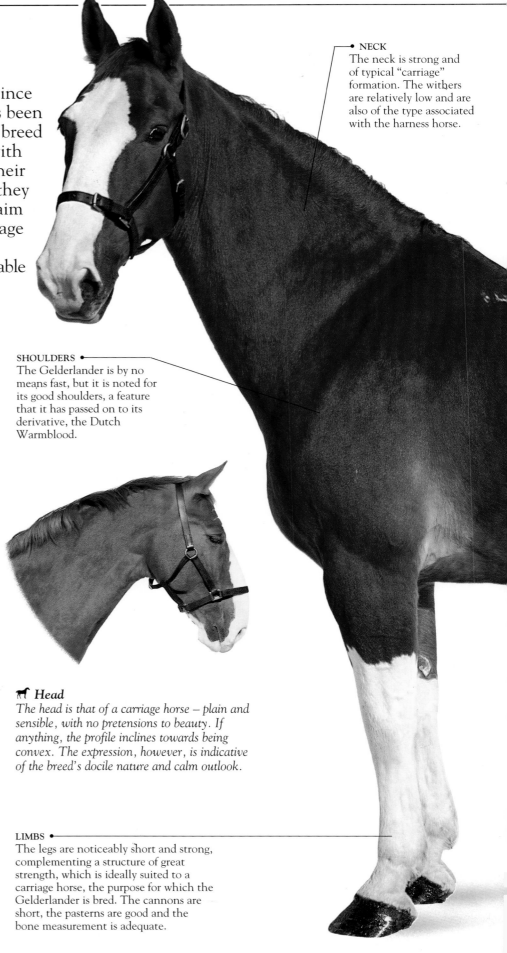

T HE BREEDERS OF THE GELDER province in the Netherlands have always been innovative and market-wise. They breed horses for their own use, but also with an eye on probable demand from their neighbors. One hundred years ago, they began on the Gelderlander. Their aim was to produce an upstanding carriage horse with presence and action, capable of light draft work and suitable as a heavy stamp of riding horse.

HISTORY

To obtain such a horse, while retaining the docile temperament that was considered essential, they crossed the dull, rather common, native mares with stallions from Britain, Egypt, Hungary, Germany, Poland and Russia. Then they interbred the best of the progeny until they obtained a fixed type. Later, they introduced Oldenburg blood and some of the lighter East Friesian Horses. Around 1900, a Hackney was used to add a spark to the breed. Since then, a little use has been made of French Anglo-Normans.

Much later, the upstanding, good-fronted Gelderlander was used with its heavier neighbor, the Groningen, as a base for the successful Dutch Warmblood (pp.84–5). The modern Gelderlander is still a high-class carriage horse, but, when broken to saddle, it has proved to be a reliable show jumper as well.

NECK
The neck is strong and of typical "carriage" formation. The withers are relatively low and are also of the type associated with the harness horse.

SHOULDERS
The Gelderlander is by no means fast, but it is noted for its good shoulders, a feature that it has passed on to its derivative, the Dutch Warmblood.

🐎 Head
The head is that of a carriage horse – plain and sensible, with no pretensions to beauty. If anything, the profile inclines towards being convex. The expression, however, is indicative of the breed's docile nature and calm outlook.

LIMBS
The legs are noticeably short and strong, complementing a structure of great strength, which is ideally suited to a carriage horse, the purpose for which the Gelderlander is bred. The cannons are short, the pasterns are good and the bone measurement is adequate.

🐎 Freedom of movement
Gelderlanders enjoying a canter around the field. Essentially carriage horses, they have the action needed for that usage but they also have good shoulders and move freely.

 Working as a team
An impressive team of powerful Gelderlanders, seen at the World Driving Championships. Gelderlanders excel in this field of competition.

BACK
The back, as is usual and desirable in the carriage horse, is a little longer than in a riding animal. It is strong and there is no suspicion of slackness in the loin.

QUARTERS
The croup is straight with the tail set high, a characteristic inherited by some European warmbloods. The quarters are structured for power, but are not conducive to speed.

Horse sleigh on ice
A scene of a Dutch horse sleigh gliding over the ice. Dutch breeders, particularly those of the Gelder, Groningen and Friesian provinces, took great pains to breed to the market requirements.

OUTLINE
The outline of the Gelderlander exemplifies the desirable carriage horse pattern. Strength, a proud bearing and a lofty, rhythmical action add to the presence of this attractive horse.

BODY
Good depth through the girth indicates stamina and endurance. The hind leg is well made and correct in its proportions, as well as being ideally suited for carriage work.

COLOR
The predominant color, and the one most associated with the breed, is chestnut, often with some white on the legs, as shown here, but grays are also found and once – long ago – a spotted horse or two.

HOOVES
The hooves are good. The old-type Gelderlander would have had more feather on the heel. The modern counterpart has practically none.

HEIGHT
The height can be between 15.2 and 16.2hh.

Dutch Warmblood

No OTHER EUROPEAN WARMBLOOD has been so skillfully promoted as the Dutch Warmblood but, in fairness, it has been produced with equal skill. There have been some notable performers, for example, the show jumper Calypso and the immortal Marius, sire of the charismatic Milton. There are also dressage horses such as Dutch Courage, which are of the classical warmblood breeding pattern.

🐎 **Active horse** (above)
The Dutch breeders were skillful in producing horses suited to the market needs. This elegant carriage, typical of the nineteenth century, is drawn by a surprisingly active, little horse.

ORIGINS

The Dutch Warmblood is essentially the product of two of Holland's indigenous breeds – the Gelderlander (see pp.82–3) and the heavier Groningen. Then it was refined by Thoroughbred blood and adjusted as necessary by using French and German warmbloods. The Gelderlander was created in the last century by the marketwise breeders of the Gelder province.

The heavier Groningen was derived from the Friesian and Oldenburg. It had powerful quarters but its front was not as good as that of the Gelderlander. The two were put together and the mix was adjusted by outcrosses to create a base for a competition horse. The carriage-horse action and the long, harness back were eliminated by the Thoroughbred and temperamental deviations were corrected by a return to the related warmbloods.

QUARTERS •
The powerful draft quarters of the old Groningen farm horse have been refined by the extensive use of the Thoroughbred.

COLOR •
Any color is acceptable but bay, as here, and brown are probably the most common. (There was once a skewbald strain in the Gelderlander but it does not appear in the Dutch Warmblood.)

LIMBS •
Dutch breeders have succeeded in producing a horse with good, sound limbs and hooves, and one with bone and substance. The short cannon is a noticeable feature.

🐎 **Dutch Courage**
One of the greatest promoters of the Dutch Warmblood is Jennie Loriston-Clarke, the British dressage rider, who has competed so successfully on Dutch Courage. Her displays in long reins, as here, and under saddle established the breed's reputation in Britain.

🐎 **Performance**
The Dutch Warmblood is already a proven performer in the show-jumping ring and the dressage arena although, like so many warmbloods, it is far less successful as a cross-country horse. The Gelderlander, from which in part it derives, is an excellent carriage horse that makes its mark in international events.

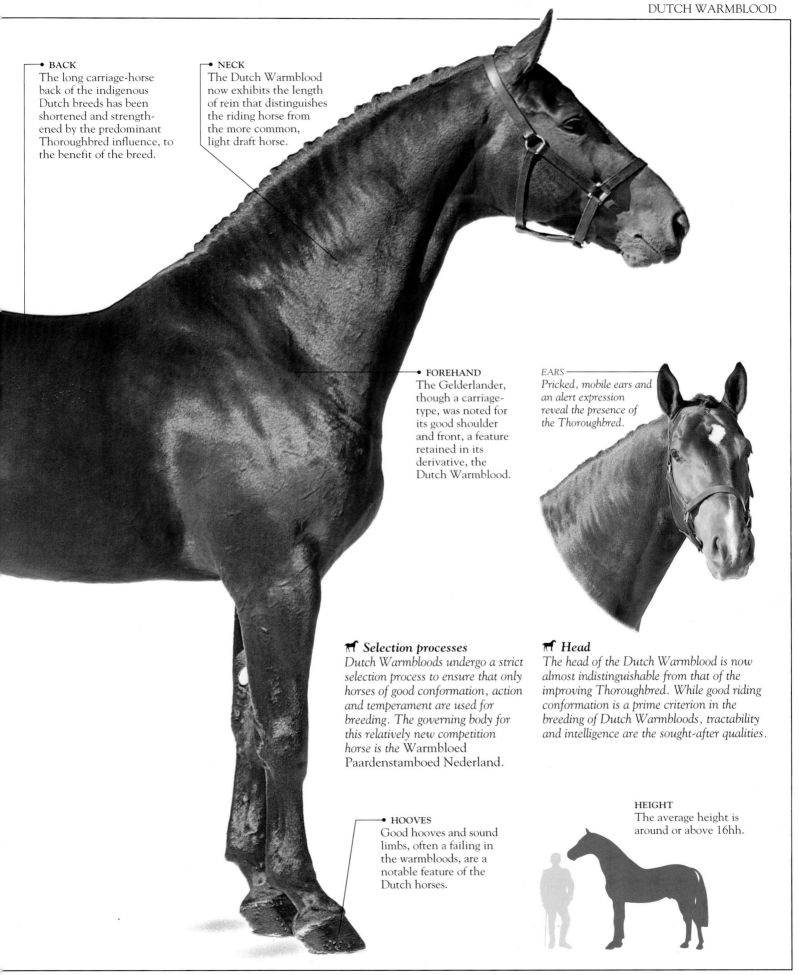

• BACK
The long carriage-horse back of the indigenous Dutch breeds has been shortened and strengthened by the predominant Thoroughbred influence, to the benefit of the breed.

• NECK
The Dutch Warmblood now exhibits the length of rein that distinguishes the riding horse from the more common, light draft horse.

• FOREHAND
The Gelderlander, though a carriage-type, was noted for its good shoulder and front, a feature retained in its derivative, the Dutch Warmblood.

EARS
Pricked, mobile ears and an alert expression reveal the presence of the Thoroughbred.

🐎 Selection processes
Dutch Warmbloods undergo a strict selection process to ensure that only horses of good conformation, action and temperament are used for breeding. The governing body for this relatively new competition horse is the Warmbloed Paardenstamboed Nederland.

🐎 Head
The head of the Dutch Warmblood is now almost indistinguishable from that of the improving Thoroughbred. While good riding conformation is a prime criterion in the breeding of Dutch Warmbloods, tractability and intelligence are the sought-after qualities.

• HOOVES
Good hooves and sound limbs, often a failing in the warmbloods, are a notable feature of the Dutch horses.

HEIGHT
The average height is around or above 16hh.

Frederiksborg

I N THE SIXTEENTH CENTURY, Denmark was a principal source of horses for the courts of Europe. Its product was the Frederiksborg, bred at the stud founded by King Frederick II in 1562. The stud aimed to breed elegant, active horses that would be suited to the disciplines of the *manège* and with sufficient spirit and quality to be used as military chargers.

ORIGINS

The foundation stock for the Frederiksborg was initially Spanish, then, and for centuries after, the foremost riding horse of Europe. Later, imports were made of Neapolitans, close relations of the Spanish Horse. By the nineteenth century, the breed had been outcrossed to eastern and British halfbred stallions. The result was a lively, riding horse of impressive appearance and scope and with an excellent, vigorous action. The Frederiksborg was admired throughout Europe for what Count Wrangel in *Die Rasen des Pferdes* (1908–9) described as his "elegant conformation, his lively and kindly temperament and his strong, sweeping and high action."

The breed was much used to improve other stock, such as the Jutland to increase its activity. One Frederiksborg from the Royal Danish Court Stud, the white Pluto, born in 1765, founded the important Lipizzaner line, which still exists today. In fact, the popularity of the Frederiksborg proved to be its undoing. Exports of the Frederiksborg became so numerous that the old breeding stock was seriously depleted and the stud turned to the breeding of Thoroughbred-type stock in 1839. Private breeders continued to raise Frederiksborgs to use as light draft/carriage horses. Recently, Thoroughbreds have been used on the breed with the object of producing competition horses, and it is unlikely that many of the old Frederiksborgs still exist.

🐎 Harness horse
The Frederiksborg conformation is predominantly that of an upstanding, quality harness horse of considerable strength. After the closure of the Court Stud, the Frederiksborg was used increasingly in harness.

FOREHAND •
The breed is broad in the chest, relatively short and upright in the neck and with an intelligent but plain head. The shoulders are powerful but somewhat upright and are more suited to harness than riding.

🐎 Traveling carriage
This typical, Danish, traveling carriage of the last century is drawn by a pair of strong, plain horses, which would probably have been related to the Frederiksborg. It seems unlikely, however, that they would have been purebred, as they can hardly be described as elegant.

• BACK
The back is strong and the neck runs into the fairly flat withers that are characteristic of the harness horse.

• COLOR
The characteristic coloring of the Frederiksborg is predominantly chestnut, as here. Other colors are rarely, if ever, seen.

🐎 **Influences on other breeds**
Locally bred mares of Frederiksborg character have formed the base stock for the Danish Warmblood (see pp.90–91). Outcrosses have been made to a number of European warmbloods as well as to the Thoroughbred and half-bred Danish horses.

• QUARTERS
The quarters are not of a structure associated with speed. The croup is typically level with the tail set high and carried well.

🐎 **Pleasing outline**
The outline of this Frederiksborg is pleasing. It can be seen that the strength of the frame would make the Frederiksborg a good basis for crossing with breeds like the Thoroughbred and Trakehner, both of which have been used in developing the Danish Warmblood.

BODY •
The body of the Frederiksborg can occasionally be a little long and, though the girth measurement is adequate, the horse seems to stand far off the ground. The joints are usually acceptable.

🐎 **Action**
The action is straight and high as befits a carriage horse. The trot is the Frederiksborg's best pace.

HOOVES •
The hooves of the Frederiksborg are strong and well shaped and are a good feature of the breed.

HEIGHT
The Frederiksborg stands between 15.3 and 16hh.

Selle Français

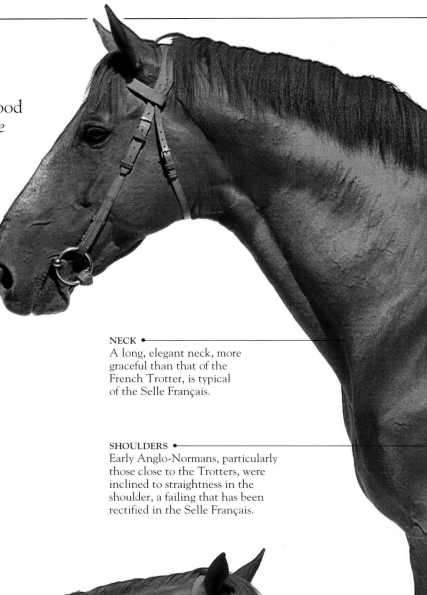

Since 1958, the French warmblood has been called *le cheval de Selle Français* (French Saddle Horse). It is as versatile as the Trakehner (see pp.92–3), and no breed is tougher or more agile. Like all warmbloods, it is a mix of breeds, but unlike them it owes much to fast trotting blood.

ORIGINS

In the nineteenth century, the skillful Normandy breeders imported English Thoroughbred stallions and half-bred stallions to cross with their tough but common, all-purpose Norman stock. Most of those half-bred stallions had a background of robust Norfolk Roadster. They produced two crossbreds, the fast harness horse, which was to become the French Trotter (see pp.58–9) and the Anglo-Norman, which was sub-divided into a riding horse and a draft cob. The former was the prototype for the Selle Français.

After the Second World War, the production of a riding horse possessing speed, stamina and ability was accelerated. Trotters, Thoroughbreds and Arabians have all contributed to the development of the type. Primarily, it is a show jumper, but it is also bred to race as AQPSA (*autres que pur sang association*, meaning "other than Thoroughbred"); many also participate in cross-country racing and eventing.

Of the existing breed, 33 percent are by Thoroughbred sires, 20 percent by Anglo-Arabs, 2 percent by French Trotters and 45 percent are by Selle Français stallions, some of whom have trotting connections.

NECK
A long, elegant neck, more graceful than that of the French Trotter, is typical of the Selle Français.

SHOULDERS
Early Anglo-Normans, particularly those close to the Trotters, were inclined to straightness in the shoulder, a failing that has been rectified in the Selle Français.

JOWL
There is no fleshiness in the jowl.

HEIGHT
Mediumweight Small: to 15.3hh; Medium: 15.3–16.1hh; Large: over 16.1hh. *Heavyweight* Small: below 16hh; Large: over 16hh.

🐎 Head

The head has now lost the coarseness of the breed's Norman predecessors. This increased refinement has come from the Thoroughbred and Arabian influence. Despite increased quality, the head of the Selle Français remains reminiscent of the French Trotter.

BONE
The Selle Français should have a very good bone measurement, no less than 8in (20cm). The old fault of small knees in the breed has been eliminated.

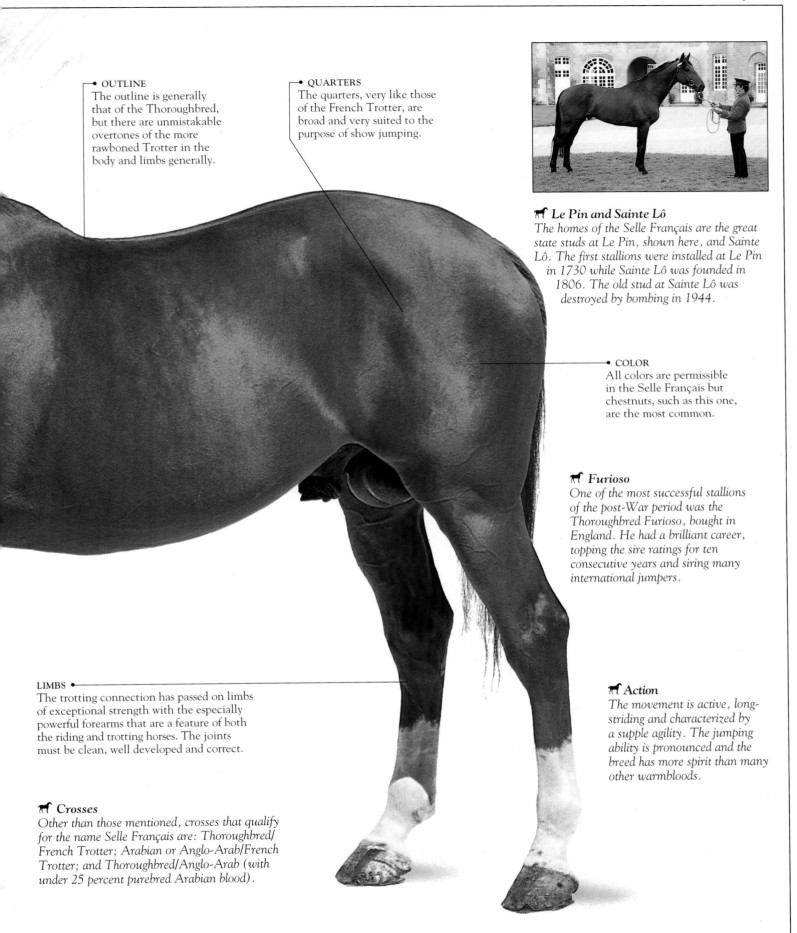

OUTLINE
The outline is generally that of the Thoroughbred, but there are unmistakable overtones of the more rawboned Trotter in the body and limbs generally.

QUARTERS
The quarters, very like those of the French Trotter, are broad and very suited to the purpose of show jumping.

🐎 Le Pin and Sainte Lô
The homes of the Selle Français are the great state studs at Le Pin, shown here, and Sainte Lô. The first stallions were installed at Le Pin in 1730 while Sainte Lô was founded in 1806. The old stud at Sainte Lô was destroyed by bombing in 1944.

COLOR
All colors are permissible in the Selle Français but chestnuts, such as this one, are the most common.

🐎 Furioso
One of the most successful stallions of the post-War period was the Thoroughbred Furioso, bought in England. He had a brilliant career, topping the sire ratings for ten consecutive years and siring many international jumpers.

LIMBS
The trotting connection has passed on limbs of exceptional strength with the especially powerful forearms that are a feature of both the riding and trotting horses. The joints must be clean, well developed and correct.

🐎 Action
The movement is active, long-striding and characterized by a supple agility. The jumping ability is pronounced and the breed has more spirit than many other warmbloods.

🐎 Crosses
Other than those mentioned, crosses that qualify for the name Selle Français are: Thoroughbred/French Trotter; Arabian or Anglo-Arab/French Trotter; and Thoroughbred/Anglo-Arab (with under 25 percent purebred Arabian blood).

Danish Warmblood

DENMARK HAS an ancient equestrian tradition. Early in the fourteenth century, the Cistercian monasteries of Holstein (a Danish Duchy until 1864) had established breeding studs, where they crossed large, North German mares with the best Spanish stallions obtainable. The modern Holstein and subsequent Danish breeds, like the Frederiksborg, evolved from this early breeding policy.

ORIGINS

Nonetheless, the Danes were late-comers to competitive sport. A National Equestrian Federation was formed in 1918, but only in the 1960s was a stud book opened for a national riding horse, first known as the Danish Sports Horse and now termed the Danish Warmblood.

The breed was developed by crossing locally bred mares with pedigree stallions from a variety of breeds and countries. The mares were half-breds, usually of Frederiksborg/Thoroughbred origin. They provided a sound enough base for breeding an all-around competition horse that was in increasing demand at the time. The stallions used were Anglo-Norman, Thoroughbred, and Trakehner, as well as Polish horses, like those once generally known as Malapolski and Wielkopolski. The Hanoverian influence is, however, notably absent in what can now be looked upon as Denmark's national breed.

⚲ Modern competition horse
The Danish Warmblood is one of the best examples of a modern competition horse currently being bred in Europe. It retains an excellent temperament while still possessing spirit and courage.

• OUTLINE
The outline can hardly be faulted and displays all the desirable attributes of the competition horse. The Danish Warmblood excels as a dressage horse, being naturally balanced, and is also an excellent cross country performer. This specimen would not come amiss in the show ring either.

COLOR •
All colors occur in the Danish Warmblood although bay, as here, is the most usual.

• HOOVES
The slope of the hoof and pastern, and the length of the pastern is exactly right in this superlative example of a modern riding horse.

⚲ Swedish Warmblood
The Swedish Warmblood originated some 300 years ago at the Royal Stud at Flyinge, and a stud book opened in 1874. It was based on a wide variety of imported horses. In this century, increased use of the Trakehner, Thoroughbred, and Hanoverian has been made to breed event and dressage horses of the highest quality.

WITHERS
Well-placed, prominent withers, blending into the slope of the riding shoulder, ensure the best possible placement for the saddle.

LENGTH OF REIN
There is an impressive and reassuring length of rein in this good example of the breed.

JOWL
The throat is clean and there is no suggestion of fleshiness in the jowl.

Head
The head shows clearly the Thoroughbred influence. The expression is at once kind, intelligent, bold and shows common sense. The overall effect is one of great beauty.

LIMBS
The limbs are powerful, the joints big and well-defined and there is ample bone to carry the horse's body weight and that of its rider. The forelegs are particularly well-made. The forearms are long and muscular, and the knees big, broad and flat.

HEIGHT
The height varies between 16.1 and 16.2hh.

Trakehner

THE TRAKEHNER is a breed of great antiquity. Of all the horses known as warmbloods, it is arguably the nearest to the ideal of the modern competition horse. Trakehner blood is often used to upgrade other breeds.

ORIGINS

The Trakehner originated in what used to be East Prussia and is now a part of Poland. In the early thirteenth century, the province was colonized by the Order of Teutonic Knights. They established the Trakehnen studs using the indigenous Schweiken as a base. These ponies were plain and often common, but they were also tough and hardy. Schweiken Ponies descend from the Konik Pony – a direct derivative of the primitive Tarpan. They inherit the Tarpan's extraordinary natural vigor and powers of endurance.

In 1732, Friedrich Wilhelm I of Prussia founded the Royal Trakehner Stud Administration. This stud was the main source of stallions for all Prussia and the area quickly established a reputation for elegant coach horses. Within 50 years, the emphasis shifted to producing army chargers and remounts of a quality unsurpassed in Europe. Thereafter, increasing use was made of English Thoroughbred and Arabian blood, which balanced deficiencies of temperament and constitution.

By 1913, most Trakehner stallions were Thoroughbred. The greatest influence was Perfectionist, son of Persimmon, who won the English Derby and the St. Leger in 1896. The best of his sons, Tempelhuter, provided a powerful line that is recognized as the foundation for the modern Trakehner.

HEIGHT
The height can vary between 16 and 17.2hh.

NECK
There is ample length to the elegant neck.

SHOULDERS
The ideal Trakehner has good, well-shaped shoulders.

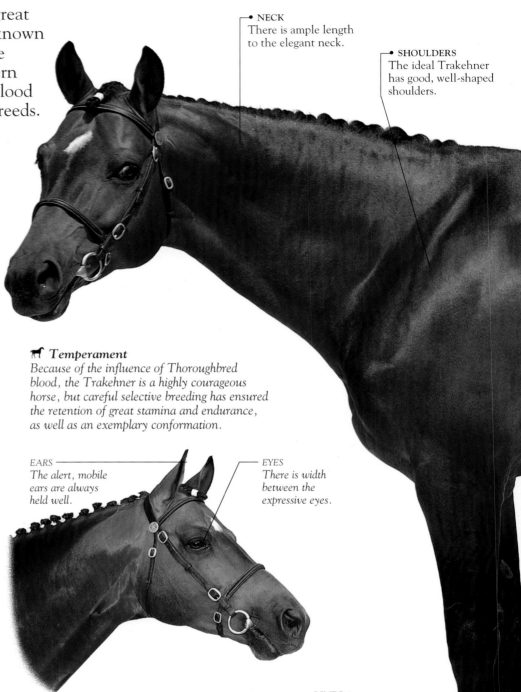

🐴 *Temperament*
Because of the influence of Thoroughbred blood, the Trakehner is a highly courageous horse, but careful selective breeding has ensured the retention of great stamina and endurance, as well as an exemplary conformation.

EARS
The alert, mobile ears are always held well.

EYES
There is width between the expressive eyes.

LIMBS
Good, strong limbs and joints are a feature of the Trakehner. It stands close to the ground on short legs and cannons.

🐴 *Head*
The refined head of the Trakehner exemplifies the background of English Thoroughbred and Arabian blood. It is full of the quality that has earned the breed the title of "noble" – a word much used in describing what may be regarded as Europe's finest warmblood. It also has an unmistakeable character and expression, not always so evident in other warmbloods.

🐴 Performance

The Trakehner has an impressive record in international sport. Trakehners dominated the 1936 German Olympic team, which won every medal at Berlin. Since then there have been many notable Trakehners in the fields of dressage, jumping and cross-country.

🐴 Tempelhuter

When the famous stallion Tempelhuter died in 1932, his progeny at Trakehnen included 54 stallions and 60 brood mares. The other important line of Dingo owes much to Tempelhuter's daughters.

🐴 Elk-horn brand

This elk-horn brand is the traditional marking of the Trakehner Horse, which was also called the East Prussian. The horse is branded on its quarter and the headstall is frequently engraved with elk-horns.

QUARTERS
The quarters are particularly powerful – it is interesting that the field for the *Gran Pardubice* steeplechase in Czechoslovakia is largely Trakehner.

COLOR
The Trakehner coat can be of any solid color. This Trakehner is bay.

🐴 Conformation

The Trakehner has an excellent conformation, which, overall, is like that of a Thoroughbred of substance. It is a wonderfully balanced specimen – athletic, agile and having great freedom of movement at all paces.

HOOVES
Notably good, hard hooves in comparison to some other warmblood breeds.

🐴 Out in the fields

These mares enjoy the freedom of their pasture. Half a century ago mares like these, with their foals at foot, trekked 900 miles (1,450km), across war-stricken Europe to escape the Russian troops. Only 1,200 survived, from a registration of 25,000, to continue the breed in West Germany where the governing body, the Trakehner Verband, was formed in 1947.

Hanoverian

Probably the most successful of the European warmbloods is the Hanoverian, which has a worldwide reputation as a show jumper and dressage horse. It is the result of a meticulous mix of compatible bloods supported by a strict process of selection.

ORIGINS

The Hanoverian breed was founded in 1735 on the stud at Celle, established by George II, Elector of Hanover and King of England. The object was to create a nucleus of strong stallions that, when mated with the heavy local mares, would produce all-purpose agricultural horses.

Initially, Celle relied upon 14 black Holsteins. These were powerful coach horses, based on native mares crossed with oriental, Spanish and Neapolitan blood. Then the Thoroughbred was introduced, which at that time was more oriental in character than otherwise. The result was a lighter, better quality horse that could be used in harness and as a cavalry remount, as well as for general farm work. The Thoroughbred influence was continued, but it was carefully monitored lest the Hanoverian should become too light.

By 1924 the stallion population at Celle was 500. After the Second World War, the policy was directed to the production of the riding competition horse. Trakehners – refugees from East Prussia – were used to reinforce the stallion band. Some Trakehners, as well as Thoroughbreds, remain at Celle and still exert a beneficial influence on the continuing development of the Hanoverian breed.

CHARACTERISTICS

The selection of Hanoverian breeding stock includes controlled performance testing and takes into account the temperament of the individual horses. Hanoverians are bred very carefully for their equable and willing temperament, and for their reliability. Much emphasis is given to these qualities.

NECK •
The neck of the Hanoverian is noticeably long and fine. It runs into large, sloping shoulders and the withers are particularly pronounced.

COLOR •
This Hanoverian is a bright bay. Every sort of solid color is found in the breed, no single color being predominant. The original Holstein foundation stallions were black.

🐎 Head
The introduction of Thoroughbred blood has given quality to the formerly heavy and somewhat coarse head of the old-type, all-purpose agricultural Hanoverian. Modern Hanoverians have a lighter head of medium size which is clean-cut and expressive, with a large and lively eye.

Brand mark *(left)*
The stylized back to back "H" motif has been the distinctive brand of the stallion depot at Celle since the latter's formation by George II in 1735. It is estimated that over 8,000 mares are served each year by selected Celle stallions.

BACK
The back is of medium length and is a strong structure with the loins being particularly powerful as befits a jumper.

QUARTERS
The quarters are exceptionally muscular and sometimes there is a characteristic flattening at the croup.

TAIL
The tail is always well set on the quarters and sometimes, indeed, appears to be set noticeably high.

Hanoverian foal
This powerful black foal was bred in England from imported and English warmblood stock. The color is reminiscent of that of the old, black, Holstein coach stallions on which the breed was founded at Celle. Hanoverian warmbloods are well represented in England.

Westphalian
Though the Hanoverian is associated with Celle, it is used in the production of another warmblood strain, the Westphalian, notably at Warendorf. The Westphalian is, to all intents, a Hanoverian bred in Westphalia.

BODY
Depth through the girth and an exemplary rib formation are a feature of the Hanoverian. The structure is one of great strength but it is not one associated with speed.

Action
The action of the breed is impressive. It is straight, true, very energetic and has a particular elastic quality. There is little or no knee action and the stride is long.

LIMBS
Powerful, symmetrical limbs with large, well-pronounced joints, short cannons and an ample measurement of bone below the knee on the forelimbs are expected.

HOOVES
The modern breed should have hard, well-formed hooves. The tendency to poor hooves has been largely eliminated.

HEIGHT
Height is approximately between 15.3 and 16.2hh.

Holsteiner

A MIX OF GERMAN, Neapolitan, Spanish and oriental blood, the Holsteiner was in great demand by its European neighbors. They valued it because of its ability as a tough and powerful, but not inelegant, carriage or coach horse, and as a strong riding horse.

HISTORY

The greatest influences on the Holsteiner breed were the English Thoroughbred and Yorkshire Coach Horse. The Thoroughbred refined the common, Roman-nosed Holsteiner and improved its galloping ability while the Yorkshire Coach Horse gave the breed a typical, high, wide action and an excellent temperament. Renowned as a strong riding horse, it was developed more and more as an army remount.

Since the Second World War, Thoroughbreds have been used to produce a lighter, competition horse with more speed and scope. The modern Holsteiner resembles a quality hunter and is successful as a show jumper, dressage horse and eventer.

FOREHAND •
The chest is wide and deep but the sloping shoulder of the modern Holsteiner and the long, slightly arched neck conform entirely to the riding horse requirement, and do not reflect the coaching background.

EYES
Large, bright eyes are characteristic of the breed.

🐎 *Dressage horse*
Its temperament and regularity of paces make the impressive Holsteiner a natural choice for dressage. Probably the best eventing prospect of the German breeds, Holsteiners have also produced some of the post-war period's finest show jumpers, like Fritz Thiedemann's Meteor.

🐎 **Head**
The old Holsteiner was plain and heavy around the head, and often had a convex profile. The infusions of Thoroughbred have given refinement to the head of the present-day Holsteiner, which is now that of a quality hunter; expressive, with large, bright eyes and well-placed ears. The tendency toward heaviness in the lower jaw, a failing in the past, has now been almost entirely eliminated.

BONE •
Pasterns correspond to the slope of the shoulder, while the bone measurement under the knee is expected to be 8–9½in (20–24cm).

🐎 The paces
Much emphasis is given to the quality of the paces. The walk is long, free and elastic, and the action straight. The trot is active, very balanced and rhythmic, and covers a lot of ground; a little knee action (inherited from the carriage type) is permissible. The canter is smooth, straight and, again, in easy balance.

BODY
Body structure is one of strength combined with quality. The withers are of pronounced riding type, the chest is deep, and the back and loins are strong and muscular.

COLOR
All colors are permissible. The most typical are bay, with black points, and brown, as here. Grays are quite common, but chestnuts less so.

🐎 Tandem team
In the nineteenth century, the Holsteiner was used extensively as a harness horse. This illustration shows Holsteiners harnessed in tandem. As a carriage horse, the Holsteiner had strength and presence, as well as a tractable disposition. The pronounced knee action has been reduced to a slight bend in modern horses, and the coaching shoulder has disappeared.

LIMBS
The limbs are exemplary with big, flat knees, well-formed hocks and short cannons. The forelegs are set well apart and the elbows are clear of the body.

QUARTERS
The tail is always carried well but it is not set over-high in the powerful quarters, which run into strongly muscular stifles, thighs and gaskins.

HOOVES
The Thoroughbred influence has improved the hooves, a failing of the old coaching breeds of mainland Europe. Breeders of the Holsteiner pay careful attention to the correctness of size, shape and density of horn.

HEIGHT
Holsteiners are 16–17hh. (For registration, 3 year old fillies should be 16hh and premium stallions of 2$\frac{1}{2}$ years should be 16.1–16.2hh.)

Maremmana

THE MAREMMANA IS BRED in the Tuscan province of Maremma. Although there has been a steep decline in the horse population of Italy over the past 50 years, riding horses, often of mixed blood, are still bred in Maremma, the Po valley, Sicily and Sardinia.

HISTORY

In ancient times, there were probably no horses or ponies indigenous to Italy, the early stock being that brought in from Spain, Persia, and Noricum, a vassal state of the Roman Empire. Nonetheless, Italy and its breeds have been influential for over 2,000 years. In the seventeenth century, Italy was foremost among the horse-breeding countries of Europe. Its breeds, the most notable being the Neapolitan, derived from Spanish, Barb and Arabian stock. In more recent times, Italy has been best known for producing some of the world's greatest Thorough-breds. As harness racing is a hugely popular sport in Italy, some first class trotters have also been bred.

Much outcrossing has obscured the background of the Maremmana, which is neither indigenous to Italy nor of a definite type. Nonetheless, in the nineteenth century the local horses would have benefited by crosses with English stock, notably the Norfolk Roadster. There must also be a background of Neapolitan blood. The result was a rustic animal. Solid and by no means handsome, it is, nonetheless, steady, enduring and versatile. It is used in agriculture as a light draft horse and was a reliable troop horse for the military and the police. The Maremmana is also much favored as a cattle horse by the local *butteri*, the Italian version of the cowpoke.

🐎 Appearance
"Rustic" is a good description for the Maremmana. Like its ancestor, the important but not very pretty Neapolitan, it is common in appearance.

COLOR •
There is no restriction on color in this horse of mixed background. All solid colors are acceptable and none is dominant. This horse is bay.

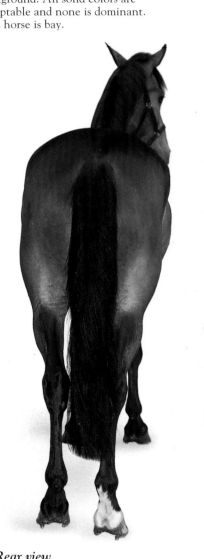

HEIGHT
The height is variable but averages around 15.2 –15.3hh.

🐎 Rear view
The quarters are not built for speed, but they are strong and serviceable, and the hock joints are well defined. In this example, the quarters and the line of the hind leg are better than would usually be found in a Maremmana. In general, they would be expected to be coarse and with the tail set fairly low.

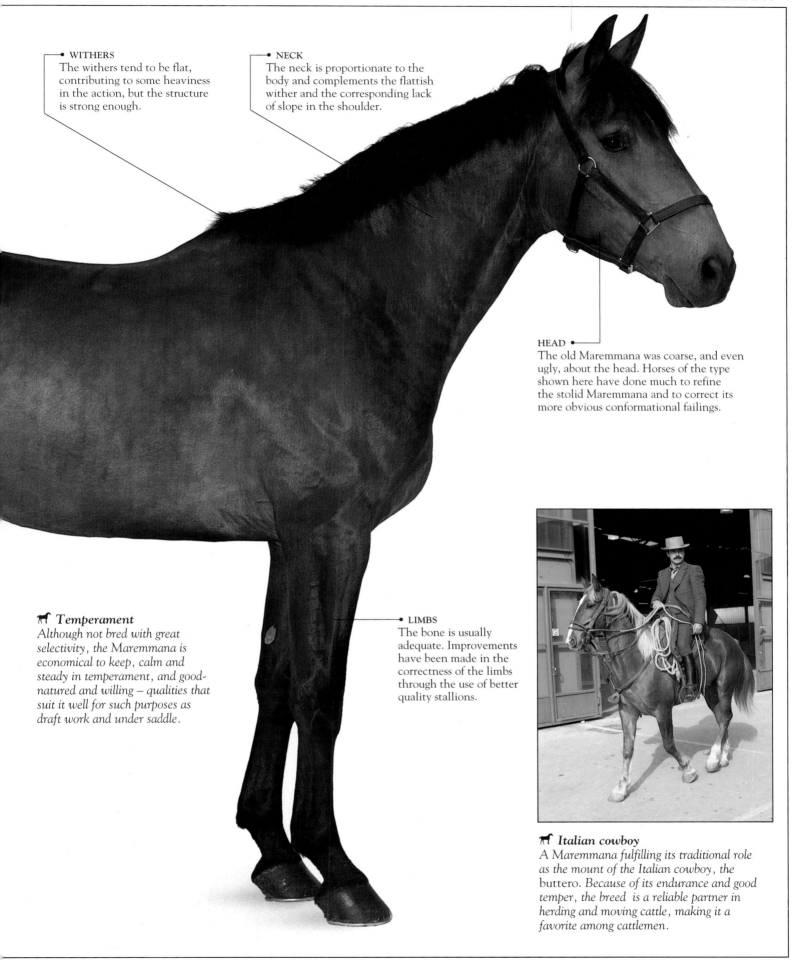

• WITHERS
The withers tend to be flat, contributing to some heaviness in the action, but the structure is strong enough.

• NECK
The neck is proportionate to the body and complements the flattish wither and the corresponding lack of slope in the shoulder.

HEAD •
The old Maremmana was coarse, and even ugly, about the head. Horses of the type shown here have done much to refine the stolid Maremmana and to correct its more obvious conformational failings.

🐎 Temperament
Although not bred with great selectivity, the Maremmana is economical to keep, calm and steady in temperament, and good-natured and willing – qualities that suit it well for such purposes as draft work and under saddle.

• LIMBS
The bone is usually adequate. Improvements have been made in the correctness of the limbs through the use of better quality stallions.

🐎 Italian cowboy
A Maremmana fulfilling its traditional role as the mount of the Italian cowboy, the buttero. Because of its endurance and good temper, the breed is a reliable partner in herding and moving cattle, making it a favorite among cattlemen.

Murgese

I TALY'S PREOCCUPATION with the Thoroughbred and the country's excellent Trotters has resulted in some neglect of the riding horse and light draft strains. Nonetheless, there are some very typical Italian horses that are well-suited to the requirements of the areas in which they are bred. As well as the Avelignese and the basic riding types like the Salerno, the far less attractive San Fratello and some more acceptable Anglo-Arabs, there is the breed of the Murge, the district near Puglia once noted for its high-quality horses.

HISTORY

The Murge is a dry, hilly region that produces animals with good bone and hard hooves. In the fifteenth and early sixteenth centuries, the horses of the Murge, the Murgese, were very much in demand for use as cavalry remounts. Since that time, in a manner that seems characteristic of Italian horse-breeding history, the Murgese Horse has suffered from a lack of interest.

MODERN HORSES

The old Murgese Horse, whatever it may have been, is now extinct and the new version, which dates from the 1920s, probably bears little resemblance to it. The present Murgese is basically a light draft horse, an inferior sort of Irish Draft. There is a lack of uniformity in the Murgese, but the best are acceptable and they can be used to fulfil a number of purposes. The Murgese can perfom a useful role in agriculture and, probably, is even more valuable as a base stock for outside crosses. A good stamp of riding horse can be produced by putting Murgese mares to a Thoroughbred or good quality, halfbred stallion. The resulting progeny will not approach the quality of the Irish Draft but will be, nonetheless, a practical animal in the required respects, suitable for light draft work, riding and as a good all-around horse. The Murgese mares can also be used to breed the strong mules so essential to the rural economy of Italy for agriculture and transport.

🐎 Mountain horse
The Murgese is not a distinctive horse. At its best, it is suitable for use as a light draft animal. It could be ridden, but is better suited as a base for crossing. Because of the rocky environment in which it is bred, it inclines more to a mountain horse type than to the massive draft animal.

EYES
The eyes are placed to the outside of the face.

🐎 Head
The head is plain and has no outstanding feature, but the expression is honest and genuine. There is some fleshiness in the jowl, and the eyes are placed somewhat to the outside of the face. The whole reveals the presence of a coldblood base, which has yet to be refined by selective outcrossing. The horse is, nonetheless, active and energetic and is said to be even tempered and economical to keep, and suits the needs of the country well.

LIMBS
The limbs are straight but the knees have a tendency to be too small and rounded.

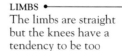

BONE
The bone below the knee is variable as might be expected of a horse of unfixed character. In the Murgese, the pasterns are often a little upright.

☙ Annual competitions
Breeding of the Murgese is not subject to strict control or breed society regulations. At one time, however, it was usual for an annual competition to be held in the town of Martina Franca to assess the potential of the young stallions.

☙ Action
The movement of the Murgese is fairly active but the stride is short and the engagement of the hind legs under the body is limited by the overall conformation. In draft, that is not a serious disadvantage.

WITHERS
The withers are inclined to be overloaded with muscle, inhibiting free movement, but the back is strong and the tendency to undue length has been checked.

QUARTERS
Quarters are not always a good feature of the Murgese, the tail may be low, and some horses lack sufficient muscling through the second thigh.

☙ Salerno
The Salerno evolved at the stud farm at Persano, which was founded by Charles III of Naples and then of Spain, in 1763. The foundation stock was Neapolitan with a powerful admixture of Andalusian blood. Later crosses to the Arabian, and particularly to the Thoroughbred, produced quality riding horses with a pronounced jumping ability. The Salerno is probably the best of the Italian riding horses and was, at one time, used extensively as a cavalry horse. Generally, it has good conformation. There is much quality about the head, a well-sloped, riding shoulder and powerfully built quarters, while the limbs are notably correct. The Salerno may be of any solid color and stands at 16hh.

COLOR
Although this horse is black, the principal color is chestnut, like the Avelignese and the Italian Draft, either of which might have had some slight influence on the Murgese.

HOOVES
The hooves of the Murgese should be hard and well formed.

HEIGHT
The Murgese can be between 15 and 16hh.

Oldenburg

THE OLDENBURG, the heaviest of the German warmbloods, was established in the 1600s, largely through the efforts of Count Anton Gunther von Oldenburg (1603–67). He used the halfbred stallion, Kranich, and a base of Friesians.

HISTORY

To this Friesian base were added Spanish Horses, Barbs, Neapolitans and English halfbreds, and during the nineteenth century the breeders introduced Thoroughbreds, Cleveland Bays, Hanoverians and French Norman strains. The resultant coach horse, or *karossierpferd*, was 17hh and heavily built. Despite its size and build, it was noted for its early maturity. With the decline in demand for heavy coach horses, the breed developed as a general-purpose farm horse. When demand changed again, after 1945, more Thoroughbred and Norman blood was introduced to make the Oldenburg closer to a riding type. Today it is an all-purpose riding horse, still big and powerful and retaining some of the harness horses' knee action, but much freer than its ancestors.

NECK
The neck is long and very strong but still reflects the coaching background.

🐎 Head
The head can be described as plain but honest. The profile is straight but a tendency toward a Roman nose is not unknown. There is occasionally some thickness of the jowl. Nonetheless, the expression is essentially kind and genuine and the eye has a hint of boldness.

LIMBS
To carry so big a frame, the limbs are strong and short with large, well-developed joints, short cannons and a bone measurement below the knee that is upward of 9in (23cm). The placement and length of the humerus in respect of the scapula accounts for the fairly high knee action.

HOOVES
When stallions are tested before licensing, particular attention is paid to the hooves. In so big an animal, they must be well open at the heels, large enough in proportion to the horse and of sound quality.

🐎 Impressive and versatile
The modern Oldenburg is lighter than its forebears and moves with greater freedom. A big, impressive horse, it is well suited to the dressage discipline on account of its kind temperament and regular paces, but it still retains its ability as a powerful harness horse.

• BUILD
Of all the warmblood riding horses, the Oldenburg is the most powerfully built. The chest is exceptionally deep, which contributes to the action. The shoulder does not approach that of the Thoroughbred in length and shape and, combined with the width of the chest, is not conducive to speed. However, the paces are rhythmical and even elastic, the horse moving very correctly.

• QUARTERS
The quarters and the hindlimbs are very strong. Although the Oldenburg is not built for speed, it is known as a powerful jumper, as well as being a good performer in dressage competitions.

• TAIL
The tail is set and carried noticeably high in the strong quarters.

The Dutch Groningen
An offshoot of the Oldenburg, the Dutch Groningen played its part in the evolution of the Dutch Warmblood. It derives from crosses between the Oldenburg and its close relation, the East Friesian, which was once indistinguishable, and the heavier Friesian mares. It was a strong, steady carriage horse, noted for its good quarters, that could be used for farm work and as a useful, if undistinguished, heavyweight riding horse. The old pure type, which was very similar to the Oldenburg of the period, probably does not exist today.

Society of Breeders
Under Acts of 1819, amended in 1897 and again in 1923, the responsibility for the breed and licensing of stallions lies with the Society of Breeders of the Oldenburg Horse, in the area of Oldenburg. The Society pursues a policy of careful selection, resulting in uniformity of type. Its stallions are performance-tested at 3 years of age.

Characteristics
The coach horse characteristics, particularly in respect of shoulders and the length of the back, have been largely eliminated in the modern Oldenburg riding horse by the use of Thoroughbred blood. The German breeders, however, have ensured that the Oldenburg retains its reputation for being temperamentally reliable.

• COLOR
Colors in the breed are mostly brown, black and bay, as here. Chestnuts and grays are unusual if, indeed, they are seen at all.

HEIGHT
The height is upward of 16.2 to 17.2hh.

Camargue

I NDIGENOUS TO THE RHONE DELTA in southern France, which is its natural habitat, the Camargue breed bears a strong resemblance to the Lascaux cave drawings of horses dated around 15,000 B.C. It is also thought that the much older remains of prehistoric horses, discovered at Solutré in the last century, may be those of the breed's ancestors.

INFLUENCES

The indigenous horse was influenced by the Barb (see pp.30–31), brought over by the Moorish invaders. Since then, the isolation of the Camargue has ensured that the *manades*, the wild herds of white horses, have remained untouched by outside influences.

The harsh environment is responsible for the incredible hardiness of the breed, which exists solely on what it can scavenge from the reed beds. The area is extremely inhospitable, hot in summer and covered in a sheet of cold, salt water the rest of the year. The landscape is dominated by the mistral, the salt-laden wind, which stunts the sparse growth. Yet the local people are fiercely loyal to their heritage and call it "the most noble conquered territory of man." The mounts of the Camargue cowboy (*gardian*) are called "white horses of the sea," and have been immortalized in verse and story over the centuries.

🐎 Riding on the marshes
The Moorish influence on the Rhone delta is evident in the saddlery, which is traditional to the gardian *and the* Camargue.

FOREHAND •
The neck is generally short, running into fairly straight, upright shoulders, which accentuates the impression of a primitive horse with overtones of the North African Barb. The forehand and the set of the foreleg to shoulder is responsible for the action peculiar to the breed.

🐎 Head
The head of the Camargue Horse, with a distinctive head rope made of twined horse hair, hardly accords with romantic legend. Though showing a North African influence, it is usually coarse and heavy and with more than a suggestion of their far-off ancestors of pre-history. Still, the Camargue is an intelligent animal and generous by nature.

HOOVES •
Although the hooves are wide to correspond with the marsh environment, they are incredibly hard and strong, so much so that Camargue Horses are rarely shod.

🐎 Temperament
The Camargue is an independent horse but fiery and most courageous under saddle. Agile and sure-footed, the breed has an innate instinct for working the Camargue's black bulls.

🐎 Action
The action is peculiar to the breed. The walk is active, long-striding and high-stepping. The trot is rarely employed and is short, stilted and jarring. The canter and gallop are both amazingly free.

COLOR
Color is the Camargue's greatest visual asset. The coat is white, like sea-foam, and strangely silky.

TAIL
Both the mane and the tail are luxurious.

🐎 Increased tourism
Today, the wild waste of the Camargue, which has supported the manades – the wild herds – for thousands of years, is being drained. However, the new tourist industry is creating a further use for the Camargue region, by allowing tourists to ride around the nature reserve on the "horses of the sea."

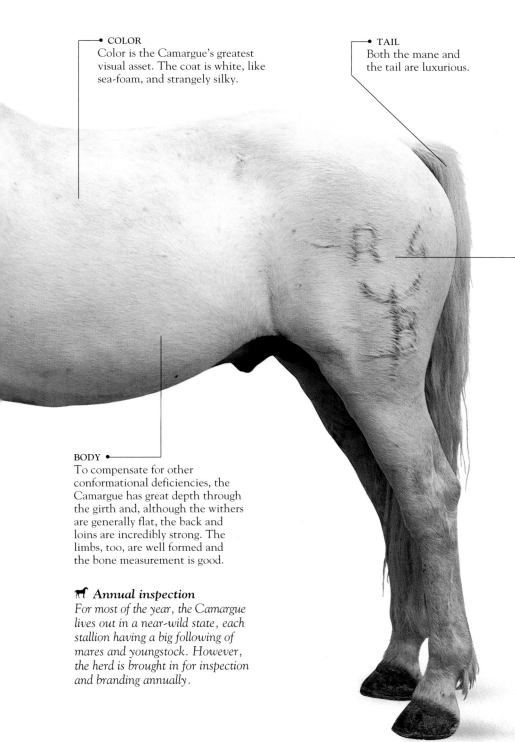

QUARTERS
The croup is often sloped, with the tail set low, but it is invariably muscular and strong. The quarters, displaying the brand mark, are generally powerful, if otherwise unprepossessing.

BODY
To compensate for other conformational deficiencies, the Camargue has great depth through the girth and, although the withers are generally flat, the back and loins are incredibly strong. The limbs, too, are well formed and the bone measurement is good.

🐎 Exceptional longevity
The Camargue develops slowly and is not full-grown until it is five to seven years old, but it has great stamina and is exceptionally long-lived.

🐎 Annual inspection
For most of the year, the Camargue lives out in a near-wild state, each stallion having a big following of mares and youngstock. However, the herd is brought in for inspection and branding annually.

HEIGHT
Variable but usually between 13.1–14.1hh.

Rocky Mountain Horse

THE ROCKY MOUNTAIN HORSE shows the American genius for innovation and adaptation. Its development has occurred over a remarkably short time; so short, that it is not yet considered to have sufficiently fixed characteristics to qualify for recognition as a breed. A registry opened in 1986 and now 200 are registered.

ORIGINS

Its origins are, like those of many American horses, with the early Spanish imports and the subsequent Mustang stock. The credit for this distinctive animal, however, belongs to Sam Tuttle of Stout Springs, Kentucky, who ran the riding concession at Natural Bridge State Resort Park. Mr. Tuttle had a stallion, Old Tobe, who was a favorite with the riders, and ideally suited to the rugged foothills of the Appalachians. Old Tobe, still active at 37, was a prepotent sire who passed on his good temperament, sure-footedness and natural, ambling gait, which was a legacy of his Spanish forebears.

The Rocky Moutain Horse is judged largely on the quality of its gait, which produces speeds of between 7mph (11kph) for comfortable traveling and 16mph (26kph) on good going and for shorter distances. The type is said to be hardy and well able to tolerate cold, mountain winters.

Spanish origin
A medium-sized animal, the outline of the Rocky Mountain Horse reflects its Spanish origins, although there is no evidence to indicate that the chocolate coat occurred among Spanish Horses.

OUTLINE
The outline of the Rocky Mountain Horse is pleasingly rounded and the proportions uniformly good.

Gait
The usual and natural gait of the Rocky Mountain Horse is an easy, very comfortable amble – a lateral gait rather than the conventional trot. This gait was common among the early Spanish Horses, and it has been greatly favored for easy travel since the Middle Ages.

Rear view
The full, flaxen tail and mane is a distinctive feature of the Rocky Mountain Horse, and is the perfect complement to the unusual, rich chocolate coat. This tone of brown is a very rare, equine coloring.

• HEAD
The head is handsome and is joined to a graceful neck that is longer than might be expected. This feature contributes significantly to the good overall balance.

• WITHERS
The withers are not sharply defined but the structure of the back and its gentle ascent to the croup is commendable.

All-around pony
It is customary for gaited American horses to be shown stretched out, which makes it easier for the pose to be held but is considered artificial in Europe. The Rocky Mountain Horse will do work on the farm and in harness as well as being a good performer under saddle.

Temperament
The temperament of the Rocky Mountain Horse is said to be both calm and kind, but the horse is not without spirit and is a remarkably good mover over rough ground.

Action
The natural, traveling gait is the amble, which covers about 7mph (11kph). Because of its smoothness, long distances can be covered without the rider becoming fatigued.

• LIMBS
The limbs are well made and the hooves hard and nicely shaped. The Rocky Mountain Horse is noted for its sure-footedness and easy way of going.

HEIGHT
Though not fixed, the height tends to be 14.2–15hh.

Furioso

THE FURIOSO is one of the many breeds that evolved during the period when the Austro-Hungarian Empire was the dominant force in Europe. The stud at Mezöhegyes was founded in 1785 by the Hapsburg Emperor, Joseph II. It became the center for the breeding of the Nonius (see pp.110–11) and then the Furioso.

Appearance (left)
The pronounced oriental influence in the Hungarian horse is clearly demonstrated by this attractive charger. The Hungarian light horsemen were considered to be among the best in the world.

ORIGINS

The Furioso breed was formed following the importation of two English horses. They were called Furioso and North Star – the breed is also often termed Furioso-North Star. Both stallions were used on Nonius mares whose foundation stallion was Nonius Senior, who in turn was by an English half-bred stallion out of a Norman mare.

Furioso, an English Thoroughbred, was imported by Count Karolyi around 1840. At Mezöhegyes, he produced no less than 95 stallions. These were used at many of the Imperial studs. North Star was imported three years later. He had a background of Norfolk Roadster, however, he was also a son of Touchstone, winner of the 1834 St. Leger and twice winner of the Ascot Gold Cup. North Star sired many good harness racers as did his great grand-sire Waxy, the 1793 Derby winner. Later in the evolution of the Furioso breed, more Thoroughbred blood was introduced, most notably was that of Buccaneer, who sired Kisber, the Hungarian-bred winner of the 1876 Derby.

Initially, the two lines of North Star and Furioso were kept separate. In 1885 they were intercrossed and, thereafter, the Furioso strain became the more predominant.

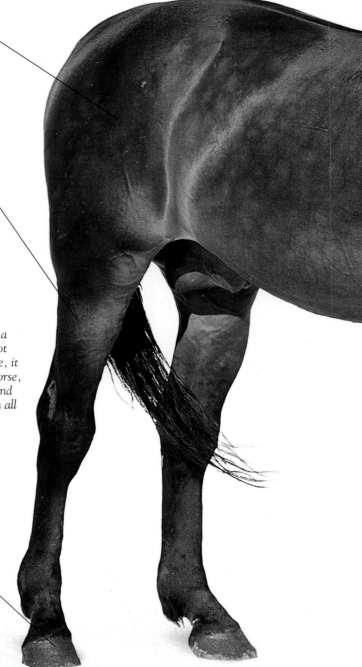

QUARTERS •
Although a good stamp of riding horse, the quarters slope down from the croup, betraying the presence of the more plebeian Nonius.

HIND LIMBS •
The hind limbs are strong and the hocks are low to the ground but they are not of the sort associated with speed and scope.

Character
The Furioso is intelligent with a most amenable disposition. Not only is it exceptionally versatile, it is a good, all-around, riding horse, which will go well in harness and is able to compete creditably in all disciplines, including steeplechasing at the standard in Central European countries.

HEIGHT
The height is around 16hh or a little above.

HOOVES •
Overall, the hooves are good and better than most of the fashionable warmblood breeds.

SHOULDERS
The shoulders and withers are of indubitable riding-type, but the action retains something of the exaggerated coaching lift of the breed's Nonius ancestors.

HEAD
The head is almost that of a Thoroughbred, although the ears are more prominent. The expression is intelligent and kindly. A relatively straight profile is characteristic.

MUZZLE
The Furioso has a somewhat squared muzzle and large nostrils.

COLOR
Most colors are acceptable but the Furioso is usually black, dark brown or dark bay, as here. White markings are the exception.

Bridle
The traditional bridle on this Furioso reflects the Asian influence of the Magyar horsemen. These were a people of the steppes, descendants of the Huns, who finally settled in the Carpathian basin 1,000 years ago. They inherited a horse culture that began in Central Asia 6,000 years ago and, as Hussars of the Hapsburg Empire, they were acknowledged as the supreme light horsemen of all time.

Coaching-horse legacy
Although the Thoroughbred is much in evidence, the legacy of the coaching horse is still present in the Furioso.

LIMBS
The limbs are good and the joints clean, large and well defined. If anything, the pasterns are a little too upright – an inheritance from the carriage antecedents.

Austro-Hungarian dominance
There were no studs in the world that exceeded in size and architectural merit those purpose-built establishments created by the Hapsburg Emperors of the Austro-Hungarian dynasty. Even today, the Hungarian studs carry large breeding herds under the care of the czikos horsemen of the great puzsta. The Furioso was first bred at Mezöhegyes; today it is bred all the way from Austria to Poland. The Hungarian Furioso is now centered on the Apajpuszta Stud, between the rivers Danube and Tisza.

Nonius

B Y THE END of the nineteenth century, Hungary had a horse population of over two million, and sold cavalry remounts throughout Europe. It also had some of the world's greatest studs, including Mezőhegyes, founded by Emperor Joseph I in 1785. At one time, it housed over 12,000 horses.

HISTORY

The stud of Mezőhegyes was the center for the breeding of the Nonius and the related Furioso (see pp.108–09). The Nonius was founded on the stallion, Nonius Senior. He was foaled at Calvados, Normandy in 1910 and captured by Hungarian cavalry at the Rosières Stud after Napoleon's defeat at Leipzig in 1813.

According to the records, Nonius Senior was out of a common Norman mare by the English halfbred stallion Orion, who without much doubt carried Norfolk Roadster blood. Nonius Senior was by no means an attractive horse. Standing 16.1$\frac{1}{2}$hh, he was described as having a coarse, heavy head with small eyes and long, "mule" ears. His other characteristics were a short neck, long back, narrow pelvis and low-set tail. Despite these qualities, Nonius Senior was a prolific sire and quickly found to be a successful one. He was used on a wide variety of mares and consistently produced good stock, far superior to himself in both conformation and action. The progeny of Nonius Senior included no less than 15 outstanding stallions.

CHARACTERISTICS

In the 1860s, more Thoroughbred blood was introduced to improve the conformation, and the breed was sub-divided into two types – large and small. The large type is a carriage or light farm horse and the small type, carrying more Arabian blood, is an all-arounder, which performs well under saddle and in harness. When bred back to Thoroughbreds, Nonius mares produce competition horses of scope and quality and with good jumping ability.

WITHERS
The withers are well defined and the shoulder is sufficiently sloped.

NECK
Though not long and elegant, the neck is, nonetheless, well-formed and complementary to the overall frame.

🐎 *Foal*
This big-limbed, Nonius foal will not be mature until he is 6 years old, but he will be commensurately long-lived. Today, Nonius breeding in Hungary is centered at the Hortobagy stud, while in Czechoslovakia, where the Nonius is also bred in quite large numbers, the center is at Topolcianky.

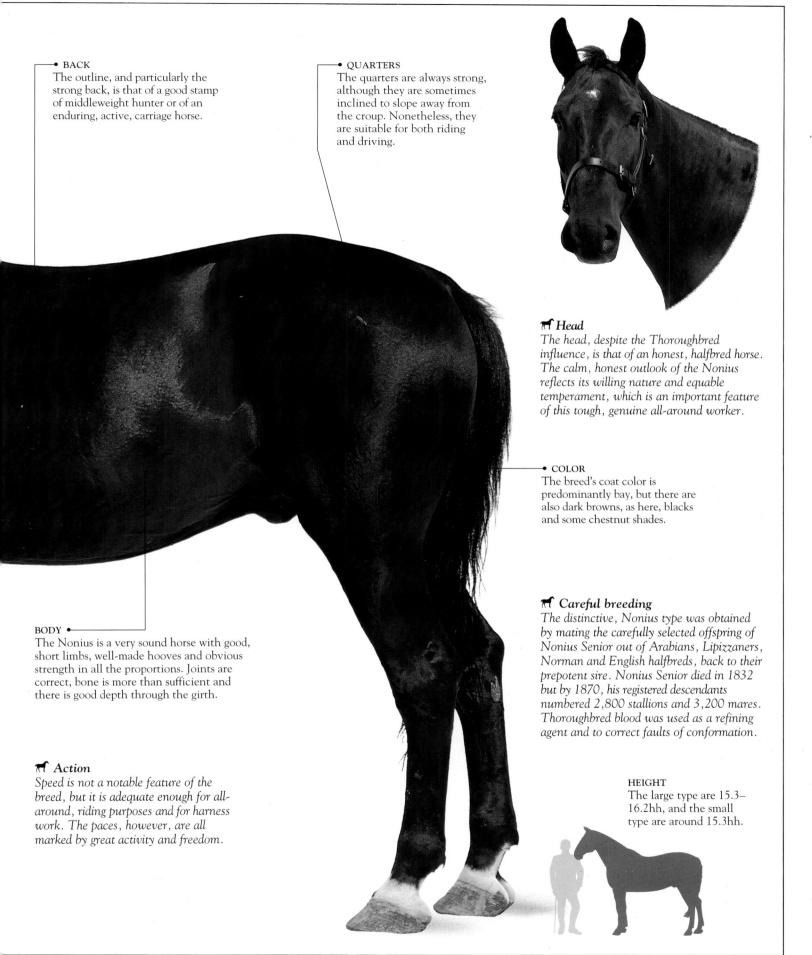

BACK
The outline, and particularly the strong back, is that of a good stamp of middleweight hunter or of an enduring, active, carriage horse.

QUARTERS
The quarters are always strong, although they are sometimes inclined to slope away from the croup. Nonetheless, they are suitable for both riding and driving.

🐎 **Head**
The head, despite the Thoroughbred influence, is that of an honest, halfbred horse. The calm, honest outlook of the Nonius reflects its willing nature and equable temperament, which is an important feature of this tough, genuine all-around worker.

COLOR
The breed's coat color is predominantly bay, but there are also dark browns, as here, blacks and some chestnut shades.

BODY
The Nonius is a very sound horse with good, short limbs, well-made hooves and obvious strength in all the proportions. Joints are correct, bone is more than sufficient and there is good depth through the girth.

🐎 **Careful breeding**
The distinctive, Nonius type was obtained by mating the carefully selected offspring of Nonius Senior out of Arabians, Lipizzaners, Norman and English halfbreds, back to their prepotent sire. Nonius Senior died in 1832 but by 1870, his registered descendants numbered 2,800 stallions and 3,200 mares. Thoroughbred blood was used as a refining agent and to correct faults of conformation.

🐎 **Action**
Speed is not a notable feature of the breed, but it is adequate enough for all-around, riding purposes and for harness work. The paces, however, are all marked by great activity and freedom.

HEIGHT
The large type are 15.3–16.2hh, and the small type are around 15.3hh.

Knabstrup

Denmark was once famous for its Frederiksborg horses, which were bred at the Royal Danish Stud, and for the eye-catching spotted Knabstrup. In their old form, both have almost disappeared. The early Knabstrups were white with brown or black spots of varying size, occurring all over the head, body and legs. The modern Knabstrup now looks more like an American Appaloosa (see pp.120–21) than otherwise.

ORIGINS

The Knabstrup breed dates from the Napoleonic Wars and is based on a spotted mare of Spanish ancestry, Flaebehoppen. Spotted strains were common in Spanish Horses up to the nineteenth century. Flaebehoppen was bought from a Spanish officer by a butcher named Flaebe (hence Flaebehoppen – Flaebe's horse), who in turn sold her to Judge Lunn, who may be said to have founded the breed.

Flaebehoppen was noted for speed and endurance, and Judge Lunn bred her to Frederiksborg stallions at his Knabstrup estate in Denmark. She founded a line of spotted horses, not so substantial as the Frederiksborg, but much in demand for their color and ability. Her grandson, Mikkel, is recognized as a foundation sire.

CONFORMATION

In terms of conformation, Knabstrups were rawboned. They were, nonetheless, constitutionally tough, sound, tractable and quick to learn, and so were in great demand as circus horses. Injudicious breeding for color resulted in the breed's deterioration late in the last century. The present-day Knabstrupers, however far removed from the original, are much improved. They have substance, more quality and a greater range of colors.

HEIGHT
The Knabstrup is about 15.2–15.3hh.

🐴 **Heavenly horses**
For the Heavenly horses of Ferghana, spotted horses not unlike the Spanish-based Knabstrup, the Emperor Wu Ti of China was prepared to wage war for upward of a quarter of a century, in the second century B.C. Such horses, much revered in the ancient world, were frequently buried with their royal masters.

🐴 **Rear view**
The sparse mane and tail of the Knabstrup seems to accompany spotted coat patterns, being a characteristic of the Appaloosa and also found in the old and the modern Knabstrup. The best of the breed has good, well-rounded quarters with substantial muscular development. The older type was probably more "ragged" across the hips.

🐎 **Conformational improvements**
This modern Knabstrup stallion is a more substantial animal with better conformation than that of the Knabstrups of 50 years ago. They had suffered some degeneration and would not have displayed the quality of this attractive horse.

• TOPLINE
The line of the back from the withers appears to be peculiar to the Knabstrup and to some Appaloosa strains.

• MANE
The mane is sparse. Here it is braided.

HEAD •
The kindly head of the Knabstrup reflects the breed's intelligence. Almost all spotted strains are easily managed, cooperative and quick to learn. These qualities, together with the striking color, ensured the breed's popularity as a circus horse.

LIMBS •
The spotted coloring extends down the legs to the hooves. The conformational defects in the limbs produced during the period of the breed's deterioration have now been largely corrected.

• COLOR
The original coloration of the Knabstrup was white, with brown or black spots covering the whole body. The roan coloring, as here, is a more recent introduction.

• HOOVES
The horn of the hooves often has vertical stripes.

🐎 **Old Knabstrup**
The old stamp of Knabstrup was strong and had more of a harness conformation, particularly in respect of the shoulder and the short neck. It was reputed to be a tough and enduring horse and the foundation mare, Flaebehoppen, was said to be a good performer and easily trained. The Knabstrup was, nonetheless, coarse in many respects and undistinguished other than by its color.

Pinto

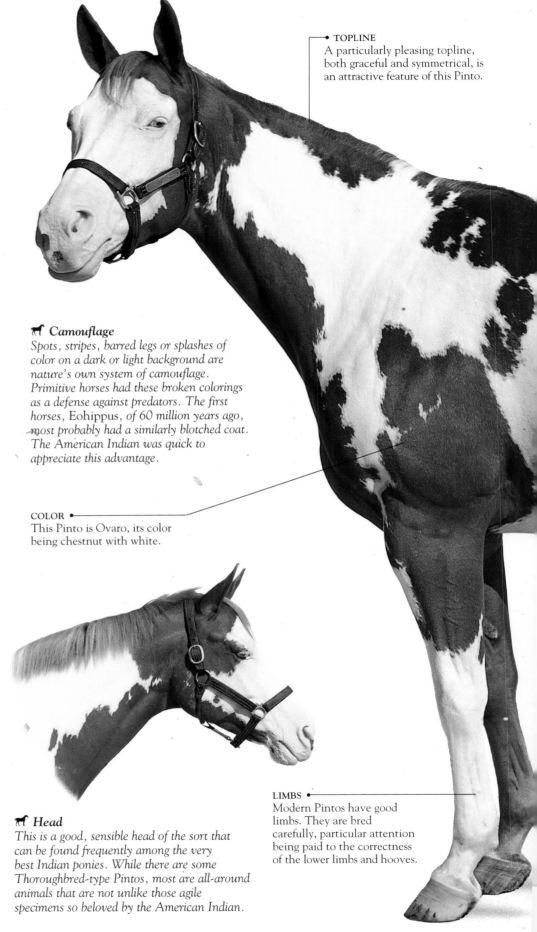

THE PINTO descends from the Spanish Horses exported to America in the sixteenth century (see also Mustang pp.74–5). The Pinto, called a Paint Horse if it is a purebred Quarter Horse or Thoroughbred, is a type of horse distinguished by its coloration and is found all over the world. It only has breed status in America.

TYPES

The Pinto Horse Association of America was established in Ellington, Connecticut, in 1956 and recognized the Pinto as a breed in 1963. There is also the American Paint Horse Association in Fort Worth, Texas.

The Pinto Association recognizes four types of colored horse: 1. Stock-type; 2. Hunters, predominantly Thoroughbred; 3. Pleasure-type; and 4. Saddle-type. It also has a similar classification for colored ponies.

COLORING

The American Indian favored the Pinto for its unusual coloring and also because the blotched coat was a natural camouflage. The Pinto was also popular with the western cowboys.

The Pinto has two types of coloring: Ovaro and Tobiano. The first is a recessive gene, predominant in South America, and the second a dominant one, more pronounced in North America. The Ovaro has a basic solid coat with large, irregular splashes of white over it. The Tobiano has a white base coat with large irregular patches of a solid color.

HEIGHT
Since the Pinto is not a breed in the accepted sense, there is no uniformity of height. Paints, however, conform to breed standard similar to Quarter Horses and stand 15–16hh.

● TOPLINE
A particularly pleasing topline, both graceful and symmetrical, is an attractive feature of this Pinto.

🐎 *Camouflage*
Spots, stripes, barred legs or splashes of color on a dark or light background are nature's own system of camouflage. Primitive horses had these broken colorings as a defense against predators. The first horses, Eohippus, of 60 million years ago, most probably had a similarly blotched coat. The American Indian was quick to appreciate this advantage.

COLOR ●
This Pinto is Ovaro, its color being chestnut with white.

🐎 *Head*
This is a good, sensible head of the sort that can be found frequently among the very best Indian ponies. While there are some Thoroughbred-type Pintos, most are all-around animals that are not unlike those agile specimens so beloved by the American Indian.

LIMBS ●
Modern Pintos have good limbs. They are bred carefully, particular attention being paid to the correctness of the lower limbs and hooves.

• OUTLINE
This Pinto inclines towards the stock horse type and has the associated conformation. This is a good example of that sort of animal for it is a powerful horse, very strong in the quarters and well proportioned.

Action
The majority of Pintos of the type illustrated here are noted for their easy, comfortable paces that can be maintained over long distances, an important requirement in days gone by.

Indian ideal (above)
The American Indians, like the ancient steppe horsemen of Asia with whom they had much in common, loved color and decoration. They painted their own bodies and did not hesitate to paint their horses, if Nature had been less than generous in the coloration. This picture epitomizes the ideal of the American Indian and his relationship with the tough, intelligent, yet graceful, Pinto Pony, who became part of the Indian way of life.

• TAIL
The sparse tail of the Pinto is also a characteristic of the Appaloosa (see pp.120–21). Tails like this were encouraged by selective breeding because they did not get entangled with undergrowth in rough and wooded country.

Cowboy
The cowboy, who was not averse to ornamentation in his dress and equipment, favored the colorful Pinto, which set him apart from his more soberly mounted fellows.

Pony of the Americas
The first Pony of the Americas was foaled in 1954 and was the result of a cross between a Shetland stallion and an Appaloosa mare. There are now stringent standards for this breed of pony, with Appaloosa coloring and characteristics, whose conformation is between that of a Quarter Horse and an Arabian. The height is set at between 11.2 and 13.2hh.

Palomino

T HE STRIKING, golden coat color known as palomino occurs in very early artifacts of Europe and Asia and is also prominent in Japanese and Chinese art prior to the Ch'in period (221–206BC). The color is also found in many horse and pony breeds. For that reason, the palomino is a "color type" and not really a "breed."

BREEDING

In America, however, where the palomino is bred extensively, it has acquired virtual breed status through the efforts of the Palomino Horse Association Inc., a body formed in 1936 "for the perpetuation and improvement of the Palomino horse through the recording of blood lines and issuing of certificates of registration to qualifying horses." The Association defines the desirable characteristics of the palomino in its official standard, allowing the height to be 14.1 to 16hh.

The Spaniards introduced the palomino color to America in the horses they brought with them, and it is now found in many American breeds and types. It occurs frequently in the Quarter Horse and the Saddlebred but it does not appear in purebred Arabians or Thoroughbreds.

Palominos are much in demand in Western riding activities and not only as showy "parade" horses. They can be seen at horse shows, they are used for pleasure and trail rides and, of course, palomino horses are attractive and exciting to watch in parades.

HEIGHT
The American Palomino Horse Association gives the height as between 14.1 and 16hh.

🐎 **Isabella**
In Spain, the palomino color is often called Isabella, after the Queen who encouraged the breeding of that color.

🐎 **Conformation**
The conformation is that of the predominant cross, and may incline toward the stock horse type or the finer parade type, as here.

🐎 **Registration**
The American register asks for progeny to have one registered parent and the other to be of Quarter Horse, Arabian or Thoroughbred blood lines.

🐎 **Head**
The head, whether the horse inclines toward the Quarter Horse or to the Arabian or Thoroughbred, must be one of quality. No horse is considered for registration that "shows coarse, draft horse, Shetland or Paint breeding." Eyes should be dark or hazel and both of the same color. White markings on the face are limited to a blaze, snip or star.

COLOR
The body color is defined as being the gold of a newly minted coin and may be no more than three shades lighter or darker. Mane and tail are shining white and must not contain more than 15 percent dark hair. Smudge or smut marks on the coat are not desirable.

Judging requirements
Color is obviously a prime requirement in the palomino, but judges will not reward poor conformation even if it is under a dazzling coat.

Arabian crosses
Although purebred Arabians are never palomino, they are frequently used as a cross to produce that color.

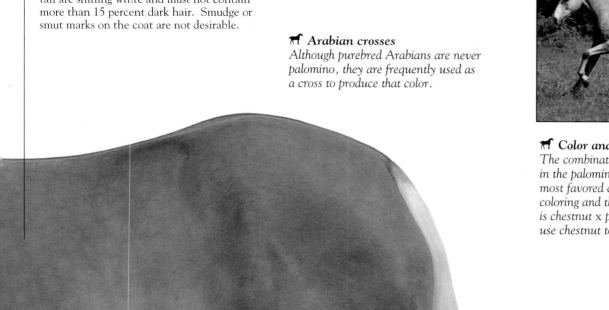

Color and fluid movement
The combination of color and fluid movement in the palomino is irresistibly attractive. The most favored cross to produce the palomino coloring and the one that gives the richest color is chestnut x palomino. It is also possible to use chestnut to cream or albino.

Origins of the name
It has been suggested that the name palomino is derived from that of a Spanish Don, Juan de Palomino, who received such a horse from Hernan Cortes. Another explanation is that it takes the name of a golden Spanish grape.

MARKINGS
White markings often occur on the legs, but they must not extend above the knees or hocks. The horse should stand on well-set legs. Skin pigmentation is either dark or of a golden color.

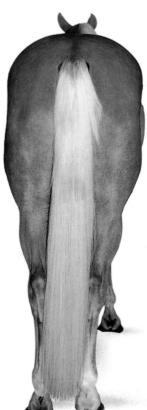

Rear view
The tail must be full and white and there should be no suspicion of a dorsal stripe on the back, as found in the dun coloration. Zebra marks on the legs, the unmistakable sign of primitive origin, are similarly unacceptable.

Australian Stock Horse

THE FIRST HORSES were imported into the settled districts of New South Wales some two hundred years ago. First they came from South Africa and then increasingly from Europe, with the favored breeds being Thoroughbreds and Arabians. The stock bred locally soon became known as Walers, after their province, a name that persisted until recently.

HISTORY

During and after the First World War, the Walers were recognized as being the finest cavalry horses in the world because they were sound, had stamina and could carry weight – no other horse performed as well. Despite their excellent merits, many Walers never returned to Australia, being destroyed at the end of the war by the order of the Australian government. What is now called the Australian Stock Horse – essentially an Anglo-Arab type infused with Percheron, Quarter Horse and even a little pony blood – is based on the Waler.

The Australian Stock Horse is used widely on cattle stations, chiefly because of its endurance. Though not fast, it is a remarkably good all-around mount with great stamina. The Australian Stock Horse Society works to promote and standardize the breed but, as yet, it has no set type and its appearance varies enormously. Therefore, the horse has no standards of conformation, although the Thoroughbred type is favored.

HEIGHT
The Australian Stock Horse stands between 15 and16.2hh.

🐎 Action
To gallop through the bush after sheep or cattle requires a horse with good balance, and a well-proportioned neck and shoulder.

HEAD •
The head inclines toward Thoroughbred refinement but there is often a suggestion of the more chunky, thicker and squarer Quarter Horse influence.

SHOULDERS AND CHEST •
The adequate slope to the shoulders and the deep chest are those of a good, all-around saddle horse.

🐎 Riding horses
The Australians have always been very successful in producing admirable riding horses that not only stand up to hard work but are capable of doing every job on the vast sheep stations of the country. They are tough, hard and yet have plenty of quality about them.

⚘ Early transport (above)
Cobb and Co. operated coaches over 6,000 miles (9,654km) in New South Wales and Queensland during the 1880s. The horses they used were Walers, often driven in seven-horse teams to the famous Concord coaches.

⚘ A perfect cavalry horse
If there was still a call for cavalry horses today, the Australian Stock Horse would be in great demand because of its ability to carry weight, its capacity for endurance and its innate hardiness, as well as its amenable temperament.

COLOR
The Australian Stock Horse is usually bay but other colors occur, although gray is rare. This horse is black.

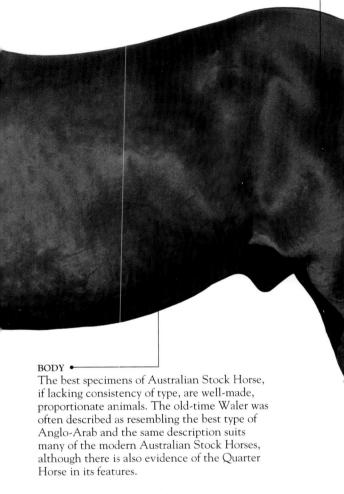

BODY
The best specimens of Australian Stock Horse, if lacking consistency of type, are well-made, proportionate animals. The old-time Waler was often described as resembling the best type of Anglo-Arab and the same description suits many of the modern Australian Stock Horses, although there is also evidence of the Quarter Horse in its features.

LIMBS
Australian-bred horses have always been noted for their excellent limbs and hooves, as well as for their enduring qualities and level tempers.

⚘ Australia's Brumbies
After the great Australian Gold Rush in the early 1850s, numerous horses – the imported forebears of the Walers and Stock Horses – were turned loose in the bush. Over the years, these horses ran wild and the herds grew ever larger while the animals degenerated in type and quality. These Brumbies, the Australian equivalent of the American Mustang, became so numerous that in the 1960s it was necessary to begin an extensive culling operation. The methods employed, however, were often inhumane and so unacceptable that Australia earned world-wide condemnation. In this picture, a Brumby exercises no little ingenuity in digging for water in a dried river bed in the harsh Northern Territory.

⚘ Endurance
The Australian Stock Horse, like its predecessors, is capable of great endurance, although it is nowhere near as fast as the Thoroughbred. In 1917, the Australian horsemen of Allenby's Mounted Corps marched 170 miles (274km) in four days in temperatures of 100°F (37.8°C). Even today, station hands cover long distances under the heat of the Australian sun.

Appaloosa

THE APPALOOSA is the American version of the spotted horse and is a distinctive and popular breed in the USA. The spotted gene in horses is as old as the equine race.

HISTORY

The cave art of Cro-Magnon man, executed as long as 20,000 years ago, depicts horses with spotted coat patterns. Spotted horses, under a variety of names, were known and often highly esteemed throughout Europe and Asia. There was the Knabstruper of Denmark (see pp.112–13), and in France such horses were termed *tigres*. In Britain, where they were once bred in a Royal stud, they were called Blagdon, or Chubbarie, a Romany name. There is now a thriving British Appaloosa Society, but their product has not yet attained breed status.

The American Appaloosa was developed by the Nez Percé Indians in the eighteenth century, using as a foundation the Spanish stock imported by the conquistadores, some of which carried the hereditary spotting genes. The Nez Percé lived in the northeast of Oregon and their lands included fertile, sheltered river valleys, principal among which was the Palouse river – Appaloosa is a corruption of "a Palouse horse." They were skillful horse breeders and practiced a strict, selective policy. The result was a distinctive, practical, work horse that had the advantage of color.

In 1876, the tribe and its horses were virtually wiped out as US troops seized tribal lands. In 1938 the breed was revived when the Appaloosa Horse Club was formed in Moscow, Idaho.

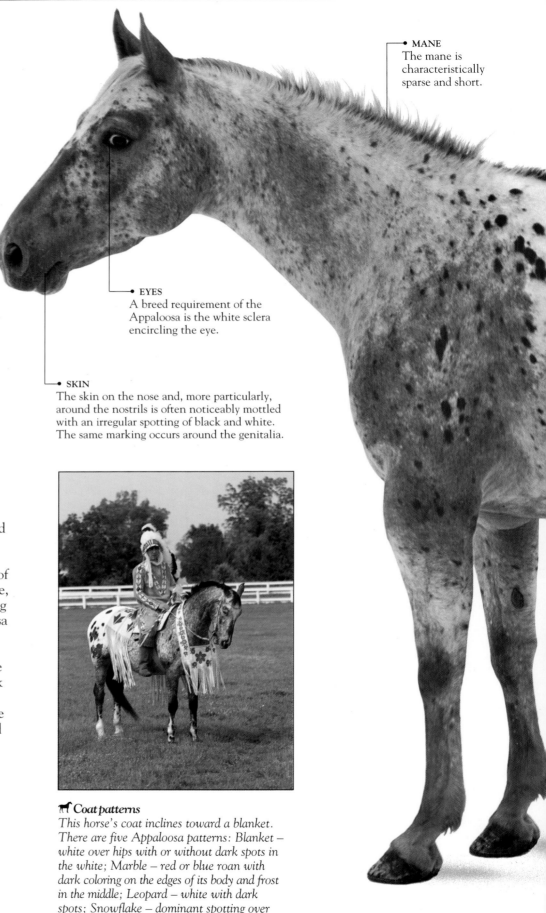

MANE
The mane is characteristically sparse and short.

EYES
A breed requirement of the Appaloosa is the white sclera encircling the eye.

SKIN
The skin on the nose and, more particularly, around the nostrils is often noticeably mottled with an irregular spotting of black and white. The same marking occurs around the genitalia.

🐎 **Coat patterns**
This horse's coat inclines toward a blanket. There are five Appaloosa patterns: Blanket – white over hips with or without dark spots in the white; Marble – red or blue roan with dark coloring on the edges of its body and frost in the middle; Leopard – white with dark spots; Snowflake – dominant spotting over hips; Frost – white specks with a dark ground.

HEIGHT
Usually 14.2–15.2hh but sometimes more in the European types.

🐎 **Divergence of types**
There is a certain divergence in type in the Appaloosa in America and Europe. The best, however, should have the appearance of a well-bred Quarter Horse, compact and with good limbs.

QUARTERS
In the USA, Appaloosas have been crossed with the Quarter Horse, and many have acquired the exaggerated development in the quarters of that breed. This is not the case in European Appaloosas, as here, which probably more closely resemble warmbloods. This type, suited for jumping and dressage, is gaining popularity in the USA.

🐎 **Athletic and agile** (above)
The Appaloosa is used as a stock and pleasure horse, as a parade horse and for jumping and racing. Not only is it athletic and agile, it is also a willing performer.

TAIL
The classic Appaloosa tail is thin, short and sparse. The Nez Percé saw this as a practical feature, for it prevented the tail being caught on sharp-thorned, close-growing shrubs and thickets.

🐎 **Appaloosa Horse Club**
The Appaloosa Horse Club was formed in 1938 from a few descendants of the original Nez Percé horses. Its object was the preservation of the breed. Now its breed registry is the third largest in the world, with over 65,000 registrations.

🐎 **Temperament**
The Nez Percé Indians bred their horses as practical, hardy and versatile mounts for war and hunting. They were also very concerned to breed horses that were sensible and had a tractable temperament. Finally, the Appaloosa had to possess endless stamina and endurance.

HOOVES
The hooves are notably good and hard, and are often distinguished by black and white vertical stripes. The Nez Percé Appaloosas were never shod.

121

Bashkir Curly

THE BASHKIR CURLY, or Bashkirsky, evolved centuries ago in Bashkiria, around the southern foothills of the Urals. There it is bred as a pack, draft and riding animal and to provide meat, milk, and clothing. In a 7- to 8-month lactation period, one mare yields 330–350 imperial gallons (1,500–1,600 litres). Moreover, the peculiarly thick, curly coat can be spun into cloth.

CHARACTERISTICS

The hardy Bashkir Curly is kept outdoors and can survive winter temperatures of -22 to -40°F (-30 to -40°C), and find food under 3ft (1m) of snow. A pair of Bashkir Curlys are said to be able to draw a sleigh 75–85 miles (120–140km) in 24 hours without being fed.

TYPES

Two types have developed within the USSR, the Mountain and the Steppe Bashkir Curly. The former has been crossed with Dons and Budonnys, and the latter, a harness type, with both Trotters and Ardennais stallions.

The pony pictured here is one of the 1,100 or so Bashkir Curlys registered in America. It has been claimed that they arrived on the American continent across the land bridge that is now the Bering Strait. However, that takes no account of the fact that the species *Equus* was extinct on the American continent after the Ice Age, which swept away the land bridge across the Bering Strait, and the horse was not reintroduced until the arrival of the Spanish conquistadores some 10,000 years later.

COAT
A principal feature of the Bashkir Curly, which is described as being docile and intelligent, is the very thick, curly, winter coat that enables it to survive in sub-zero temperatures.

COLOR
The principal colors of the Bashkir Curly are a red chestnut, as here, bay and light brown.

HOOVES
The practice of shoeing is not carried out in the Bashkir Curly's natural habitat, the animals' hard hooves allowing them to work under all kinds of conditions without shoes.

HEIGHT
The Bashkir Curly stands at 14hh.

MANE
In the Bashkir Curly, the mane and tail, as might be expected, should be exceptionally thick.

HEAD
The head of the Russian Bashkir Curly is massive and set on a short, fleshy neck that runs into flat withers. The American version has been improved in these respects, and in recent years selective crosses have produced a better quality animal in the USSR.

BODY
The Bashkir Curly is described in the official standard as being small with a wide body and a flat, straightish back. The measurement around the girth for stallions is 71in (180cm).

🐎 **The American Bashkir Curly**
In America, Bashkir-type ponies are found in the Northwest. They are reputed to have been popular with the American Indian, who used them in the same way as the Bashkir people. It is claimed that the ponies were first seen running wild in the 1800s.

LIMBS
The limbs of this solid little horse are comparatively short, and the official Russian breed standard quotes a remarkable bone measurement of 8in (20cm) below the knee.

🐎 **Living in luxury**
The breed is well able to fend for itself in the most severe climatic conditions and is, in consequence, among the most hardy in the world. This American Bashkir Curly is indulging in the luxury of a Kentucky paddock.

Landais

THE LANDAIS was originally a semi-wild pony that lived in the heavily wooded Landes region, south of Bordeaux and running down the Cote d'Argent to Biarritz and the barrier of the Pyrénées. It may have descended from the Tarpan and possibly the same is true of the bigger Landais, often called Barthais, which used to be found on the better grazing of the Chalosse plain.

INFLUENCES

In the nineteenth century, Arabian blood was introduced and repeated in 1913, when there were some 2,000 ponies in the area. After the Second World War, the Landais came near to extinction; at one time there were no more than 150 ponies. To avoid the dangers of in-breeding, the breed enthusiasts outcrossed to Welsh Section B stallions, strongly supported by the Arabian.

The formation of French pony clubs in the early 1970s encouraged the breeding of the Landais for use by children. The breed represents a significant base stock in the French Riding Pony (*Poney Français de Selle*), which, it is hoped, will one day rival its British counterpart.

The present-day Landais is a pony of improved quality, showing Arabian character and retaining the neat, pointed ears of the Welsh breeds. It remains a hardy breed and adapts easily to varying temperatures. Economical to keep, the Landais is, it is claimed, both docile and intelligent.

TOPLINE
The topline of the pony is acceptable in terms of the length of rein – from the withers over the neck to the poll. This counteracts, to a degree, the failings in the shoulders.

NECK
The neck is relatively long and thickens significantly at its base to join a somewhat loaded shoulder.

HEIGHT
The height is between 11.3 and 13.1hh.

🐎 Head
The Landais head is small, neat and finely chiselled, showing the strong Arabian influence. The short, pointed ears are entirely Welsh in character, and the eyes are widely spaced. The profile is straight but the overall appearance is not unattractive. Generally, the head joins smoothly to the neck without there being fleshiness through the jowl.

BACK
There is usually a straightness of the back, which, combined with the flat withers, poses a problem in regard to the fitting of the saddle. In general, the conformation tends to place the pony on its forehand.

COLOR
Predominant colors are dark bay, brown, black and chestnut. This pony is liver-chestnut.

QUARTERS
The quarters slope downward from the croup and have insufficient length, a matter now being corrected by outcrosses of better quality. The tail is held high in movement.

🐎 Pottock (*above*)
The semi-wild Pottock belongs to the mountainous, Basque region. It is one of the few remaining, indigenous ponies of France. It has been improved by crosses to Welsh Section B stallions and Arabians. There are three types: the Standard and the Piebald, which are between 11.1 and 13hh, and the Double, a bigger pony of 12.2–14.2hh. The Pottock is less refined than the Landais, but very tough.

LIMBS
The pony appears to be very light of limb, although the breed standard stipulates 6 1/2 – 7in (16.5–18cm) of bone on the forelimbs as being desirable. There is a tendency for the elbow to be "tied-in", restricting the freedom of movement.

HOOVES
On the whole, the hooves remain indicative of the Landais' primitive ancestry, being hard and well shaped.

🐎 Rear view
Thick manes and tails and a silky coat are a feature of the Landais; the tails are often grown very long. Generally, the quarters are inclined to be weak, the hind leg often inheriting this worst characteristic of the Arabian.

Ariègeois

T HE ARIÈGEOIS, sometimes called *cheval de Mérens*, has its home on the eastern edge of the Pyrenean chain that divides France from Spain. It takes its name from the Ariège river. The old-type of Ariègeois, so accurately described in Caesar's *Commentaries on the Gallic Wars*, is found only in the high valleys of the Spanish border toward Andorra.

HISTORY

Carvings and wall pictures at Niaux in the Ariège, made about 30,000 years ago, show the black, mountain pony in winter order, characteristic "beard" and all. Its substance was probably achieved by crossings with the Romans' heavy pack mares, and oriental blood was added to the pony at various times. The Ariègeois' home is not unlike the high fells of Cumbria in northern England. Indeed, the black Ariègeois is very similar to the British Fell (see pp.152–3) and almost an exact replica of the Dales (see pp.150–51).

Primarily a pack pony, the Ariègeois is employed on upland farms for cultivating steep slopes, where tractors are impractical. When smuggling was an accepted occupation along the Spanish border, the movement of contraband depended on the sure-footed Ariègeois – and it may still be so.

🐎 *Impervious to the cold*
The Ariègeois is impervious to the severe winters and is quite at home in its steep mountain home. However, it is not resistant to heat and needs shelter from the summer sun.

• OUTLINE
The outline is similar to that of the British Dales Pony. As befits an animal used for pack transport, the back is long but strong. Usually, the croup is sloped and the tail set somewhat low in consequence.

TAIL •
Like most inhabitants of the high mountains, the Ariègeois grows a thick, harsh mane and tail as protection against the cold winter weather.

LIMBS •
The limbs are less massive than might be expected, and there is a tendency to cow-hocks – so often a characteristic of the mountain-bred pony.

HOOVES •
The breed is exceptionally sure-footed and traverses the steep and icy mountain paths without difficulty. The density of the horn is exceptional and makes shoeing unnecessary.

NECK
The neck is fairly short and straight, and lacks any elegance.

MANE
The mane is exceptionally heavy and adds to the impression of coarseness about the head.

BODY
Despite the broad chest, straight and upright shoulders and flat withers that have considerable width between the shoulder blades, the girth of the Ariègeois is fairly deep.

COLOR
The coat is solid black with reddish highlights in winter. White markings are exceptional. The flanks, however, may be lightly flecked with white.

🐎 *Head*
The head can be coarse but it is light-boned and expressive. The forehead is flat, the ears fairly short and very hairy and the profile straight. The eyes are bright and alert with a gentle expression. In winter, a hairy "beard" growth covers the jawbones.

🐎 *Hardy breed*
The breed is versatile, easily managed and constitutionally hardy. It can work on minimum rations of relatively poor quality.

HEIGHT
The Ariègeois is between 13.1 and 14.3hh. The latter is attained only on lowland pastures.

Haflinger

The Haflinger has its mountain homeland in the southern Austrian Tyrol, around the village of Hafling in the Etschlander Mountains. The principal Haflinger stud is at Jenesien. The pony has an innate ability to work on the steep mountain slopes, and is used for both riding and driving.

ORIGINS
The modern Haflinger, although a coldblood, has an eastern foundation through the Arabian stallion El Bedavi XXII, to whom all purebred Haflingers can be traced back. Otherwise the base stock originates in the indigenous, but now extinct, Alpine Heavy Horse and a related pony breed. There are later infusions of smaller Norik Horses and Hucul, Bosnian and Konic Ponies, which may be regarded as being of a similar genetic background.

CHARACTER
The close-knit character of the Haflinger family and the mountain environment ensures a fixed type of unmistakable appearance. The breed is enormously sound and hardy, the young stock being raised on the Alpine pastures (a practice known as *alpung*) where the thin air develops their hearts and lungs.

HEAD
The large eyes, big, open nostrils and small ears give the Haflinger a lively, intelligent appearance and reflect its kindly temperament.

COLOR
The color is always chestnut or palomino with a characteristic flaxen mane and tail. This makes the Haflinger one of the world's most attractive ponies.

Avelignese (left)
The Avelignese is the Italian version of the Haflinger and is often bigger than its cousin over the mountain (up to 14.3hh). They share a common ancestor in El Bedavi XXII, and have much the same background and an almost identical appearance. A mountain horse used in draft and pack work, the Avelignese is bred in the mountainous areas of northern, central and southern Italy.

🐎 **Edelweiss brand** (right)
The Haflinger is sometimes called the Edelweiss Pony. All Haflinger-bred ponies bear a brand mark featuring Austria's native flower with a letter H at its center.

BACK
The Haflinger is strong and notably muscular. The back is inclined to be long as befits a pony that is often used for pack purposes.

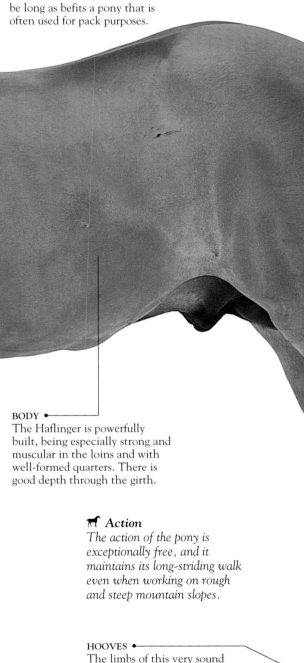

BODY
The Haflinger is powerfully built, being especially strong and muscular in the loins and with well-formed quarters. There is good depth through the girth.

🐎 **Action**
The action of the pony is exceptionally free, and it maintains its long-striding walk even when working on rough and steep mountain slopes.

HOOVES
The limbs of this very sound pony are well made, and the hooves are excellent. Bred and reared on mountain slopes, it is naturally sure-footed.

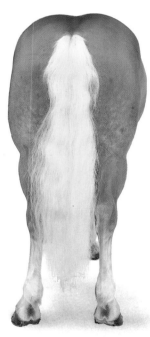

🐎 **Willing worker**
The Haflinger is a versatile and willing worker. It will draw a sleigh, pull wheeled vehicles or work in forestry or on the farm. In Austria, ponies are not worked until they are 4 years old, but it is not unknown for them to be fit and active at 40 years of age.

🐎 **Rear view**
A full and flowing, flaxen tail that is well set into strong quarters is a feature of Austria's hard-working Haflinger Pony.

HEIGHT
The Haflinger Pony stands up to 13.3hh.

Italian Heavy Draft

T HE MOST POPULAR HEAVY HORSE in Italy is the Heavy Draft Horse, sometimes called the Italian Agricultural Horse. A third of the stallions standing at stud in Italy are of this breed. It is bred throughout northern and central Italy but chiefly in the region around Venice. A feature of the breed is that it matures early, a distinct advantage in a horse that is now produced for its carcass potential in the European meat market as well as for its working qualities.

HISTORY

There was a time when Italy imported the massive Brabant – the Belgian Draft – initially using these very heavy horses to improve their local strains. Thereafter, the more active Boulonnais and Percheron were tried, but none really fulfilled the Italian requirement for a quick-moving horse of smaller proportions. The answer was found eventually in outcrossing heavily to the lighter, clean-legged Breton Postier (see pp.174–5). Because of the Breton's connection with the Norfolk Trotter or Roadster, it was renowned for its speed at trot and was the ideal type for the light draft and farm work required in Italian agriculture. They crossed well with the more common Italian Draft mares, and the progeny were powerful animals with kind, docile temperaments. Their speed in action accounts for the Italian breed title, *Tiro Pesante Rapido* – Quick Heavy Draft.

🐎 Conformation
The Italian Draft, though not so attractive as the Breton from which it derives, is, nonetheless, a compact, symmetrical animal retaining some of the Breton's good, conformational features.

FOREHAND •
Like that of the Breton, the chest is exceptionally deep, the forelegs being spaced well apart. Some coarseness is apparent, the legacy of the common and less well-made Italian mares.

LIMBS •
The limbs are fairly muscular but the joints are inclined to roundness, another characteristic of the poor-quality base stock.

🐎 Bardigiano (left)
The Bardigiano is a mountain-pony strain from the northern Appenine region. It owes something to the heavier mountain strains as well as to the Avelignese, a pony almost identical to the Haflinger (see pp.128–9). A pronounced oriental influence is also discernible. This is a strong, well-made pony of character, hardy and quick-moving. Despite the unusual mixed background, it appears to be bred with greater care than is usually the case with Italian breeds, other than the Trotter, the Thoroughbred and the Salerno. It is certainly one of the most attractive of Italy's equines.

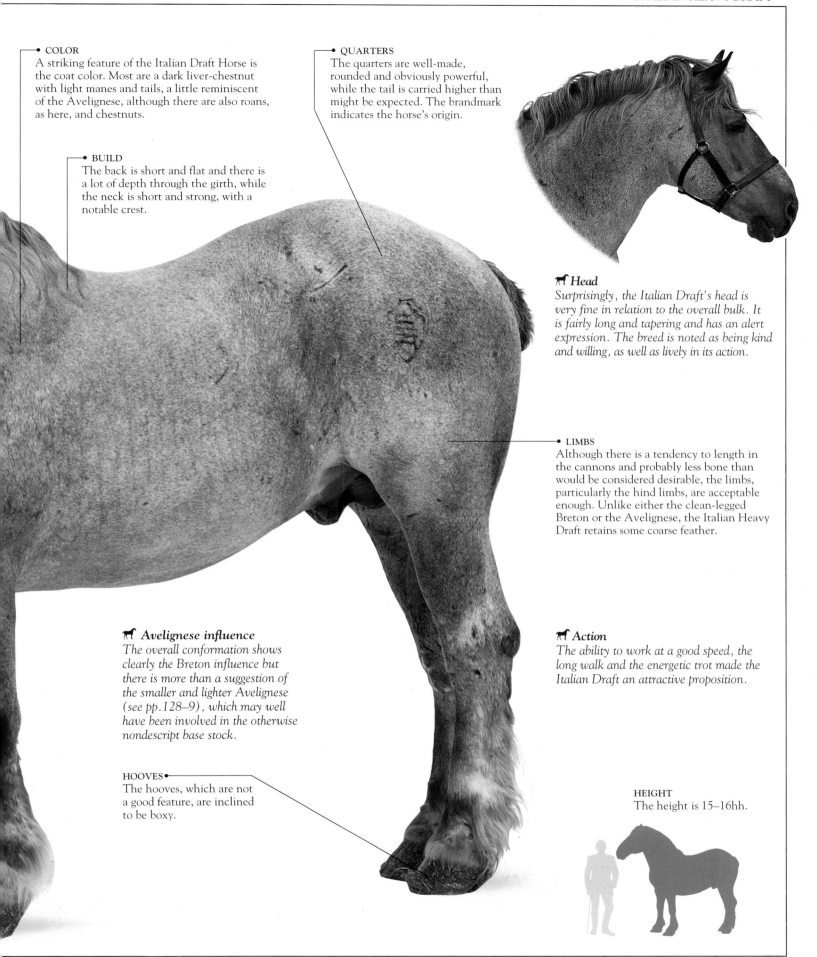

COLOR
A striking feature of the Italian Draft Horse is the coat color. Most are a dark liver-chestnut with light manes and tails, a little reminiscent of the Avelignese, although there are also roans, as here, and chestnuts.

BUILD
The back is short and flat and there is a lot of depth through the girth, while the neck is short and strong, with a notable crest.

QUARTERS
The quarters are well-made, rounded and obviously powerful, while the tail is carried higher than might be expected. The brandmark indicates the horse's origin.

🐎 Head
Surprisingly, the Italian Draft's head is very fine in relation to the overall bulk. It is fairly long and tapering and has an alert expression. The breed is noted as being kind and willing, as well as lively in its action.

LIMBS
Although there is a tendency to length in the cannons and probably less bone than would be considered desirable, the limbs, particularly the hind limbs, are acceptable enough. Unlike either the clean-legged Breton or the Avelignese, the Italian Heavy Draft retains some coarse feather.

🐎 Avelignese influence
The overall conformation shows clearly the Breton influence but there is more than a suggestion of the smaller and lighter Avelignese (see pp.128–9), which may well have been involved in the otherwise nondescript base stock.

HOOVES
The hooves, which are not a good feature, are inclined to be boxy.

🐎 Action
The ability to work at a good speed, the long walk and the energetic trot made the Italian Draft an attractive proposition.

HEIGHT
The height is 15–16hh.

Norwegian Fjord

OF THE MODERN HORSES, none bears so striking a resemblance to the Asiatic Wild Horse as the attractive Norwegian Fjord, which may also have a connection with the Tarpan, as it retains both their coat color and much of their primitive vigor. The Fjord was the Vikings' horse and is recognizable in their runestone carvings in Norway, many of which depict fights between stallions, perhaps an early form of performance testing. The Fjord went with the warriors in their longboats when they raided Scotland's Western Isles. Its influence remains in Scotland's Highland Pony and in the ancient Icelandic Horse.

CHARACTERISTICS

In its native land, the powerful Fjord carries out every sort of work, taking the place of the tractor on mountain farms. It will draw a plough, and carry a pack load though rivers and along precipitous, mountain tracks. It is also used under saddle and excels in long-distance events, which suit its courage and boundless stamina. It is a brilliant performer in harness and can hold its own in demanding, competitive events.

The Fjord is found in variant types throughout Scandinavia but is bred principally in Norway. A great number are exported to Germany, Denmark and Central European countries, where their qualities have made them popular.

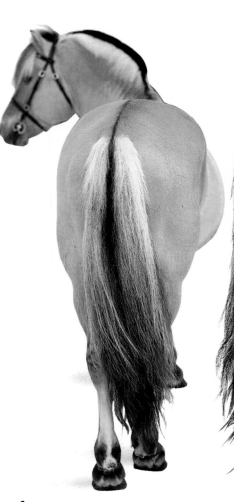

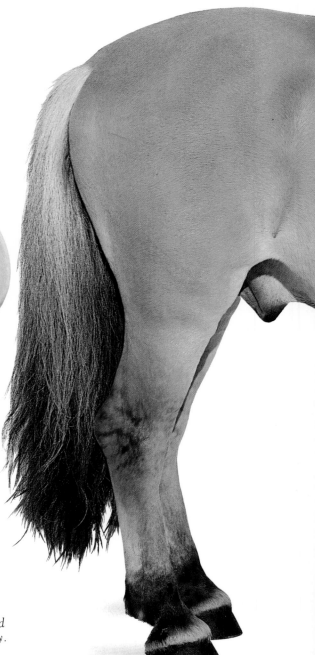

🐎 Eastern blood
Although the Fjord is primitive in type, selective breeding has produced a suggestion of eastern blood, possibly from the Tarpan, and limbs of great strength and substance.

🐎 Gotland Pony
On the Swedish island of Gotland in the Baltic Sea, the Gotland Pony has existed since the Stone Age and is probably Scandinavia's oldest breed. At one time it ran wild, and there is still a wild herd in the Lojsta Forest. Like the Fjord, it is possibly a descendant of the Tarpan. It walks and trots well but is no galloper.

🐎 Rear view
The tail is often silver and is thick and full but is occasionally low-set. The dorsal eel-stripe is typical of the breed and revealing of the Fjord's primitive ancestry. The quarters reflect the short, compact conformation and the overall strength of build. Light feather occurs on the heels.

MANE
From early Viking times, it has been the custom to cut the coarse mane so that it stands erect, the crescent shape giving a pronounced crest to the neck. The black hair at the center of the mane stands out above the rest.

HEAD
The head is wide and pony-like with small, sharp ears. There is some thickness through the jowl, but the profile is never convex.

COLOR
The Fjord color is dun, in all its shades, accompanied by a dorsal eel-stripe running from the forelock to the tip of the tail. There are often zebra bars on the legs, as here.

LIMBS
The limbs are an outstanding feature of the Fjord – powerful, short and straight with excellent joints. Selective breeding has ensured a substantial bone measurement below the knee and short cannons.

BODY
The body is rounded in the barrel and very well muscled. A powerful, fairly broad chest is typical. There is no discernible wither and no great slope to the shoulders.

🐎 *At work*
The Fjord excels as a sure-footed, enduring worker in difficult conditions of terrain and climate. It makes an excellent harness pony, able to carry out all sorts of farm, pack and harness work on the upland holdings.

HOOVES
The hooves are exemplary in every way, being sound, hard and properly shaped.

🐎 *A will of its own*
The Fjord is an economical feeder and is tough, hardy and long-lived. It is a willing, courageous worker but has a will of its own.

HEIGHT
The Norwegian Fjord stands between 13 and 14hh.

Icelandic Horse

MANE
Both mane and tail
are full and abundant.

ALTHOUGH THE ICELANDIC HORSE stands no more than 13.2hh, it is never referred to as a pony by the Icelanders. The horses came to this volcanic island in the longboats of the Norsemen, who settled there between A.D.860 and 935. It has occupied a central place in the lives of the Icelanders for over 1,000 years.

HISTORY

The strong, Icelandic horse culture has an extreme purity of stock as it has received no outside blood for over 800 years. There was an attempt to add eastern blood but it proved so disastrous that the *Althing*, the world's oldest parliament, prohibited the import of horses in A.D.930.

From an early date, selective breeding seems to have been practiced, using fights between stallions as a basis for selection. Selective breeding on a practical scale began in 1879 in the most famous breeding area, Skagafjördur in northern Iceland. The programs were largely based on the quality of the five gaits peculiar to the Icelandic Horse. Many studs breed strictly to a specific color, of which there are 15 basic types and combinations.

The Icelandic Horse, often kept in semi-feral conditions, is used for every sort of work. Sport is equally important. Competitive events are held frequently and include racing, cross-country and even dressage competitions. As cattle cannot be wintered out in Iceland and the Icelandic Horses can, horse herds are also kept for meat; horse flesh has always been a staple of Icelandic diet.

HEAD
The head is distinctive but plain and heavy in proportion to the short, stocky body.

FOREHAND
The shoulders appear to be relatively straight rather than otherwise. The neck is short and carried well but is usually thick through the jowl.

HEIGHT
The Icelandic Horse stands between 12.3 and 13.2hh.

🐎 *Semi-feral horses*
About half of Iceland's horses live outdoors all year in a semi-feral state, without receiving any supplementary feed to sustain them through the harsh winters. Occasionally, however, the horses are given the highly nutritious herring, with which the Icelandic seas abound.

COLOR
Color is a feature of the Icelandic breed and there are 15 recognized combinations. Chestnut accompanied by a flaxen mane and tail, as here, is popular. There are also duns, bays, grays and blacks. Sometimes palomino and albino are found as well as piebald and skewbald.

BODY
The girth is always deep and the back is short.

QUARTERS
The quarters of the Icelandic Horse are peculiarly wedge-shaped and sloping but are, nonetheless, very strong and muscular. The animal has a notable ability to engage the hind legs well under the body.

Tolt
The tolt, pictured here, is the specialized four-beat running walk used by the Icelandic Horse to cross broken ground swiftly. It is a "gait which with unaltered footfall can escalate its swiftness from a mere stop to great speed" (Icelandic Pony Society breed standard).

LIMBS
Although small, the Icelandic Horse is able to carry full-grown men at speed over long distances and difficult terrain. Its compact body is carried on strong limbs, notable for their short cannons and strong hocks.

Five-gaited horse
The five Icelandic gaits are: fetgangur (walk) used under pack; brokk (trot) for crossing rough country; stökk (gallop) and the two gaits of antiquity, the skeid (pace), which covers short distances at speed and the tolt, the famous running walk.

HOOVES
The hooves are exemplary and the breed is noted for its agility and sure-footedness over rough country.

Racing the Icelandic Horse
The first modern race-meeting of Icelandic Horses was held at Akureyri in 1874. Racing takes place at different venues between April and June, the biggest being at Reykjavik on Whit Monday.

Caspian

I T WAS A MATTER of enormous scientific and historical importance when the Caspian Miniature Horse, now termed a "pony" on account of its size, was discovered by Mrs. Louise L. Firouz at Amol on the Caspian littoral in 1965. The Caspian is certainly the most ancient breed in existence.

HISTORY

It is generally accepted that just prior to the domestication of the horse, four sub-species were in existence (see Origins pp.10–11). There were two pony types and two horse types, the last of these, Horse Type 4, was the smallest of all, standing no more than perhaps 9hh, but it was a horse in respect of its proportions. It was the most refined of the four, had a high-set tail and a distinctly concave profile. Its habitat was in western Asia and it is suggested that this was the Arabian prototype. The trilingual seal of Darius the Great (c.500B.C.) shows very small horses pulling the royal chariot, and Egyptian artefacts, dated 1,000 years before Darius, depict similar horses of small stature but full of quality.

Research seems to point to the Caspian as being the far-off ancestor, far off by some 3,000 years possibly, of the Arabian horse. It has physical characteristics different to other equines. There is an extra molar in the upper jaw, a pronounced difference in the shape of the scapula and a different formation of parietal bones of the head.

There are thriving Caspian societies in Britain, Australia, New Zealand and the USA. Studs exist in Iran.

HEIGHT
The height is between 10 and 12hh (the ancient pony was smaller).

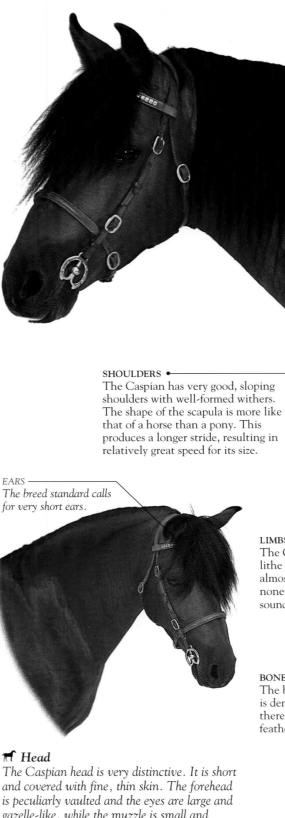

NECK
The neck is usually arched and graceful, flowing into the fairly sharp withers formation.

SHOULDERS
The Caspian has very good, sloping shoulders with well-formed withers. The shape of the scapula is more like that of a horse than a pony. This produces a longer stride, resulting in relatively great speed for its size.

EARS
The breed standard calls for very short ears.

LIMBS
The Caspian has slim, lithe legs that look almost fragile but are, nonetheless, inherently sound and strong.

BONE
The bone below the knee is dense and strong and there is little or no feathering at the fetlock.

🐎 **Head**
The Caspian head is very distinctive. It is short and covered with fine, thin skin. The forehead is peculiarly vaulted and the eyes are large and gazelle-like, while the muzzle is small and tapered with the large nostrils set low. The breed standard calls for very short ears, actually stipulating that they should not be more than 4¹/₂in (11.4cm) long.

⚘ Temperament

The Caspian is a kind, highly intelligent and willing animal. It is spirited but never unruly, and the stallions can be both handled and ridden by small children.

COLOR
Principal colors are bay, as here, gray and chestnut with occasional blacks and creams. White markings can occur on head and legs.

BACK
The back is straight and the tail is usually carried high, like that of the Arabian.

⚘ Arabian prototype (above)

The well-proportioned Arabian may have originated with the Caspian and it has many of the latter's characteristics. The Caspian has a similar symmetry and is more a miniature horse in its proportions than a pony. Although the Arabian is an ancient breed, it has been claimed that it could have been preceded by the Caspian.

BODY
The body is slim and narrow with no hint of heaviness. Because of this narrow build, children find the Caspian easy to ride.

⚘ Action

The action is natural and floating. The walk and trot are long-striding, the canter is smooth and the gallop very rapid. Despite its size, the Caspian can keep up with an average horse at all gaits other than the full gallop. It is a natural jumper of exceptional and extraordinary ability.

HOOVES
The hooves of the Caspian are very strong, small and oval-shaped.

⚘ Rear view

Narrow and light, the quick-moving Caspian is built for speed, although it is also a very capable performer in harness. The breed has a full and flowing mane and tail, the latter being carried high.

Falabella

MINIATURE HORSES have been bred as pets and for their curiosity value at various periods of equine history, but the best known is the Falabella. Despite its size, the Falabella is not a pony but a miniature horse, having the horse's characteristics and proportions. The "breed" is named after the Falabella family, who developed the little animals on its Recreo de Roca Ranch, outside Buenos Aires in Argentina.

🐎 *Julio Cesar Falabella*
Julio Cesar Falabella is a member of the family that first developed the miniature "breed." He is pictured here with a mare and foal that still bear some resemblance to the original Shetland foundation.

ORIGINS

The basis of the Falabella was the Shetland Pony and possibly a very small, freak Thoroughbred, at one time. The Falabella came about through deliberate down-breeding with crosses of the smallest animals and thereafter through close in-breeding. In the process, strength and vigor have been lost, and the animals have lost any of the Shetland's hereditary toughness.

Falabellas are popular in America and are bred in England, as well as being exported elsewhere. It is said that they can be used in harness, but they are unsuitable for riding.

🐎 *Falabella foals*
These Falabella foals are appealing, but the practice of down-breeding and in-breeding has resulted in conformational weaknesses even in these carefully reared animals. Breeders have also to consider the effects on the constitution and guard against inherited loss of vigor.

QUARTERS •
Here is a good example of a miniature horse although it lacks correctness and some strength in the quarters and hind limbs. The aim of the breeders is to produce a near-perfect specimen in miniature.

COLOR •
Most colors occur including bay, black, brown, gray and part-colors but the spotted Appaloosa-type coat pattern, as here, is increasingly sought after.

HOCKS •
The hocks tend to be weak and to be held close together, that is, cow-hocked.

TAIL •
Luxurious growth of the mane and tail is usual on the Falabella.

⚘ Sugar-Dumpling
A noted breeder of midget horses was Smith McCoy of Roderfield, West Virginia. His smallest horse was a mare called Sugar-Dumpling. She weighed a mere 30lb (13.5kg) and stood only 20in (51cm) high.

⚘ Pet
Although the Falabella has no practical use, it can be an attractive and engaging pet, and it is reputed to be a most friendly and intelligent little creature. The head and general expression are particularly pleasing.

• COAT
Falabella coats are often long and silky but they do not have the Shetland's thick, warm undercoat and they do not approach that breed in terms of hardiness or strength of constitution.

⚘ Head
This Falabella head is not unlike that of the Shetland, from which the breed was derived. In the best Falabella specimens, the head is in proportion to the small body, in the poorer ones it is large in comparison.

• LIMBS
The limbs are not always the best, a common failing being the tendency toward lack of bone and bow-legs in front – deficiencies that breeders are trying to eliminate.

• HOOVES
The hooves may be acceptable in terms of size and shape, but are occasionally inclined to be boxy.

HEIGHT
The height does not exceed 30in (76cm) at the withers.

Exmoor Pony

T HE EXMOOR PONY is the oldest of Britain's Mountain and Moorland breeds and, apart from "primitives" like the Tarpan, is probably as old as any breed. It retains features found in its main ancestor, Pony Type 1 (see Origins pp.10–11) – a particular jaw formation with a seventh molar, for instance, that is present in no other equine.

ORIGINS

The breed takes its name from the high, wild moorland in Southwest England, its natural habitat and where it has been largely isolated for centuries. It is this harsh, inhospitable environment that is responsible for the peculiar character of the incredibly strong and hardy Exmoor Pony. Efforts were made to "improve" the breed in the nineteenth century, but without any great success. It is thought that Spanish blood was introduced after 1815 through "a sort of spectre horse," who came to be known as Katerfelto, and ran on the Moor. He was eventually captured but it was never discovered from where he had come. He was described as being dun with black points and a pronounced eel-stripe down his back.

There are still herds running on Exmoor whose purity and quality are jealously safeguarded by the Exmoor Pony Society, as well as, of course, others bred off the Moor. However, ponies bred away from the Moor tend to lose type, and it is necessary for breeders to return to the original stock to maintain the original character.

Strength
The Exmoor Pony is enormously strong, well balanced and capable of carrying weight well out of proportion to its size. It has been known to carry a man for a full day's hunting.

NECK
Bronze Age harnesses compelled chariot ponies to pull largely from a strap across the neck, resulting in a muscular development on the underside. For generations, the Exmoor Pony, first used in chariots, exhibited this peculiarity.

Head
The Exmoor Pony's head is unique. The muzzle is mealy colored; the nostrils wide; the ears short, thick and pointed; the forehead is broad; and the eyes are large and prominent. They are termed toad eyes because they are hooded to provide protection against the weather. The head is a little larger than other breeds because of the length of the nasal passages, which allow the air to be warmed before inhalation.

HEIGHT
The Exmoor Pony stands between 12.2 and 12.3hh.

🐎 Brand marks (left)
Foals passed by the breed inspectors at the annual autumn "gathering" are branded with a star on the shoulder to indicate that they are purebred Exmoor Ponies. Beneath the star the herd number is branded and on the left hindquarter you find the number of the pony within the herd. Therefore, you can always identify ponies by their brand.

• COLOR
The color of the Exmoor Pony is distinctive. The ponies are bay, brown or dun with black points. They are mealy colored on the muzzle, around the eyes, on the inside of the flanks and thighs, and on the under-belly. No white markings are permissible.

🐎 Action
The action is straight, smooth and balanced without any exaggerated knee lift. Exmoor Ponies are noted for their ability to gallop and jump.

🐎 On Exmoor
Ponies have run on Exmoor since before the Ice Age, their character being formed by the harshness of the environment. In a sense, the herds of Exmoor Ponies remain wild. Although they are brought in annually for inspection, they are naturally nervous of encounters with humans. They are also nervous of dogs, possibly because encounters with them arouse atavistic memories of attacks by wolves.

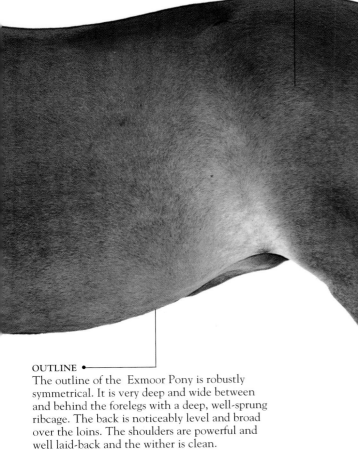

OUTLINE •
The outline of the Exmoor Pony is robustly symmetrical. It is very deep and wide between and behind the forelegs with a deep, well-sprung ribcage. The back is noticeably level and broad over the loins. The shoulders are powerful and well laid-back and the wither is clean.

LIMBS •
Features of the breed are uniformly short limbs, and well spaced forelegs set square to the body. The hind legs are set nicely apart, perpendicular from hock to fetlock, and the hock is in line with the pelvis bone.

HOOVES AND BONE •
Short cannons, good bone and hard, neat hooves are general in the breed.

🐎 Rear view
In nature, the Exmoor Pony's tail has a thick and fan-like growth at the top. This "ice" tail gives protection against rain and snow. The coat, too, is double textured and waterproof. In winter it grows thick, harsh and springy. In summer it is dense and hard and has a peculiar metallic sheen.

Dartmoor Pony

"THERE IS ON DARTMOOR a race of ponies much in request in that vicinity, being sure-footed and hardy and admirably calculated to scramble over the rough roads and dreary wilds of that mountainous district. The Dartmoor is larger than the Exmoor and, if possible, uglier." So wrote William Youatt, an equine authority, in 1820.

CHARACTERISTICS

Fifty years later, comment was made in *The Field Magazine* about the ponies' jumping ability, "they can jump as well as the moor sheep, and much after the same fashion." Today, the Dartmoor Pony still performs well over obstacles. However, Youatt would be amazed at the transformation that the original ponies have undergone to produce the modern Dartmoor Pony. It is one of the most elegant riding ponies, far removed from the stock that he observed.

ORIGINS

The breed has its origin on the rough moorland of the Dartmoor Forest intersected by the rivers Dart, Taw and Tavy. Nowadays, few ponies are bred on the Moor.

The Dartmoor Pony has been influenced by several different breeds. There is an early connection with the Old Devon Pack Horse, drawn from both Exmoor and Dartmoor Pony blood, and the Cornish Goonhilly Pony. Both are now extinct. Oriental or eastern horses may have been introduced as early as the twelfth century. Among the many breeds used in the nineteenth century were trotting Roadsters, Welsh Ponies and Cobs, Exmoor Ponies, Arabians, and small Thoroughbreds. Shetland Ponies were also used in an attempt to produce ponies for coal mining.

During the Second World War, Dartmoor Ponies came close to extinction. Between 1941 and 1943 only two males and twelve females were registered. The breed was largely saved by the Pony and Riding Society (now the National Pony Society).

NECK
The Dartmoor Pony's neck is strong but with the length associated with a riding pony.

SHOULDERS
The Dartmoor Pony is notable for the excellence of the shoulder which is wonderfully sloped to give the best sort of riding action, and ensures that the Dartmoor Pony is a first-class performer.

🐎 Head
The head, set gracefully on the neck, is "pure pony": small, full of quality and with the characteristic small and very alert ears. The temperament is excellent, and the Dartmoor Pony makes an ideal child's pony, not least because of the easy smoothness of the distinctive action.

🐎 The Leat
The greatest factors in the development of the Dartmoor Pony were the stallion, the Leat, and his owner, Sylvia Calmady-Hamlyn. She was honorary secretary of the Dartmoor Pony Society for 32 years. The Leat, a part-bred, was 12.2hh, and was described as "a magnificent pony." His sire was the desert-bred Arabian Dwarka, and his dam the black 13hh mare Blackdown by Confident George, out of a Dartmoor Pony mare.

🐎 Constitution
Like all the British native breeds, the Dartmoor Pony is hardy and constitutionally sound.

LOIN
The loin and hind leg are particularly correct. The excellence of the Dartmoor Pony's conformation gives the breed a natural balance.

🐎 Riding pony champions
Along with Welsh Ponies, the Dartmoor Pony dominates the riding pony classes and has contributed greatly to the beautiful British riding pony. It is very popular in Europe, and crosses well with Thoroughbreds or Arabians. The second cross with the Thoroughbred produces class competition horses.

COLOR
Dartmoor Ponies are bay, as here, black or brown. Skewbald or piebald are not accepted by the breed society, which also discourages any excessive white markings.

LIMBS
Limbs and hooves are the best. The cannons are short and the bone measurement under the knee of the forelimbs is ample.

🐎 Action
The Dartmoor Pony action is notable among the pony breeds for the lack of knee lift. It is low, long and economical – "typical hack or riding action."

HEIGHT
Height does not exceed 12.2hh.

Welsh Mountain Pony

THE WELSH PONY and Cob Society Stud Book was opened in 1902 and is divided into four sections: two for ponies and two for cobs. The indisputable base for the Welsh breeding is the smallest of the four pure-breds, the Welsh Mountain Pony, which occupies Section A in the Stud Book. From this foundation emanate the Welsh Pony (Section B), the Welsh Pony of Cob Type (Section C), and the powerful Welsh Cob (Section D).

ORIGINS

The Romans were the first "improvers" of the indigenous Welsh stock. They introduced eastern blood, an outcross that recurs often in the breed's history.

The first recorded influence was that of the Thoroughbred Merlin, a direct descendant of the Darley Arabian, put out on the Ruabon hills in Clwyd in the eighteenth century. Apricot, a Merioneth stallion, also had an influence. He was described as being an Arabian-Barb out of a mountain mare.

The patriarch of the modern Mountain Pony is acknowledged as being Dyoll Starlight, born in 1894, whose dam was said to have been a "miniature Arab." After Dyoll Starlight came Coed Coch Glyndwr, whose dam was Starlight's granddaughter.

CHARACTER

The modern Welsh Mountain Pony is arguably the most beautiful of all ponies but in its evolution it has, nonetheless, retained its characteristic hardiness, strength of constitution, inherent soundness, and the pony sagacity peculiar to the breed. The Mountain Pony is a splendid child's mount, a brilliant performer in harness and an unsurpassed foundation to produce bigger ponies and horses.

HEIGHT
Welsh Mountain Ponies
do not stand over 12hh.

Dyoll Starlight
Dyoll Starlight marks the watershed between the old breed and the refined modern pony. The stud prefix Dyoll is the name of his breeder Meuric Lloyd spelt backwards. Lady Wentworth, owner of the Crabbet Arab Stud, acquired Starlight when Lloyd became terminally ill, on condition that the pony should not be sold. She broke the agreement by selling him to Spain in 1925. He died there in 1929.

Mares and foals
The Mountain Ponies of today owe much to the second great progenitor of the breed, Coed Coch Glyndwr. He was the foundation stallion of the famous and influential Welsh stud, Coed Coch, founded in 1924 by Miss M. Brodrick at Dolwen, Abergele, in North Wales. His great grandsire was the Cob, Eiddwen Flyer.

🐎 On the mountain
The Welsh Mountain Pony is a product of its early environment in terms of action, conformation and constitutional hardiness. The wild terrain, the paucity of food and harsh climatic conditions have also ensured a remarkably efficient nutrient conversion – the ponies are able to thrive on minimal rations.

EARS
Tiny, pointed ears, essential in the pony breeds, are a feature of the Mountain Pony.

• BODY
The body is notably compact with great depth through the girth, allowing ample room for powerful lungs and a heart that is large in comparison to the pony's small stature. The short, powerful loin is a particular feature.

• COLOR
Dyoll Starlight was largely responsible for the predominance of grays in Section A ponies, but bays, such as this one, and chestnuts also occur, and there are notable palomino strains.

🐎 Action
The action of the Mountain Pony originates in the powerful hind leg and exemplary hock joints engaged well beneath the body. The movement from the shoulder is remarkably free but with the knee action necessary for the safe crossing of broken ground.

• HOOVES
The hooves, in common with those of most mountain breeds, are of dense, blue horn and are exceptionally hard.

🐎 Head
The head of the Welsh Mountain Pony is dominated by the large and luminous eyes, which are the glory of the Welsh breeds. The eyes and the wide, open nostrils, together with the dished face, reveal the strong influence of eastern blood in this kind but innately courageous and spirited pony, which is as beautiful as any in the world.

Welsh Pony

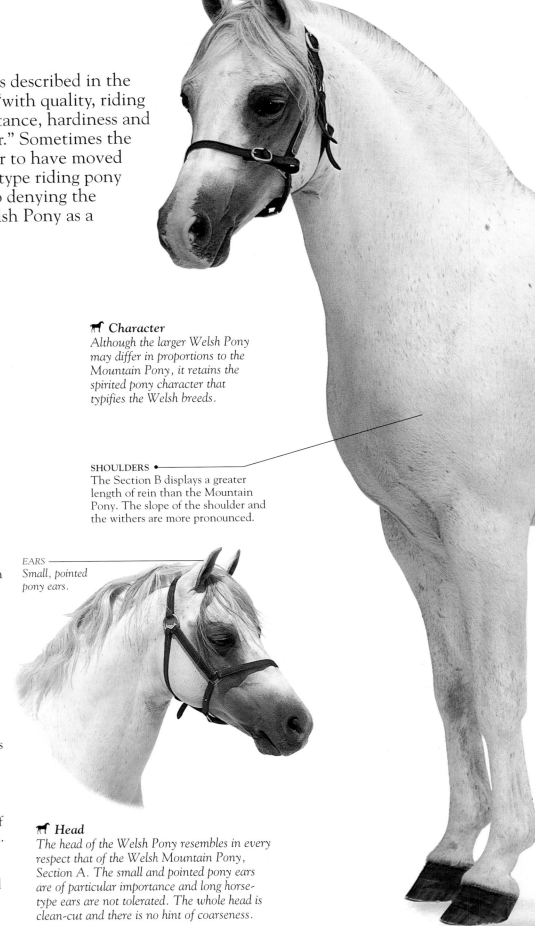

THE WELSH PONY, Section B, is described in the Stud Book as a riding pony "with quality, riding action, adequate bone and substance, hardiness and constitution and pony character." Sometimes the modern Welsh Pony may appear to have moved too close to the Thoroughbred-type riding pony (see pp.190–91), but there is no denying the commercial viability of the Welsh Pony as a competition pony.

ORIGINS
The early ponies of the "old breed" were often the result of crosses between Mountain mares and small Welsh Cob stallions, upgraded by the use of Arabians and small Thoroughbreds. They lived on the mountain and many carried men both shepherding and hunting. The modern ponies are much improved in quality, scope and action. They are unequalled as riding ponies anywhere in the world and most retain their original characteristic toughness and their typical pony qualities.

INFLUENCES
The "Abraham" of the Section B pony was Tan-y-Bwlch Berwyn, whose son Tan-y-Bwlch Berwynfa was the foundation of the famous Coed Coch Section B herd. Berwyn, and the Welsh pony in general, relied on the eastern blood that complements the Welsh stock so well. Berwyn was foaled in 1924. He was by Sahara, a Barb (or more likely Arabian) stallion bought in Gibraltar in 1913, out of a dam who was the granddaughter of the Welsh Mountain Pony sire, Dyoll Starlight.

Criban Victor, a stallion almost as notable, arrived twenty years later. He, too, displayed the essential connections with the Mountain Pony. He was by Coed Coch Glyndwr's son, Criban Winston, although his dam was by the famous Welsh Cob stallion, Mathrafal Broadcast – a classic Welsh amalgam of the Sections comprising the Stud Book. Additional evidence of the strong and permeating eastern influence is provided by the lines that have derived from the world champion, Skowronek, and the illustrious Raseem.

Character
Although the larger Welsh Pony may differ in proportions to the Mountain Pony, it retains the spirited pony character that typifies the Welsh breeds.

SHOULDERS •
The Section B displays a greater length of rein than the Mountain Pony. The slope of the shoulder and the withers are more pronounced.

EARS
Small, pointed pony ears.

Head
The head of the Welsh Pony resembles in every respect that of the Welsh Mountain Pony, Section A. The small and pointed pony ears are of particular importance and long horse-type ears are not tolerated. The whole head is clean-cut and there is no hint of coarseness.

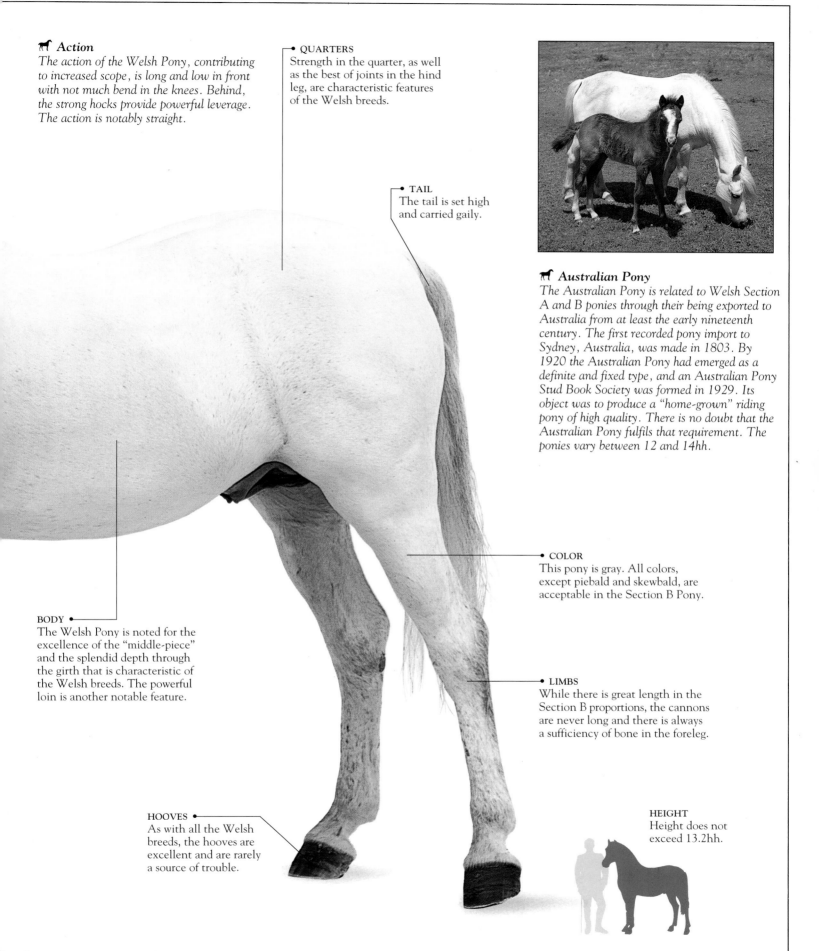

Action
The action of the Welsh Pony, contributing to increased scope, is long and low in front with not much bend in the knees. Behind, the strong hocks provide powerful leverage. The action is notably straight.

QUARTERS
Strength in the quarter, as well as the best of joints in the hind leg, are characteristic features of the Welsh breeds.

TAIL
The tail is set high and carried gaily.

Australian Pony
The Australian Pony is related to Welsh Section A and B ponies through their being exported to Australia from at least the early nineteenth century. The first recorded pony import to Sydney, Australia, was made in 1803. By 1920 the Australian Pony had emerged as a definite and fixed type, and an Australian Pony Stud Book Society was formed in 1929. Its object was to produce a "home-grown" riding pony of high quality. There is no doubt that the Australian Pony fulfils that requirement. The ponies vary between 12 and 14hh.

COLOR
This pony is gray. All colors, except piebald and skewbald, are acceptable in the Section B Pony.

BODY
The Welsh Pony is noted for the excellence of the "middle-piece" and the splendid depth through the girth that is characteristic of the Welsh breeds. The powerful loin is another notable feature.

LIMBS
While there is great length in the Section B proportions, the cannons are never long and there is always a sufficiency of bone in the foreleg.

HOOVES
As with all the Welsh breeds, the hooves are excellent and are rarely a source of trouble.

HEIGHT
Height does not exceed 13.2hh.

Welsh Cob

T HE WELSH COB is tough,
enduring and inherently
sound. It is a versatile family
horse and, though spirited,
is easily managed and
economical to keep. The
heartland of the Cob is
Cardiganshire, where it is
still integral to rural life.

ORIGINS
The Welsh Cob, called Section D in
the Stud Book, derived initially from
the crossing of Welsh Mountain Ponies
with Roman imports. Improvements
were made in the eleventh and twelfth
centuries using Spanish, Barb-type
horses. These produced the Powys Cob
– the remount of the English armies
from the twelfth century onward – and
the Welsh Cart Horse, a moderate-sized
but powerful, now extinct, animal.

THE MODERN HORSE
The modern Welsh Cob came from a
mix of the Powys stock with eighteenth
and nineteenth-century outcrosses to
Norfolk Roadsters and Yorkshire Coach
Horses. The four Cob lines stem from
all those elements with an admixture of
the ubiquitous Arabian blood. Yet the
Cob remains, in perfection, a larger
version of the base provided by the
Welsh Mountain Pony.

   In the past, the Welsh Cobs were in
demand as heavy gun horses and for
mounted infantry. There was also a
large trade with the big city companies
such as dairies and bakeries. The
modern Cob is brilliant in harness and
makes a courageous, sure-footed hunter.

HEIGHT
Technically, anything over
13.2hh but usually between
14.2 and 15.2hh.

🐎 *Thoroughbred cross*
*The Thoroughbred cross with the
Cob, particularly the second cross,
produces sound competition horses of
the necessary size, scope and speed.*

🐎 *Head*
*The arresting, quality head of the Welsh Cob
reflects exactly the base stock represented by
the Welsh Mountain Pony. Like that of the
Mountain Pony (see pp.144–5), the face of
the Welsh Cob is dished, the eyes are large
and the nostrils are wide and open.*

Performance

Before stallion licensing was introduced, breeding stock was often selected on the basis of performance over a given distance. A favorite route was 35 miles (56km) uphill from Dowlais to Cardiff, which was completed in under three hours.

Foundation sires

The foundation sires of Section D were: Trotting Comet (1840), with a background of Welsh Cart Horse and Norfolk Roadster blood; True Briton (1830), by a Yorkshire Coach Horse out of a reputed Arabian; Cymro Llwyd (1850), by the Crawshay Bailey Arabian out of a Welsh mare; and Alonzo the Brave (1866), a Norfolk Roadster.

OUTLINE
The outline of the Welsh Cob is identical to that of the Welsh Mountain Pony.

Welsh Pony of Cob Type (above)

The small (13.2hh) Welsh Pony of Cob Type, Section C in the Stud Book, is a splendid harness pony, ideal for trail riding and a wonderful riding pony and hunter for young people or small adults. It was the result of crossing Mountain mares with smaller trotting Cobs. Often called the "farm pony," it did every job on the hill farms and was used to cart slate from the mines of North Wales to the seaports. In 1949, when the type was in danger of disappearing, it was given a Section in the Stud Book. Increasingly, Section C is bred to Section C but the influence of the Welsh Mountain Pony is still strong.

COLOR
Welsh Cobs can be any color except piebald and skewbald. Blacks, bays, chestnuts and palominos abound and there are also creams and duns. This Welsh Cob is a dark liver-chestnut. Cymro Llwyd was a dun or palomino and is largely responsible for those colors in the modern animal. Gray is rare in the Welsh Cob.

Action

Welsh Cob action is free and forceful. The whole foreleg is lifted from the shoulder and then fully extended before the hoof touches down.

Driving

Welsh Cobs, because of their activity, stamina and courage, are ideal for competitive driving. A first cross to the Thoroughbred will increase the size and speed, but the Cob is the natural successor to the great trotting tradition of the Norfolk Roadster and remains a supreme harness horse in its own right.

HEELS
A moderate amount of silky feather at the heel is permissible but the hair must not be coarse and wiry.

Dales Pony

THE DALES PONY belongs to the Upper Dales of Tyne, Allen, Wear and Tees in North Yorkshire. The Dales Pony is the larger, heavier-built neighbor of the Fell Pony (see pp.152–3), with whom it shares common ancestors. Dales Ponies provided the power and sinews needed to operate the lead mines of Alston Moor and Allendale. They worked underground, once the horizontal levels were completed, and carried loads of lead ore to the Tyne sea ports. They were also used in coal mines, as general farm animals and in pack trains. They are capable of handling loads well out of proportion to their size; their packs weighed up to 224lb (100kg).

ORIGINS

The old-time Dales Pony was noted as a great trotter in harness or under saddle, and was well able to travel one mile (1.6km) in three minutes, carrying considerable weight. In order to improve on this ability, Welsh Cob blood was introduced in the nineteenth century, in particular that of the trotting stallion, Comet.

Clydesdale outcrossing was practiced to the extent that in 1917 the Dales was regarded as being two-thirds Clydesdale. Nonetheless, it was also acknowledged as being, "for Army purposes, second to none in the country" because of the strength and quality of its hooves, legs and bone.

CHARACTERISTICS

The modern Dales Pony retains that wonderful bone and limb as well as its hard, blue hooves. It is immensely strong and has a remarkable weight-carrying capacity, although its relationship with the Clydesdale is no longer apparent. A brilliant and courageous performer in harness, it is also used increasingly as a riding pony. The Dales Pony combines courage and stamina with a calm temperament. It is economical to keep, has a strong constitution and is rarely sick. Because of these qualities, it is particularly useful as a trail riding pony.

COLOR
Alone among the British native breeds, the Dales' predominant coloring is black. Occasionally bays and browns, such as this dark brown, are found and, less usually, the odd gray pony – a possible legacy of the liaison with the Clydesdale.

MUZZLE
A muzzle of medium width without coarseness is desirable.

🐎 **Head**
The head of the Dales Pony owes nothing to the Clydesdale infusion of the past. There is width between the bright and docile eyes and the small, pony ears are alert and mobile. The whole impression is one of intelligence.

• BACK
The Dales Pony has a particularly strong, short back and good conformation. This gives it a unique capacity for carrying weight, and contributes significantly to its true, powerful action, especially at the trot, a pace at which the breed excels.

Carrying bread to London
This etching of pack horses carrying provisions to London in the 1840s may hardly represent the Dales Pony accurately, but it does show the size of the load that a pack pony was able to carry over the rough tracks of the day.

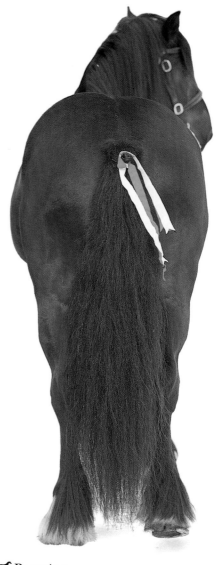

• GIRTH
An essential requirement for the breed is great depth of girth combined with well-sprung ribs.

HOOVES •
For centuries, the breed has been famed for the excellence of its hard hooves. A silky feather is carried on the heels.

Rear view
From the rear, the overall impression of the Dales Pony is that of great strength concentrated within a compact form. It is enormously active in movement, going straight and true with much propulsive power from strong hocks and quarters.

HEIGHT
Height does not exceed 14.2hh.

Fell Pony

B Y TRADITION, the Fell Pony is held to occupy the northern edges of the English Pennines and the wild moorlands of Westmorland and Cumberland, while the neighboring, and genetically related, Dales Pony (see pp.150–51) belongs to the other side of the Pennines in North Yorkshire, Northumberland and Durham. Both ponies are branches with the same root and have developed according to the uses that have been made of them.

ORIGINS

There is little doubt that the black, coldblood Friesian (see pp.64–5), descendant of Europe's primitive Forest Horse, had an early influence on these northern breeds. The Frieslanders and their black horses were employed as auxiliary cavalry by the Roman legions stationed in Northern Europe.

The greatest influence is that of the strong, swift Galloway, which remains particularly evident in the modern Fell Pony. The Galloway was the mount of the border raiders and then of the Scottish drovers. It was bred between Nithsdale and the Mull of Galloway and, although it has been extinct since the nineteenth century, the qualities it bequeathed to British stock are still evident. The Galloway stood between 13 and 14hh. It was hardy, sure-footed, possessed of great stamina and very fast under saddle and in harness. It probably also formed part of the "running horse" stock that provided a base for the eastern sires of the seventeenth and eighteenth centuries and from which sprang the English Thoroughbred.

CHARACTERISTICS

In its time, the Fell was a pack pony, like its neighbor the Dale. Most probably, however, the Fell, which is lighter than the Dales and a tremendous trotter, was as much used under saddle as in harness on the rough fells. Today, it is sought after for both purposes and is, additionally, an excellent cross to produce horses of competition potential. Through the Wilson ponies, the Fell Pony is at the base of the modern Hackney Pony (see pp.56–7).

SHOULDERS •
An important point of conformation concerns the shoulder. In the Fell Pony, it is well laid back and sloping, to give the riding action, but it is not too fine at the wither.

EARS
The Fell Pony has small, neat ears.

JOWLS
There is no coarseness around the jowls.

LIMBS •
A feature of the breed is the measurement of good flat bone below the knee. The official standard lays down a minimum of 8in (20cm).

🐎 *Profile*
The Fell Pony is noted for its small, quality head – broad across the forehead and tapering down to the muzzle – and for its large, open nostrils. Its prominent, bright eye denotes intelligence and also reveals something of the equable temperament characteristic of the breed.

🐎 "As hard as iron"
The breed standard states that "the Fell Pony should be constitutionally as hard as iron." In the eighteenth century, when Fell Ponies were used in pack trains, the average load was 224lb (95kg) and the ponies covered some 240 miles (384km) a week.

🐎 Lingcropper
The most famous of the early Fells was the eighteenth-century Lingcropper, who might have been a Galloway. He was found during the Jacobite risings "cropping the ling" at Stainmore, Westmorland, still carrying his saddle.

🐎 Carriage driving
The swift, balanced trot of the Fell Pony combined with its courage, endurance and stamina make it an ideal driving pony. In recent years, the Duke of Edinburgh has driven a Fell Pony team in competitive events.

COLOR
Fell colors are black, brown, as here, bay and gray, without white markings, although a star is occasionally seen.

TAIL
The luxuriant mane and tail of the Fell Pony are left to grow long.

🐎 Personality
The overall impression of the Fell is that of enduring strength combined with quality and a general alertness of outlook.

HOCKS
The hocks of the Fell Pony, because of their strength and ability to flex, contribute to the powerful drive of the hind leg.

🐎 Action
The movement is described as "smart and true" with good knee and hock action, the pony going from the shoulder and strongly flexed hocks and showing "great pace and endurance."

HOOVES
Hooves are characteristically hard, blue horn, round, well formed and capable of standing up to hard work over the high stony passes of the fells. Another characteristic is the generous growth of fine hair at the heels.

HEIGHT
Height does not exceed 14hh.

Highland Pony

THE MODERN HIGHLAND PONY has developed as a result of numerous outcrosses, though its origins are of great antiquity. There were ponies in northern Scotland and the Scottish islands following the Ice Age, and the pony bears an uncanny resemblance to the animals depicted 15–20,000 years ago on the cave walls at Lascaux in France.

ORIGINS

Around 1535, Louis XII of France gave horses to James V of Scotland. These horses – a type of Percheron – were used to improve the native stock, as were Spanish Horses in the seventeenth and eighteenth centuries. The Dukes of Athol, foremost among the old Highland breeders, introduced oriental horses in the sixteenth century; and John Munro-Mackenzie used the Arabian Syrian in the late nineteenth century to establish the famous Calgary strain on the Island of Mull. Patriarch of the Highland breed was Herd Laddie by Highland Laddie, foaled in 1881 and bought by the Athol Stud in 1887.

CHARACTERISTICS

The strong Highland Pony was Scotland's original all-purpose horse, and it retains this versatility. Highlands are first-rate riding ponies, up-to-weight and sure-footed in the most treacherous conditions. Hundreds are employed for trekking – a Scottish invention. They work in harness and forestry, carry game panniers and are strong enough and sufficiently unflappable to carry deer carcasses, weighing up to 18 stone (252lb/126kg), when the herds are culled.

NECK
The neck is strong, but never short, and the throat is clean.

At war
Highland Ponies featured prominently in the Jacobite risings of the eighteenth century. In the Boer War in South Africa (1899–1902), both the Lovat Scouts and the Marquis of Tullibardine's Scottish Horse were mounted on Highland Ponies.

In the Highlands
Highland Ponies are easily kept, thriving on rough pasture and needing little extra feeding. They have an ability to cross boggy land and are innately sure-footed. Sound as a bell and free from hereditary disease, the Highland Pony is a particularly long-lived breed. It is, moreover, docile and affectionate without being dull.

LIMBS
The Highland Pony has short cannons with hard, flat bone and is very strong in the forearm. The knees are large and flat. The feather on the legs is silky.

HEIGHT
The Highland Pony does not exceed 14.2hh.

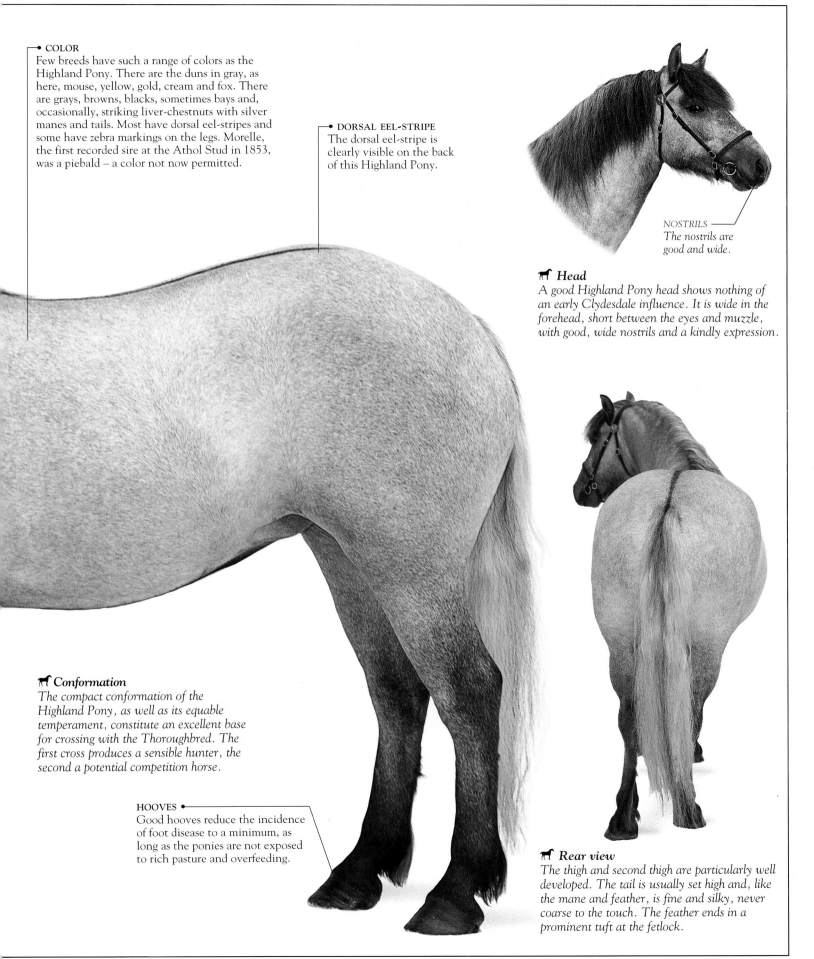

● COLOR
Few breeds have such a range of colors as the Highland Pony. There are the duns in gray, as here, mouse, yellow, gold, cream and fox. There are grays, browns, blacks, sometimes bays and, occasionally, striking liver-chestnuts with silver manes and tails. Most have dorsal eel-stripes and some have zebra markings on the legs. Morelle, the first recorded sire at the Athol Stud in 1853, was a piebald – a color not now permitted.

● DORSAL EEL-STRIPE
The dorsal eel-stripe is clearly visible on the back of this Highland Pony.

NOSTRILS ——
The nostrils are good and wide.

🐎 Head
A good Highland Pony head shows nothing of an early Clydesdale influence. It is wide in the forehead, short between the eyes and muzzle, with good, wide nostrils and a kindly expression.

🐎 Conformation
The compact conformation of the Highland Pony, as well as its equable temperament, constitute an excellent base for crossing with the Thoroughbred. The first cross produces a sensible hunter, the second a potential competition horse.

HOOVES ●
Good hooves reduce the incidence of foot disease to a minimum, as long as the ponies are not exposed to rich pasture and overfeeding.

🐎 Rear view
The thigh and second thigh are particularly well developed. The tail is usually set high and, like the mane and feather, is fine and silky, never coarse to the touch. The feather ends in a prominent tuft at the fetlock.

Shetland Pony

THE ORIGINAL HABITAT of the smallest of the British pony breeds on the Shetland Islands, about 100 nautical miles (185km) northeast of Scotland, is bleak and gale-swept. The land has no trees; it abounds with rocky outcrops and much of the soil is thin and acid, supporting little more than rough grasses and stunted heather. So heather, these grasses and mineral-rich seaweed formed the diet of the original Shetland Pony and this, together with the inhospitable environment, has governed its character and small stature.

ORIGINS
Shetland Ponies probably came to the Shetland Islands from Scandinavia perhaps as much as 10,000 years ago, before the ice fields had receded. These first ponies would have been of pronounced Tundra-type (see Origins, pp.10–11). The Shetland Pony still retains the extra large nasal cavities, which allow the air to warm before entering the lungs, that are common to equines of the northern latitudes.

CHARACTERISTICS
Shetland Ponies are naturally hardy and constitutionally strong. The ponies move with a quick, free action that is straight in front and behind and, because of the background of rough, rock-strewn terrain, has a characteristic lift in the knee and hock joints.

HEAD
The head is well shaped and sensible; the ears small and neat, and the forehead broad, denoting intelligence.

SHOULDERS
Shoulders are strong, well laid and oblique, not upright or loaded. There is great depth through the girth.

NECK
The neck is crested, particularly in stallions. It is also strong, muscular and in proportion to the pony's size.

CHEST
The Shetland Pony is broad between the forelegs – never narrow.

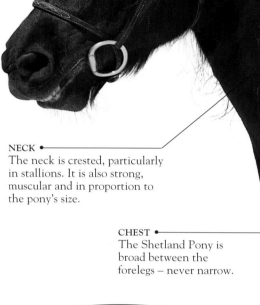

HEIGHT
The Shetland Pony is measured in inches rather than in hands. The average height is 40in (101cm), but the best in terms of conformation are usually 1–2in (2–5cm) smaller.

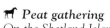 *Peat gathering*
On the Shetland Islands, Shetland Ponies did every kind of work, including carrying seaweed and gathering peat for fires. In comparison with their diminutive size, they are one of the world's most powerful equines, capable of carrying a man nimbly over rough country and able to work under the weight of heavy panniers.

• COLOR
Shetland Ponies come in a variety of colors. Black, as here, is the foundation color, but brown, chestnut, and gray can be found as well as skewbald and piebald.

• BODY
A short back with exceptionally muscular loins is characteristic of the Shetland Pony. It has a thickset, deep-ribbed body that gives an impression of strength.

• QUARTERS
The tail is well set on the broad quarters, which run into well-developed gaskins.

🐎 **Miniature Shetland Ponies** (above)
In recent years, there has been a movement toward the breeding of "miniature" Shetland Ponies even smaller than the general breed standard. They have an obvious curiosity value, but there is a danger of them losing type.

• TAIL
The tail and mane are especially full and profuse for protection against the weather.

COAT •
The coat changes according to the season. It is smooth in summer, but a thick, wiry, double coat is grown in winter.

LIMBS •
The limbs are short and set at each corner. They have large, sharply defined joints and strong, flat bone.

HOOVES •
The Shetland Pony has round, tough hooves of hard, blue horn with pasterns that are normally sloped, not upright.

🐎 **Popular and versatile**
Away from their homeland, Shetland Ponies make popular children's ponies, and go well in harness and circus work. In the past, they were often seen in public parks and private grounds, and were much in demand for pit work.

Connemara Pony

THE CONNEMARA PONY takes its name from the wild part of Ireland to the west of Loughs Corrib and Mask. It is the sole "indigenous" equine of Ireland. A variety of breeds have been used to upgrade the Connemara Pony to the point of excellence it has attained today.

ORIGINS

Crosses with Barbs and Spanish Horses resulted in the renowned Irish Hobby of the sixteenth and seventeenth centuries. The Hobby, forerunner of the Connemara Pony, was a hardy, agile pony that, like the Galloway, played a part in the evolution of the Thoroughbred. Arabians were imported in the nineteenth century, and government breeding schemes brought in Welsh Cobs, Thoroughbreds, Roadsters, or Hackneys, and the less desirable Clydesdale cross in an attempt to check the degeneration of native stock. There were also Irish Draught sires and a line to the famous purebred Arabian, Naseel. The show jumper Dundrum was by the Thoroughbred stallion Little Heaven, and belonged to the Carna Dun line.

STUD BOOK

The Connemara Pony Breeders' Society was formed in 1923, and the English Connemara Society in 1947. The first stallion to be entered in the Connemara stud book was Cannon Ball, born in 1904. Cannon Ball won the Farmers' Race at Oughterard for sixteen years in succession. Rebel, born in 1922, and Golden Gleam, foaled a decade later, also had powerful influences on the breed development.

CHARACTERISTICS

The end product is probably the most brilliant performance pony available. The Connemara Pony is fast, courageous, sensible and a remarkable jumper. Its natural environment has given the Connemara Pony hardiness, endurance and its special character.

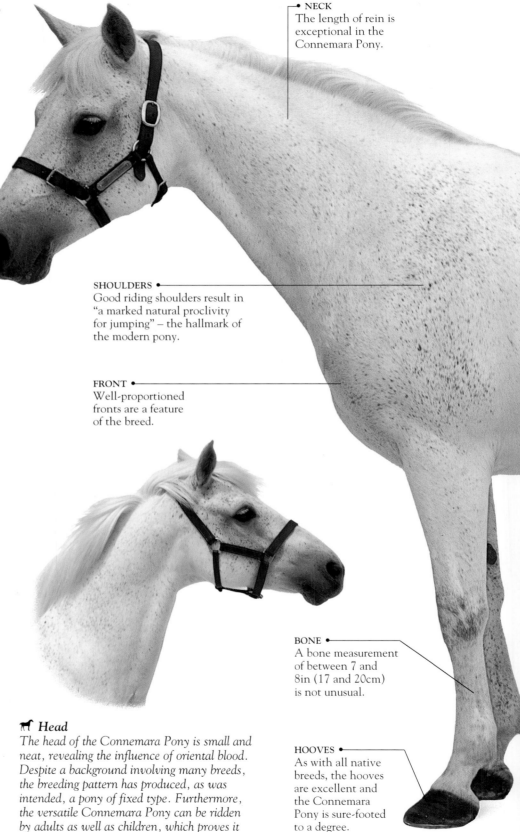

NECK
The length of rein is exceptional in the Connemara Pony.

SHOULDERS
Good riding shoulders result in "a marked natural proclivity for jumping" – the hallmark of the modern pony.

FRONT
Well-proportioned fronts are a feature of the breed.

BONE
A bone measurement of between 7 and 8in (17 and 20cm) is not unusual.

HOOVES
As with all native breeds, the hooves are excellent and the Connemara Pony is sure-footed to a degree.

🐎 *Head*
The head of the Connemara Pony is small and neat, revealing the influence of oriental blood. Despite a background involving many breeds, the breeding pattern has produced, as was intended, a pony of fixed type. Furthermore, the versatile Connemara Pony can be ridden by adults as well as children, which proves it to be a supremely tractable animal.

🐴 Top-class horses
The Connemara Pony is a natural cross with a Thoroughbred to produce a top-class competition horse.

🐴 Type
"… an extremely hard, wiry type of pony showing a great deal of Barb and/or Arab blood." Evidence of Mr Ussher C.B. to 1897 Royal Commission.

🐴 Conformation
Elegance combined with substance, good proportions throughout and true riding action summarize the qualities of this brilliant performance pony. The compact body is notable for its depth.

🐴 Farm worker
In Galway, the Connemara Pony was used for every sort of farm task as well as being employed as a pack animal to carry seaweed, potatoes, peat and corn. Of the old dun-type Connemara Pony, Professor Cossor Ewart wrote, "they are capable of living where all but wild ponies would starve… strong and hardy as mules, fertile and free from hereditary disease their extinction would be a national loss." Royal Commission report Congested Districts Board 1897.

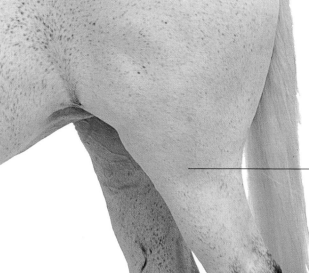

COLOR
Coat colors are gray, as here, dun, black, bay, brown and occasionally roan or chestnut. Piebalds and skewbalds are not accepted by the breed society.

🐴 Ideal competition mount
Connemara Ponies have been exported extensively to Europe, where they are now bred in considerable numbers. They are regarded as the ideal competition mount for young people, and in Germany are subject to rigorous performance testing.

HEIGHT
The Connemara Pony can stand between 13 and 14.2hh.

New Forest Pony

N EW FOREST PONIES have been subject to outside influences for centuries because of the position of the Forest in southwest Hampshire, an area crossed by the principal routes to the West.

🐎 **Thoroughbred** (*left*)
The sire of Eclipse, probably the greatest racehorse of all time, was Marske, who was used on Forest mares for a short time from 1765. Once Eclipse's reputation was established, Marske was returned to stud in Yorkshire.

ORIGINS
There have been continual efforts to improve the Forest stock ever since the proclamation of Canute's Forest Law in 1016. As early as 1208, Welsh mares were put into the Forest; in the eighteenth century the Thoroughbred stallion Marske served Forest mares for a short time; and in the nineteenth century Queen Victoria loaned Arabian and Barb stallions. However, the principal development was due to Lord Cecil and Lord Lucas, both great, if rather innovative, "improvers." Between them, they introduced Highlands, Fells, Dales, Dartmoors, Exmoors and Welsh Ponies. Lord Lucas even brought back a Basuto Pony when he fought in the Boer War. Surprisingly, a distinctive type emerged from this pot pourri of breeds.

CHARACTERISTICS
The modern, commercially viable New Forest Pony is, for the most part, stud-bred but still retains the special character and movement inherited from its natural environment. The ponies have real riding shoulders and a typically long, low action made very evident at the canter, the "Forester's" best pace. Very used to human contact, the ponies are easily handled and are less sharp, or cunning, than some native breeds. They are excellent performers and are very strong; the larger ones can easily carry adults.

HEIGHT
The upper height limit is 14.2hh. Forest-bred stock may be smaller.

🐎 **Foundation stallions**
Foundation stallions are Denny Danny, with a line to the Welsh Pony, Dyoll Starlight; Goodenough and Brookside David, both connected to Field Marshall; Brooming Slipon, and Knightwood Spitfire, grandson of the Highland, Clansman.

🐎 **Polo pony blood**
A major influence in the evolution of the Forester was the polo pony stallion Field Marshall, out of a Welsh mare. He stood in the Forest in 1918–19.

LIMBS ●
Good strong limbs. The action is free, long and low, the canter being an especially good pace. Foresters are wonderful cross-country ponies.

SHOULDERS
The shoulders, which are long and sloping, are real riding shoulders.

🐎 *Breed society*
The breed society is the New Forest Pony Breeding and Cattle Society, formed after the amalgamation of earlier societies in 1938. It produced its own stud book in 1960.

HEAD
The New Forest Pony varies in type and is occasionally somewhat "horsy" about the head. The overall impression is of intelligence, and the ponies are easily trained. The modern Forester, because of its scope and ability, is in great demand throughout Europe.

COLOR
New Forest Ponies are any color except piebald, skewbald or blue-eyed cream. Bays, as here, and browns predominate.

🐎 *Diet*
Forest-bred ponies live on the moor grasses around the numerous bogs and are particularly fond of gorse tips.

BODY
The Forester is an all-round riding pony and has plenty of depth through the girth.

HOOVES
As with most ponies, this one is very sure-footed.

🐎 *Environmental influences*
The Forest, providing sufficient if not abundant food, has influenced the essential character and the distinctive movement of the versatile and sure-footed New Forest Pony. Despite the presence of so many contributing breeds, it is the Forest that provides what Lord Cecil observed as "the mysterious power of nature to grind down and assimilate all these types to the one most suited to the land."

American Shetland

BY FAR THE MOST POPULAR PONY in America is the Shetland (see pp.156–7), which originated in the Shetland Isles of Scotland. The first import of Shetlands to America was made in 1885. The American Shetland Pony Club was formed three years later and today there are possibly as many as 50,000 Shetlands in the USA. Shetlands are also very numerous on the European mainland, most particularly in Holland. However, no other attempt has been made to cross the breed as in America.

ORIGINS

Few of the Shetlands in America today bear much resemblance to the tough Shetland Island Pony whose character was formed by its harsh environment where the winter weather is severe and sustaining feed is minimal. Indeed, the American Shetland is a purely artificial, man-made product and while it is claimed that it retains the native hardiness and constitution of the pure Shetland, that is arguable and most unlikely. The "breed" was created by first selecting the finer types of Island Shetland and then crossing them with Hackney Ponies, and topping up the mixture with a dash of Arabian and small Thoroughbred blood.

The "new-look" American Shetland is primarily a harness pony of pronounced Hackney character and with much the same brilliance of action. However, it is also raced in harness and the so-called "hunter" types are shown under saddle and are expected to demonstrate jumping ability.

🐎 Hardy forebears
The Island Sheltie can live in conditions of extreme wet and cold and thrive on poor feed. There is a vigor about this pony and the American version bears little resemblance to it.

🐎 Hooves
The hooves are grown artificially long, and heavy shoes are used to accentuate the trotting action of the American Shetland Ponies.

HIND LEG •
Greater length has been introduced in the hind leg by the use of Hackney Ponies, Arabians and small Thoroughbreds.

🐎 More like a Hackney
In essence, the American Shetland is not much more than an American variation on the Hackney Pony. It is said, however, to be intelligent, spirited, adaptable and very good natured. The action, in harness, is high, extravagant and flashy.

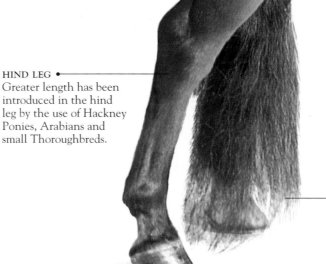

FRAME •
The overall frame of the American Shetland is narrower and longer than that of the broad-beamed, short-legged Island Shetland and there is obviously a greater refinement and structural delicacy.

• TAIL
The luxurious growth of mane and tail are reminders of the true-bred Shetland of the Islands. The harness ponies are shown with artificially set tails.

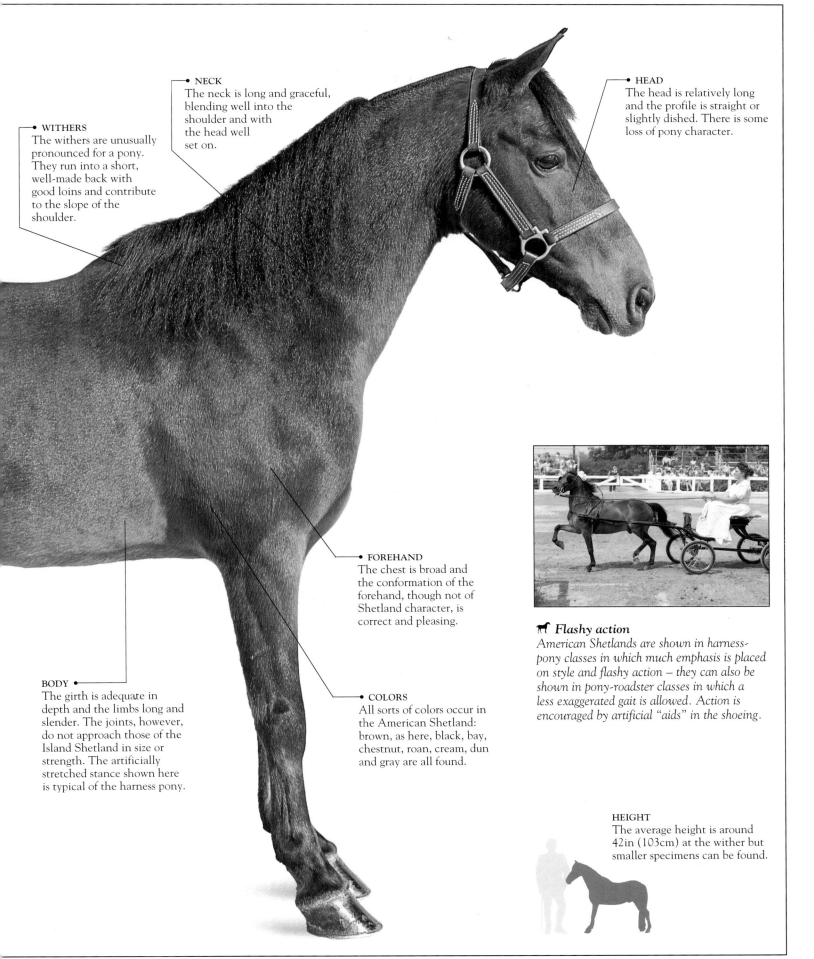

NECK
The neck is long and graceful, blending well into the shoulder and with the head well set on.

HEAD
The head is relatively long and the profile is straight or slightly dished. There is some loss of pony character.

WITHERS
The withers are unusually pronounced for a pony. They run into a short, well-made back with good loins and contribute to the slope of the shoulder.

FOREHAND
The chest is broad and the conformation of the forehand, though not of Shetland character, is correct and pleasing.

BODY
The girth is adequate in depth and the limbs long and slender. The joints, however, do not approach those of the Island Shetland in size or strength. The artificially stretched stance shown here is typical of the harness pony.

COLORS
All sorts of colors occur in the American Shetland: brown, as here, black, bay, chestnut, roan, cream, dun and gray are all found.

🐎 *Flashy action*
American Shetlands are shown in harness-pony classes in which much emphasis is placed on style and flashy action – they can also be shown in pony-roadster classes in which a less exaggerated gait is allowed. Action is encouraged by artificial "aids" in the shoeing.

HEIGHT
The average height is around 42in (103cm) at the wither but smaller specimens can be found.

Shire

THE SHIRE HORSE is as English as the British bulldog and is considered by many people to be the supreme heavy draft breed. It was called "Shire" because it was bred in the Midland shires of Lincoln, Leicester, Stafford and Derby.

ORIGINS

The breed descends from England's medieval war horse, the Great Horse. The Great Horse became known as the English Black, a name bestowed by Oliver Cromwell, in the short period when England was a Commonwealth.

The principal influence in the evolution of the massive, modern Shire was the heavy Flemish or Flanders Horse. During the sixteenth and early seventeenth centuries, Dutch contractors draining the English Fenlands brought with them their strong horses. These crossed with the English stock. The Friesian (see pp.64–5), is another influence, which gave the English Blacks a better movement. During the reign of Charles II, the King's Household Cavalry were still mounted on the Old English Black.

FOUNDATION

The foundation stallion of the Shire breed is recognized as the Packington Blind Horse, who stood at Ashby-de-la-Zouche between 1755 and 1770. He is in the first stud book published in 1878. It was not until 1884 that the name Shire came into use, when the Shire Horse Society replaced the English Cart Horse Society.

🐎 Strength
The massively built Shire weighs between 2,240 and 2,688lb (1,016–1,220kg). At the Wembley Exhibition in 1924 a pair of Shires pulling against a dynameter (an instrument for measuring power) exceeded the maximum reading. It was estimated that they had exerted a pull capable of moving 50 tons.

LIMBS
The limbs are clean and hard, the measurement of flat bone being 11–12in (28–30cm). There is heavy feather but it should be straight and silky.

🐎 Head
The head is of medium size, the nose is slightly Roman, i.e. convex, and the forehead is wide between the eyes. The eyes should be large and docile in expression, indicating the kind disposition of this breed of "Gentle Giants." For a draft horse, the neck is relatively long, running back into a deep, oblique shoulder, wide enough to carry a collar.

HEIGHT
The Shire can stand between 16.2 and 17.2hh. The average is 17hh.

• GIRTH
The average girth measurement of a Shire stallion is 6–8ft (180–240cm) and is combined with a broad, powerful chest. These are factors that denote a good, healthy constitution.

• BODY
The short back; thick, powerful musculature, particularly over the loins; and the wide, sweeping quarters exemplify the "strength" structure, combined with weight, that are essential in the draft horse.

• COLOR
The most popular Shire color is the traditional black of the breed's forebears, with white feathering. Bay, as in this case, and brown are acceptable and there are numerous grays.

🐎 Plowing matches
The Shire may no longer play a significant role in agriculture but plowing matches are still numerous and very popular. Shires can also be seen on city streets hauling heavy brewer's drays. The brewing companies are the breed's most loyal supporters.

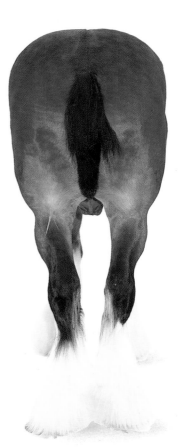

🐎 War horses
In medieval England, the English Great Horse was developed to be strong enough to carry a knight in plate armor and bearing heavy weapons, and still be agile in combat. The knight mounted his horse only just before battle was joined, otherwise it was led from the right by his squire. Hence the name Destrier for a war horse (From the Latin dextrarius *– the right side).*

🐎 Rear view
The most important parts of the draft horse are the hooves and hocks. The hooves must be open, very solid and perfectly shaped with length in the pasterns. The hocks have to be broad and flat, set at the correct angle for optimum leverage and carried close together. The action is straight in front and behind.

Suffolk Punch

THE SUFFOLK PUNCH of East Anglia is the oldest of Britain's heavy horse breeds and, perhaps, the most endearing. The English dictionary defines Punch as a variety of English horse, short-legged and barrel-bodied, "a short, fat fellow," and that fits its subject exactly. The unique feature of this pure breed is that every Suffolk traces its descent from one stallion, Thomas Crisp's Horse of Ufford (Orford), which was foaled in 1768. He was a "chesnut" horse, as are all Suffolks. (The word chestnut is spelt without the first "t" in Suffolk records.)

🐎 **On the farm**
In this etching, a pair of eighteenth-century Suffolks perform a routine farm chore. Because of their activity and great strength, Suffolks can be used in every sort of heavy draft role.

ORIGINS
The Suffolk's early origins are obscure but it is inconceivable to think that the trotting Roadsters, developed in East Anglia from the sixteenth century onward, as well as the heavier Flanders mares, did not play their part in its evolution. Both possessed much the same coloring now regarded as characteristic of the Suffolk, and Flanders Horses were robust trotters.

The Suffolk Punch was developed as a farm horse. It is a clean-legged horse (without feather) and so is admirably suited to heavy clay lands. It also possesses enormous pulling power, and in the past was much in demand for heavy draft work in towns and cities.

Maturing early and enjoying a long life, the Suffolk is an economical horse. Despite its unquestionable stamina and power, it thrives on less feed than is needed by other heavy breeds. On typical East Anglian farms, they are fed at 4:30 am. Two hours later they go to the fields, and can work, with short rests, until 2:30 pm. Other heavy breeds would have to stop mid-morning for another feed with additional time needed to allow for digestion.

HEIGHT
Suffolks stand at 16–16.3hh.

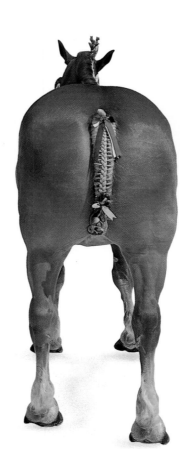

🐎 **Rear view**
The quarters are obviously of great strength, but the hind legs must be placed sufficiently close to allow the horse to walk a 9in (23cm) furrow, otherwise when going between rows of sugar beet, "he'll kick out more than he'll hoe." The long tail is, by tradition, braided for work.

• NECK
The neck is deep and conforms exactly to the position of the shoulder. Mane decoration is usual for show purposes.

• BUILD
Wonderfully deep and round-bodied, and standing on powerful, short legs, the roly poly Suffolk is among the most attractive of the heavy horse breeds.

• COLOR
Seven color shades are recognized by the Suffolk Horse Society, ranging from a pale, almost mealy color to a dark, almost brown, "chesnut." The most usual is a bright, reddish color, as here.

LIMBS •
Good bone, sloping pasterns and clean legs characterize the breed. The tractive power is assisted by the low shoulder, a feature skillfully developed by early breeders.

HOOVES •
The hooves are of medium size, smaller than those of most heavy breeds, but hard and sound. Much attention has been given in recent years to improving the quality and conformation of the Suffolk hooves.

🐴 *Head*
The head is quite large with a notably broad forehead and a straight or slightly convex profile, and alert and relatively short ears.

🐴 *Fallen-tree test*
A test, peculiar to the Suffolk fairs where Punches were offered for sale, was to hitch a horse to a heavy, fallen tree. The tree did not have to be moved but, to pass the test, the horse had to get right down on his knees in what is considered the typical, Suffolk, drawing attitude.

Clydesdale

THE CLYDESDALE IS A BREED of no great antiquity in terms of equine history, as it has only developed over little more than the past 150 years. However, with the exception of the Percheron (see pp.170–71), it is probably the most successful of the heavy breeds in respect of its export throughout the world. It is found as far afield as Germany, the USSR, Japan and South Africa, as well as in the USA, Canada, Australia and New Zealand.

ORIGINS
The breed has its foundation in Flemish Horses imported into the Clyde Valley, Lanarkshire, in the eighteenth century. There is also a strong Shire influence. Two Clydesdale breeders of the nineteenth century, Lawrence Drew and his friend David Riddell, believed the Clydesdale and the Shire to be two branches of a single breed.

CHARACTERISTICS
The Clydesdale is less massively proportioned than the Shire and has none of the Suffolk's rolypoly appeal, but of the three it is the best mover, having very active paces. It is described by the Clydesdale Horse Society, which published its first stud book in 1878, as having "a flamboyant style, a flashy, spirited bearing and a high-stepping action that makes him a singularly elegant animal among draft horses."

The Clydesdale Horse Society was formed in 1877, and in the first volume of its stud book there were listed no less than 1,000 stallions. The American Clydesdale Society was founded in the following year and the breed was soon established in the USA and Canada.

HEIGHT
Average height is about 16.2hh, but stallions may be up to or over 17hh.

🐎 Tail
Elaborately decorated tails are a feature of the heavy show horse. A best decorated horse class is held at the Royal Highland Show in Scotland.

🐎 Worldwide popularity
Clydesdales have been exported all over the world. In 1990, a Clydesdale colt standing 18.2hh was sold to Japan for the price of £20,000 from the Fairways Heavy Horse Centre at Perth, Scotland. The previous record was £9,500, paid in 1911.

HOCKS
Cow hocks, the hind legs placed close together, are a breed characteristic. They are not judged as a conformational fault.

HOOVES
The lower limbs carry heavy, silky feather and the hooves, although somewhat flat, are well formed and hard-wearing.

• NECK
The Clydesdale neck is proportionately longer than that of the Shire.

• SHOULDERS
The shoulder is sloped and the withers, higher than the croup in the interests of improved traction, are quite sharply defined.

• COLOR
The predominant Clydesdale colors are bay and brown but grays, blacks and roans, such as this blue roan, are also found. Heavy white markings often occur on the face, legs and on the underside of the body generally.

🐎 Head
The head of the Clydesdale is more elegant than that of most of the heavy horse breeds. Unlike the Shire head, in which the profile is decidedly convex, the Clydesdale profile is straight, giving the impression of quality.

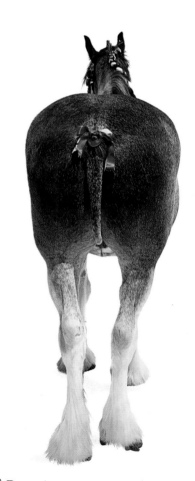

🐎 Hard workers
Clydesdale horses were used to work the prairies of Canada and America, often in teams of seven horses to the three-furrow plow. They also earned the title of "the breed that built Australia."

🐎 Draft work
The Clydesdale, weighing 1 ton (2240lb/ 1016kg) or more but having great activity as well as an extremely tractable disposition, is ideally suited for urban draft. It is said that "the glamour of the Clyde turns an ordinary beer delivery into a public event...."

🐎 Rear view
Although a big horse, the modern Clydesdale is lighter and even more active than those bred in the past. The leg often appears long, but the Clydesdale is rarely other than deep through the girth. The hock joints are very strong, although cow hocks are common.

Percheron

THE PERCHERON is a handsome, clean-legged, free-moving, heavy horse that originated in the limestone region of Le Perche in Normandy. Together with the Boulonnais (see pp.178–9), it is the most elegant of the heavy draft horse breeds and, like them, it owes much to oriental blood. A nineteenth-century authority described it as "an Arab influenced by climate and the agricultural work for which it has been used for centuries." He may have had an excess of enthusiasm for the breed but there is no doubting the strength of the eastern influence.

♞ Pulling power (above)
The Percheron holds the unofficial pulling record of 3,410lb (1,547kg). It is exceptionally biddable and will do any sort of work.

HISTORY

Some admirers of the breed hold that it was forebears of the Percheron that carried the knights of Charles Martel to victory over the Muslims at Poitiers in A.D.732 and that, as a result, the Barbs or Arabs of the enemy became available to French breeders. Certainly, eastern blood was introduced after the first Crusade in 1096–9, and by 1760 the stud at Le Pin made available Arabian sires to Percheron breeders.

The most influential Percheron lines are dominated by Arabian outcrosses represented by Godolphin and Gallipoly. Gallipoly sired the most famous of Percheron stallions, Jean le Blanc, who was foaled in 1830.

In its long history, the Percheron has been a war horse, coach horse, farm horse and heavy artillery horse and has even been used under saddle. The modern Percheron is immensely powerful as well as being hardy and versatile. Among the heavy breeds it has a distinctive and stylish action, which is long, free and low.

♞ Tail
The Percheron's full tail is usually put up in a kind of "polo bang" when the horse is worked in harness.

HEIGHT
Between 16.2 and 17hh, though many are 15.2 to 16.2hh. The world's biggest horse was the Percheron Dr Le Gear. He stood 21hh and weighed 27 cwt (3,024lb/1,372kg).

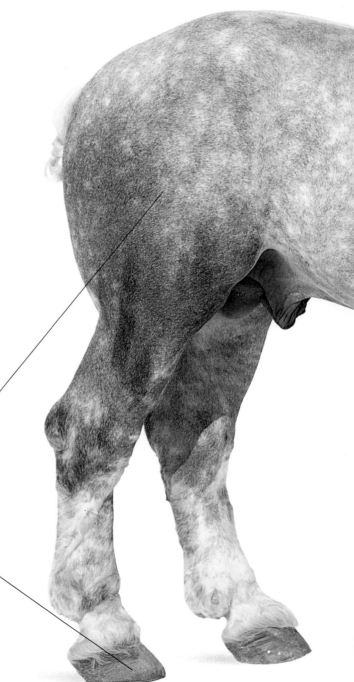

QUARTERS ●
The Percheron is noted for the excellence of the powerful hindquarters, which are sloped and unusually long for a draft breed.

HOOVES ●
The hooves are of hard, blue horn and of medium size, with no feather at the heels. They are a notable feature of this exceptionally popular breed.

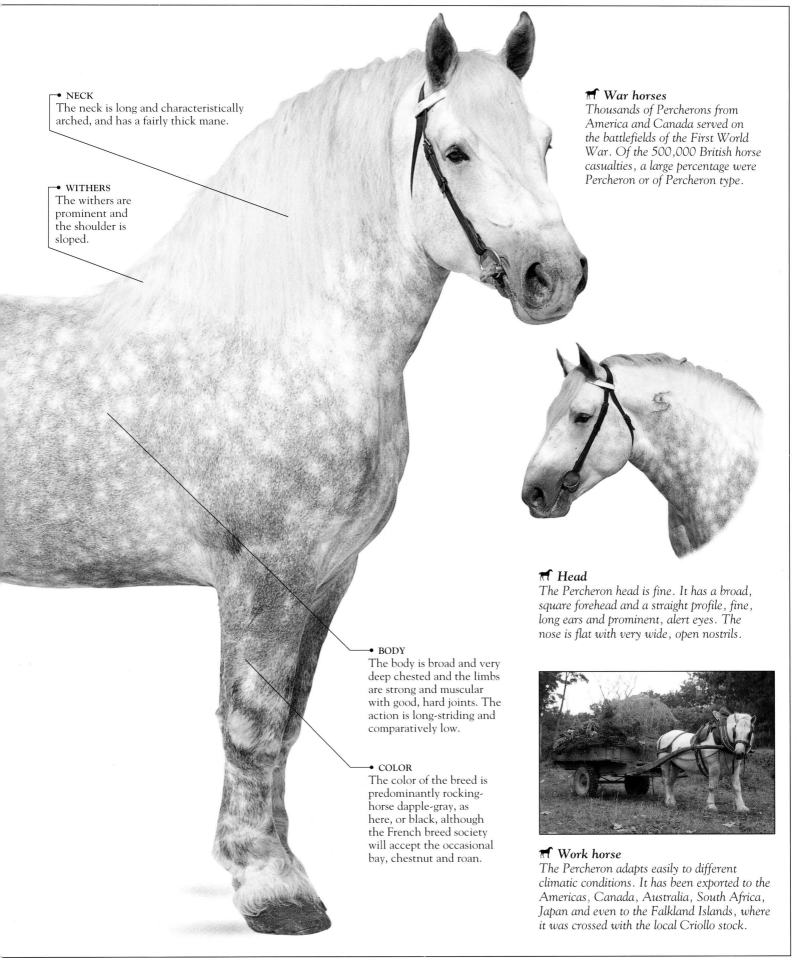

NECK
The neck is long and characteristically arched, and has a fairly thick mane.

WITHERS
The withers are prominent and the shoulder is sloped.

🐎 **War horses**
Thousands of Percherons from America and Canada served on the battlefields of the First World War. Of the 500,000 British horse casualties, a large percentage were Percheron or of Percheron type.

🐎 **Head**
The Percheron head is fine. It has a broad, square forehead and a straight profile, fine, long ears and prominent, alert eyes. The nose is flat with very wide, open nostrils.

BODY
The body is broad and very deep chested and the limbs are strong and muscular with good, hard joints. The action is long-striding and comparatively low.

COLOR
The color of the breed is predominantly rocking-horse dapple-gray, as here, or black, although the French breed society will accept the occasional bay, chestnut and roan.

🐎 **Work horse**
The Percheron adapts easily to different climatic conditions. It has been exported to the Americas, Canada, Australia, South Africa, Japan and even to the Falkland Islands, where it was crossed with the local Criollo stock.

Ardennais

T HE HEAVY HORSE of the Ardennes region of France and Belgium, the Ardennais, has to be regarded as the doyen of the European heavy breeds and one of the oldest. Its ancestors were known 2,000 years ago and they were probably the descendants of the snub-nosed, prehistoric horse whose remains were found at Solutré.

HISTORY

Before the nineteenth century, the Ardennais was less massive than it is now, and was ridden and used in light draft. At the beginning of the nineteenth century, crosses were made to the Arabian and Thoroughbred, as well as to the Percheron and Boulonnais, although not always with great success. Three types emerged: the small old-type Ardennais of about 15hh, now not so much in evidence; the Ardennais du Nord, or Trait du Nord, as shown here, a bigger horse derived from outcrosses to the Brabant (see pp.180–81); and the Auxois, a larger version of the original Ardennais and very powerful.

The climate in which the Ardennais is reared is harsh, and as a result these massively framed horses are very hardy. They are also exceptionally calm and easily handled. They are still in use as heavy draft horses but, for the most part, are raised for the meat market.

🐎 At work
The Ardennais, more thick-set than any other cart breed, short and close to the ground, is a willing, hard worker with stamina and endurance and is easily managed. Its undoubted energy derives from the oriental outcrosses, its size from the Belgian blood.

NECK
The neck is heavy but also long.

🐎 Head
A straight-profiled head is distinguished by a low, flat forehead and slightly prominent eye sockets. The neck, though heavy, muscular and arched, is longer than would be expected in so chunky a horse and it is well set into the powerful shoulders.

HOOVES
The hooves are smaller than might be expected, though strong and well formed.

COLORS
The preferred colors are roan, red-roan, as here, iron-gray, dark chestnut and bay. Light chestnuts and even palominos are admissible, but not black.

🐎 *Auxois*
Auxois, the old horse of Burgundy, has been a contemporary of the Ardennais since the Middle Ages. It is largely considered an offshoot of the Ardennais although it has retained its red-roan color. It is less massive in the legs and quarters.

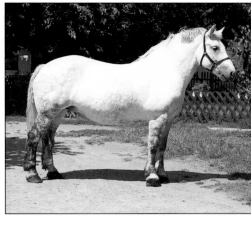

BACK
The Ardennais is compact with a more than usually short back and exceptionally muscular loins.

QUARTERS
The quarter muscles of the Ardennais are particularly short, thick and powerful.

🐎 *Murakozer* (above)
The Murakozer takes its name from the town of Murakoz in southern Hungary. During the twentieth century, the breed was developed there from native Mur-Insulan mares and was crossed with Ardennais mares, as well as Percherons and Norikers and lighter Hungarian horses of more quality. A swift-moving draft horse, it does not have the Ardennais heavy feather but has inherited something of the latter's heavy frame as well as its equable temperament.

LIMBS
"Like small oak trees," the limbs are very short and strong, and they carry heavy feather. The small, older type of Ardennais had less feather on the lower limbs and was lighter and quicker.

🐎 *"Cart horse of the north"*
The popular heavy Ardennais from Lorraine is still called "the cart horse of the north," but there is little evidence now of the lively Ardennes post horse, which brought back Napoleon's wagons from his disastrous Russian campaign.

BODY
The bone structure of the Ardennais is enormous and is accompanied by musculature of corresponding strength. The girth is naturally deep and the overall impression is of power. The withers, unlike that of most heavy breeds, are on a line with or even lower than the croup.

HEIGHT
The height is between 15 and 16hh. The average is about 15.3hh.

Breton

• OUTLINE
The outline is attractively short and square, with the body broad, strong and deep and the hindquarters showing great power.

THE BREEDERS OF BRITTANY are as skillful as any in Europe. Since the Middle Ages, the area has produced its own distinctive, Breton types based on the primitive, little, hairy horse of the Black Mountains. At one time, there were four derivatives of the Breton, two pacers or amblers, a general purpose ride-and-drive, and a heavier draft horse. The riding type, the *Cheval de Corlay*, was even raced at local meetings.

TYPES

Today two types are recognized. The Breton heavy draft is a massive, early-maturing horse much sought after in the meat markets, and has Ardennais blood. The far more active, almost clean-legged, Breton Postier is a lighter version of the Suffolk Punch (see pp.166–7) and was once the pride of the French Horse Artillery. The Postier has crosses of Boulonnais (see pp.178–9) and Percheron (see pp.170–71), both active, refined animals with the powerful Norfolk Roadster in their ancestry. The Postiers inherit the exceptional energy at trot from the Percheron and Boulonnais, and are ideal for light draft and farm work. Breton Postiers, sharing the same stud book with the heavy drafts since 1926, are selectively bred, and are required to pass performance tests in harness – traditional events at festival days. The Breton Postier is still popular in France, and is exported to North Africa, Japan, Spain and Italy to be used as an improver of less-developed stock.

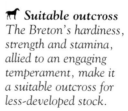

🐎 **Tail**
It is customary for the tail of the Breton, like that of the Norman Cob (see pp.78–9), to be docked. It is thought to give the horse a jaunty look and prevents the rein becoming caught up under the tail.

🐎 **Suitable outcross**
The Breton's hardiness, strength and stamina, allied to an engaging temperament, make it a suitable outcross for less-developed stock.

🐎 **Agricultural employment**
A quick, active horse suited for all sorts of agricultural work, the Breton is also employed extensively in the French vineyards of the Midi.

NECK
The neck follows the general outline of the body, being short, arched and thick. It runs into the shoulders that, although sloping, are shorter than might be expected. Nonetheless, the Breton is active, fast and free at the walk and trot.

COLOR
The typical coloration is red-roan but chestnuts, as here, bays and grays are also found. Black is not a breed color.

🐎 Head
The square head of the Breton has a straight profile and should have large, open nostrils and bright, kindly eyes. The mobile ears are small and set rather low on the head.

LIMBS
The limbs are short, strong and very muscular in the thighs and forearms.

HOOVES
The hooves are well shaped, hard and not too large. The legs are virtually "clean," carrying little or no feather.

HEIGHT
The height is 15–16.1hh. The Postier is smaller than the heavy draft.

Jutland

Denmark's heavy horse, the Jutland, has been bred on the Jutland Peninsula from time immemorial. In the twelfth century it was a war horse, noted for its sturdy build, capable of carrying an armored knight and enduring the hardships of campaigning.

ORIGINS

The Jutland seems to have been largely responsible for Germany's Schleswig Horse and infusions of Danish blood were being made into that breed well into the twentieth century.

At some point in the development of the modern Jutland, there were crossings with Cleveland Bays and their derivative the Yorkshire Coach Horse. However, the overwhelming influence is that of Oppenheim LXII, a dark chestnut Suffolk Punch (see Suffolk Punch pp.166–7) imported to Denmark in 1860. Even today, there is a very close resemblance between the Suffolk, the Jutland and the Schleswig. The most important blood line of the Jutland is that of Oldrup Munkedal, one of the many descendants of Oppenheim LXII.

CHARACTERISTICS

The Jutland's great endurance and its exceptionally tractable nature make it ideal for both draft and agricultural work. Unhappily, this most likeable and attractive coldblood has decreased in numbers in recent years due to mechanization. However, it is still used for city draft work and is appreciated as a most willing worker. Jutlands are also seen at horse shows and occasionally working on the land.

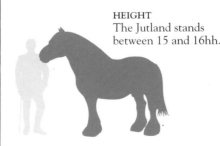

HEIGHT
The Jutland stands between 15 and 16hh.

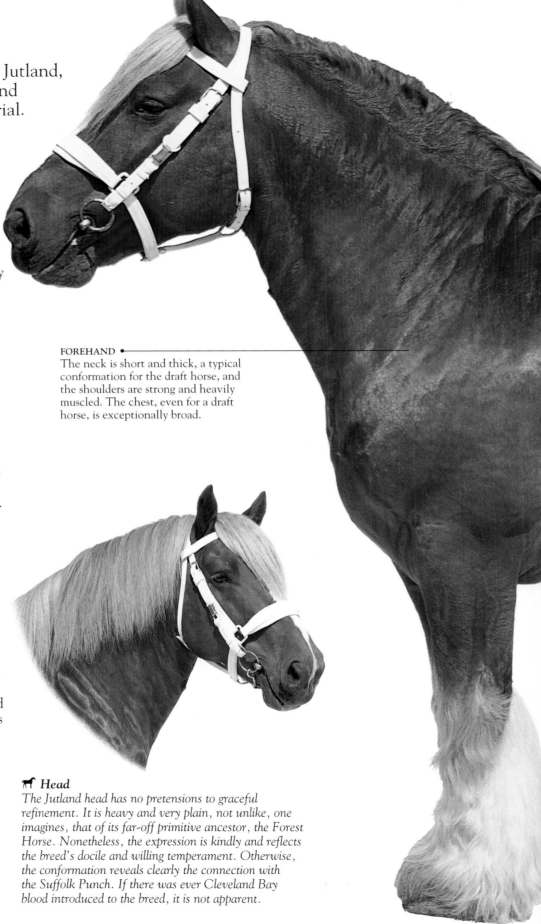

FOREHAND •
The neck is short and thick, a typical conformation for the draft horse, and the shoulders are strong and heavily muscled. The chest, even for a draft horse, is exceptionally broad.

🐎 Head
The Jutland head has no pretensions to graceful refinement. It is heavy and very plain, not unlike, one imagines, that of its far-off primitive ancestor, the Forest Horse. Nonetheless, the expression is kindly and reflects the breed's docile and willing temperament. Otherwise, the conformation reveals clearly the connection with the Suffolk Punch. If there was ever Cleveland Bay blood introduced to the breed, it is not apparent.

BODY
The compact, rolypoly body shows the breed's connection with the Suffolk Punch as clearly as anything else. It is further distinguished by an exceptional depth through the girth.

BACK
The back is short, wide and powerful, giving a compact appearance to the body. The withers are relatively flat and broad, which is not unusual in the European coldbloods.

COLOR
Without doubt, the Jutland's attractive coat color derives from the Suffolk Punch. The breed color is a dark chestnut with flaxen mane and tail and there are very few exceptions to this general rule.

QUARTERS
Like its Suffolk forebears, the quarters of the Jutland are appealingly round. They are also massive and very muscular.

LIMBS
The limbs are short and carry heavy feather, which breeders seek to eliminate. The joints in some individual animals can be criticized as being insufficiently hard and strong.

FEATHER
Heavy feathering of the lower legs can give rise to complaints in the heavy horse, notably scratches and grease heels.

HOOVES
The hooves are generally good, though they were not the best feature of some of the old Suffolks and are still far from exemplary in the Schleswig.

Draft horse
In draft, the Jutland presents a pleasing and attractive appearance and the rigs are always popular at shows and in the city streets. The hardy, easily kept Jutland is a tireless, willing worker and tractable in the extreme.

Rear view
Except for the feathering on the leg, this rear view of the Jutland could be the massive, rounded outline of the Suffolk. Although heavily built, the Jutland is a medium-sized draft horse and its action is quick and free.

Boulonnais

T HE BOULONNAIS, a native of Northwest France, has been acclaimed as the noblest draft horse of them all and it is, or perhaps unhappily it was, a most beautiful horse showing its breeding in a dozen features. It owes the fineness of its body tissues and its graceful lines to its oriental background.

ORIGINS

The breed's beginnings are with the ancient heavy horses that were native to the northwest of France before the Christian era. When Julius Caesar's Roman legions gathered there for the invasion of Britain in the first century A.D., their eastern horses were crossed with the native stock. Much later, during the Crusades, more Arabian blood was introduced, particularly through the agency of Eustache, Comte de Boulogne and Robert, Comte d'Artois, both skillful and innovative breeders.

The increased use of heavy armor in the fourteenth century enforced the use of northern heavy blood to give greater weight and size and there were also crossings with Spanish Horses. In the seventeenth century, the breed took on the name Boulonnais and two types emerged. The smaller horse measured less than 16hh and was known as the *mareyeur* (horse of the tide). It was used to make express fish deliveries from Boulogne to Paris and has almost died out. However, the large Boulonnais, which stands over 16hh, is still bred, if largely for the meat market.

FOREHAND •
The neck is thick but gracefully arched. There is more slope to the muscular shoulders than in other draft breeds and the withers are fairly prominent. The good front, or forehand, is unique among draft breeds.

HEIGHT
The Boulonnais stands between 15.3 and 16.3hh. The *mareyeur* was 15.1–15.3hh.

🐎 **Head**
The head of the Boulonnais is absolutely distinctive and shows clearly the influence of oriental outcrosses. The profile is straight, the eye sockets are prominent, the jowl is open and clean and the forehead is flat and wide. The eye is usually particularly large, the nostrils are open and the ears are very small, erect and mobile.

🐎 Action

The action is exceptional in a draft horse, being straight, relatively long and very swift and energetic. The breed has stamina and can maintain a steady speed over a long period.

• COAT
The skin is silky with prominent veining and the mane is fine and bushy. There is none of the coarseness associated with cold-blood breeds.

• QUARTERS
The Boulonnais' quarters are round and muscular with a characteristic double muscling of the croup. The tail, which is bushy, is set fairly high – very much higher than in other draft breeds.

🐎 North Swedish Horse

The North Swedish is a compact draft horse used in the forests of Sweden, where half the timber cut is still moved by horses. The stud at Wangen has a systematic breeding program that includes hauling tests and regular veterinary inspections of horses in work. Prior to the end of the nineteenth century, the North Swedish was an amalgam of breeds based on ancient native Scandinavian stock. It still bears a strong resemblance to its nearest relation, the Døle Gudbrandsal of Norway (see pp.64–5). The breed stands up to 15.3hh. It is sound and resistant to disease, noted for its longevity and an extraordinarily active gait combined with tremendous pulling power. The main colors are dun, brown, chestnut and black. Black is accompanied by white pasterns or "socks."

BODY •
The body is wonderfully compact and deep. The back is broad and straight, the chest wide and the ribs are as well sprung as those of an Arabian. Combined with the expression of elegance, the whole outline is majestic in appearance.

LIMBS •
Boulonnais limbs are strong with prominent muscular projections in both forearm and thighs. Other points are the short, thick cannons, the lack of feathering and the large, solid joints.

• COLOR
The coat color is predominantly gray in all its shades, as here, but there are occasionally bays and chestnuts, which were once much sought after.

Brabant

T HE BRABANT, also known as the Belgian Draft Horse, takes its name from one of the principal breeding areas. It is one of the world's most important breeds, having contributed to equine development well outside of its native country. The breed is little known in Britain and not sufficiently recognized in the country of its origin, but it is popular and appreciated for its sterling qualities in the USA, a number being kept at the famous Kentucky Horse Park.

ORIGINS

The breed is an ancient one. It is likely to be directly descended from the even older Ardennais (see pp.172–3) and, therefore, from the primitive foundation of the European heavy-horse breeds – the Forest or Diluvial Horse (*Equus silvaticus*). These massive horses were known to the Romans and received honorable mention in Julius Caesar's *De Bello Gallico* as most willing and untiring workers.

In the Middle Ages, the Brabant was called the Flanders Horse. As such, it was instrumental in the evolution of the English Great Horse and, later, in the development of the Shire. It was the basis of the Clydesdale (see pp.168–9), it had a large effect upon the Suffolk Punch (see pp.166–7) and it had an influence on the Irish Draft (see pp.76–7).

🐎 Brabant
Principally bred in Brabant, Belgian Draft Horses have been distinguished by that name, although they are also referred to as race de trait Belge. The breeders of this horse produced exceptional qualities through stringent selection, excluding foreign blood and occasionally in-breeding.

🐎 Three bloodlines
By 1870, there were three main Brabant groupings, based on bloodlines rather than conformational differences. The lines are those of Orange I, founder of the massive Gros de la Dendre line; Bayard, founder of the Gris du Hainaut, which produced sorrels and red-roans; and Jean I who founded the Colosses de la Mehaique.

QUARTERS
The huge, powerful quarters of the Brabant are distinctively rounded and the croup is characteristically "double-muscled."

COLOR
Colors vary from line to line. Bays, duns and grays occur, but red-roan with black points, sorrels and chestnuts, such as here, predominate.

HOOVES
Short, extremely strong legs usually terminate in a good deal of feather. The hooves are of medium size and well formed.

• BACK
The Brabant is thick set and compact. The Colosses de la Mehaique line is particularly noted for the great strength of the short back and loins.

HEAD •
The head is small in proportion to the body, square and somewhat plain, but the expression is intelligent and kindly.

• NECK
A short, thick, powerful neck joining withers and shoulders of similar proportions is an ideal combination for every sort of heavy draft purpose.

• BODY
Power is the hallmark of this massive breed and it is exemplified in the deep-girthed, compact body that goes with the Brabant's traditional strength of constitution.

♞ Working the land
The Brabant was bred with great care to suit the traditional agricultural skills of the country, its climate, its rich, heavy soil and the economic and social reliance upon the land. The action of the breed is not "brilliant" but it is practical in relation to its purpose.

• LIMBS
The Brabant is noted for the extreme strength and hardness of its short limbs. Soundness of limb was a feature in all the three principal lines.

HEIGHT
Brabants stand between 16.2 and 17hh.

Hunter

BY DEFINITION, A HUNTER is any horse used for the purpose of riding to hounds. It is a type of horse and may vary according to the requirements of the country in which it is hunted. It does not share common, fixed characteristics, such as those of size or color, and so it cannot be defined as a breed.

ORIGINS

The best hunters are those bred in Ireland, Britain and, to a degree, America, where the Thoroughbred element is equally paramount. The Irish hunter is often based on the Irish Draft/Thoroughbred cross, as is sometimes the case with those bred in Britain. Any cross is permissible, and many good hunters have a background of pony blood such as Connemara, New Forest, Fell, Highland or Welsh Cob. However, the best hunters will always carry a good proportion of Thoroughbred blood.

CHARACTERISTICS

A good hunter is sound, well proportioned and with all the conformational attributes of the top-class riding horse. It is well balanced, with easy, comfortable paces, and fast enough to keep with hounds. The hunter requires courage, agility, stamina and jumping ability to cope with every sort of obstacle during a long day in the field. Temperate and well mannered, the hunter must have a robust constitution that allows it to hunt up to two days a week throughout the hunting season.

HEIGHT
Height in the hunter is variable. The average, except for small hunters, is around 16–16.2hh.

SHOULDERS
A well-sloped shoulder is an essential attribute of the well-bred hunter. It enables the horse to gallop easily over broken terrain and to jump all kinds of obstacles.

 Conformation
A quality hunter has all the attributes of a riding horse combined with substance, strength and good bone. A well-made horse stays sound for longer than one of poor conformation.

COLOR
All colors are acceptable in the hunter. This one is dark bay.

LIMBS
Weight-carrying capacity depends upon general build and the bone measurement below the knee.

The hunter and his hunter
For 300 years, hunting has been the sport of the countryside. "Go anywhere in England where there are natural, wholesome, contented and really nice English people; and what do you always find? That the stables are the real center of the household." G.B. Shaw.

The second horse (left)
This nineteenth-century etching illustrates the practice of employing "second horses," a practice continued today in the fast, galloping grass countries of the English shires. The owner rides his first horse in the morning and changes to his fresh "second horse" for the afternoon's hunting. The groom, or second horseman, follows the hunt quietly on lanes and tracks until the replacement horse is required.

Head
Hunters are not always as beautiful as this one, but they should show some quality and give the impression of being workmanlike and honest. The good ones have a look about them that denotes intelligence and an equable disposition.

BODY •
The hunter must be both compact and deep through the girth to allow for full expansion of the lungs.

HOOVES •
"Armies may march on their stomachs, horses walk, trot, canter, gallop and go hunting on their feet."

Rear view
An exemplary back-end view of a quality horse. Quarters and gaskins are powerful, joints clean and hard, and the cannons of the hind legs are straight, not being offset below the hock joints. The overall impression is that of strength and of galloping potential.

Polo Pony

THE POLO PONY is not regarded as a breed, although the type of polo pony that has evolved in Argentina, and which is superior to any other, is very close to being a breed. Indeed, its character is more fixed in detail than many of the established breeds.

HISTORY

Britain was the first western country to play polo and used to have a Polo Pony Stud Book based on native pony mares with small Thoroughbreds. After 1914, the height limit of 14.1hh, set by the Americans in 1895, was abandoned. It was raised to 14.2hh, and Argentinian ponies increasingly dominated the game. The scale of horse breeding in Argentina and the availability of indigenous skills in horsemanship allowed ponies to be sold more cheaply than elsewhere. Moreover, the Argentinian ponies were tougher and had better bone than the English and American Thoroughbreds. The Argentinians imported the best Thoroughbred stallions, crossed them with the tough, part-bred Criollo stock and then again to the Thoroughbred in the second cross. This produced the ideal pony of about 15.1hh, distinctly Thoroughbred in appearance, but shorter strided.

NECK
For the sake of balance, a fairly long, well-muscled neck that is in no way heavy is an absolute essential for a polo pony.

QUALITY
Although the polo pony is Thoroughbred in appearance, it has a typical, wiry quality of its own.

🐎 **Head**
A roached mane is customary on the polo pony to avoid interference with the stick. Otherwise, the head is similar to that of a Thoroughbred. The polo pony is lively, intelligent and full of character. The Argentinian ponies seem to have an inbred talent for the game in much the same way that a cow pony works cattle instinctively.

🐎 **Before the match**
Preparations for the game include braiding of the pony's tail in a polo bang so that the stick does not get caught in it; the placing of protective boots on all four legs; and meticulous inspection of all tack to prevent accidents during play.

HOOVES
Hooves need to be completely sound, as polo grounds are often hard and the game is played at a full gallop.

🐎 Essential characteristics

The requirements of a polo pony are speed, stamina (for his work is done at the gallop), courage and very good balance. In addition, the temperament must be bold and lively without being excitable.

• BODY
Prominent withers with good, strong shoulders are an essential attribute if the pony is to be sufficiently handy. The back needs to be short and the ribs well sprung.

• QUARTERS
Good quarters are an obvious requirement – the pony must be able to gallop flat out, stop in a second and turn on a dime.

🐎 Criollo

The Criollo, the native horse of Argentina, is derived from early Spanish stock and is probably as tough and sound as any other horse in the world. It is the cow pony of the legendary gauchos and, when crossed with the Thoroughbred, became the base for the Argentinian polo pony. Although not necessarily beautiful, it is unsurpassed in many ways. It has plenty of bone, very strong joints and wonderful hooves. It is rarely unsound on any of these counts.

• COLOR
The polo pony can be any color. This one is bay.

• LIMBS
Limbs and joints must be strong and correctly made for the pony to endure the rigorous game, and be able to accelerate, turn and stop quickly. Short cannons and good bone characterize the top-class pony. An unduly long, low stride is not, however, an essential attribute.

🐎 Morning walk

Polo ponies taking their morning exercise on the exercise track at the Kentucky Horse Park. The Park, with some of the best grounds in the USA, regularly stages high-goal polo. The American game maintains consistently high standards.

HEIGHT
The ideal height is around 15.1hh. Argentinian polo ponies are always called ponies, whatever their height.

Hack

I N TIMES GONE BY, grooms rode their masters' hunters quietly to the meet and the owners, after breakfasting, followed in their dog-carts or carriages, or they cut a dash on a "covert hack." This was a Thoroughbred riding horse, elegant, well mannered, and comfortable to ride at a smooth "hack canter." The covert hack was an attractive, showy horse, lighter than a hunter. It did not have to carry weight for a full day's hunt nor, therefore, have to have the substance and bone essential for the hunting field.

PARK HACK

Even more refined than the covert hack was the beautiful and highly schooled "park hack." In the fashionable days of riding in Rotten Row in London's Hyde Park, the park hack paraded its well-tailored owner, who often might be escorting a lady, before the appraising and sometimes critical public eye. To show off its rider to full advantage the park hack was brimful of presence, moving in all the paces with lightness and with great gaiety and freedom. Its manners, like its appearance, could not be less than absolutely impeccable.

MODERN HACK

The same qualities are required of the modern show ring hack, which must be a model of good conformation. While light and graceful, a modern hack is not a "blood weed" and it is expected to have not less than 8in (20cm) of bone under the knee.

The majority of entrants in hack classes are Thoroughbred, or nearly so, and are far closer to the park hack than to the stronger covert type. Some, however, may be part-bred Arabians and one or two very good ones are Anglo-Arabs. Show classes are for small hacks (14.2–15hh), large hacks (15–15.3hh), and ladies' hacks (14.2–15.3hh). Ladies' hacks are shown under sidesaddle. Hacks are shown at walk, trot and canter. They are not required to gallop but must give an individual display. In British shows, entries are also ridden by the judge.

🐴 Action
Hack action must be straight, true and low to the ground with no tendency toward cheating or lifting the knee. The trot is smooth and floating, the canter is slow, light and in perfect balance, and the movement is distinguished by a particular brilliance. While the hack is schooled to perfection, the performance is not expected to resemble the disciplined accuracy of the dressage horse.

🐴 Rear view
Viewed from behind, the immediate impression is one of graceful symmetry combined with strength. No deviation is tolerated in the straightness of the hind limbs or in the construction of the joints. A good, second thigh and enough width over the quarters is just as much a requirement of the hack as of any equine. The hooves must be of the highest quality.

• OUTLINE
The overall outline of the hack is that of the Thoroughbred, the structure being designed for speed. The proportions are as near to perfect as possible and the musculature is long, never short and thick.

• MANE
When shown, hacks have their manes braided to show off the neck. The tail is either thinned by pulling or it, too, is braided.

EARS
Ears should be mobile and enquiring.

🐎 Head
A quality head denotes well-bred antecedents, and is essential in the hack. No show class was ever won by a horse that was common in this respect. Big, bold and generous eyes are a feature, along with the enquiring, mobile ears.

COLOR •
The hack can be any solid color. This one is a dark bay.

🐎 Definition
One telling definition of a hack describes it as a horse to be ridden with one hand while its owner flirts with a lady companion.

• HOOVES
Hacks are shown in lightweight shoes to enhance the action.

HEIGHT
Hacks are between 14.2 and 15.3hh, depending on the class requirement.

Cob

STOCKY LITTLE HORSES, big bodied and standing solidly on short, powerful legs, cobs are quite unmistakable in their appearance. Their overall conformation and short, thick musculature, is that of a structure far more disposed to strength and weight carrying capacity than to speed. For all that, the true cob is able to gallop and the action is more low than high.

ORIGINS
The cob is a type, not a recognized breed, and there is, indeed, no set pattern to its production. Some of the very best cobs have been produced as the result of crossing an Irish Draft or a heavyweight hunter with a Thoroughbred, and some recent champions have been pure Irish Draft Horses. Occasionally, there have been examples of cobs bred from or by Shires and Welsh Cobs. However, their breeding is rarely deliberate and often accidental.

CHARACTERISTICS
Until the passing of the Docking and Nicking Act 1948, which made the practices illegal in Britain, it was traditional to dock the tails of cobs. This gave a jaunty, sporting appearance, but it was a cruel and unnecessary custom.

The word most frequently applied to cobs is "bomb-proof" and it suits them admirably. Their job is to provide a steady, unflappable ride for a heavyweight rider who may have passed the first flush of youth. Their manners, therefore, have to be very good and they should certainly never hot up. Most cobs, indeed, have a particular intelligence and are usually full of character.

In the past, the cob was a dual-purpose animal, going as well in harness as under saddle. Today, a cob is more likely to be kept as a general family all-arounder, and many of them make great hunters that are easy and economical to keep.

COLOR
Cobs are of any color, but many are gray due to the Irish Draft influence, but no objection would be made to a skewbald or even a spotted one, although this is extremely rare. This cob is bay.

QUARTERS
Big, strongly muscled and well-formed quarters are a characteristic of the cob, whose job is to carry weight. They are too thickset for any great speed, but can usually jump well.

Rear view
The cob does not always have a head "like a lady's maid" but he certainly has "the bottom of a cook." The back-end may not be conducive to speed but there is no doubting its strength.

BACK
The back is short and fairly broad as befits a weight-carrying structure, and the loins are thick and powerful. A long back, particularly if accompanied by slackness in the loin, is an unacceptable conformational fault in the cob.

SHOULDERS
The shoulders are strong but are sufficiently sloped for low, economical movement and to prohibit any exaggerated action from the knee.

🐎 *Impression*
The cob is a gentleman's gentleman.

NECK
The neck, in accordance with the cob's build, is relatively short. It is, however, strong and it is always arched.

MANE
The mane is always roached.

GIRTH
Cobs stand on short, powerful limbs, but the great depth of girth gives them the appearance of being even shorter than they are in reality.

KNEES
The knees are large and flat, and the forearms are strongly muscled and quite free where they join the body at the elbow.

🐎 *Head*
The cob head is well formed, workmanlike and honest rather than an example of refinement and quality. However, it is not coarse and has an intelligent look, accentuated by the mobile, alert ears and the generous, widely spaced eyes.

LIMBS
The cannon bone below the knee is short and the bone measurement, which is taken below the knee and governs the weight-carrying capacity, can be as much as 9in (23cm).

HOOVES
The cob has broad, open hooves of a size in proportion to its build.

HEIGHT
Cobs may stand as much as 15.3hh.

Riding Pony

T HE RIDING PONY was developed specifically for the show ring. In essence, it is the juvenile rider's equivalent of the elegant Thoroughbred show hack. At its best, it is probably the most perfectly proportioned equine in the world, particularly in the middle height limit from 12.2 to 13.2hh.

ORIGINS

The evolution of the riding pony over a period of no more than a half century is an object lesson in the judicious melding of selected bloods to produce an end product entirely suited to the purpose required. The riding pony is based on a mix of native British blood (notably Welsh, and to a lesser degree Dartmoor), Arabian and Thoroughbred. The establishment of so unique a pony may not be classed as an achievement in quite the same category as that of the "invention" of the English Thoroughbred, but it remains, nonetheless, a remarkable and largely unparalleled accomplishment in the history of horse breeding.

CHARACTERISTICS

The riding pony moves gracefully and in perfect balance from the shoulder with the free, long, low action of the English Thoroughbred. It has inherited all the presence of its hotblood ancestors, but it has to be perfectly mannered and retain the bone, substance and good sense of its native forebears. For that to be accomplished in riding pony stock represents the pinnacle of the breeder's art.

HEIGHT
Average height is 13.2hh. Show classes have three height divisions: up to 12.2hh, 12.2–13.2hh and 13.2–14.2hh.

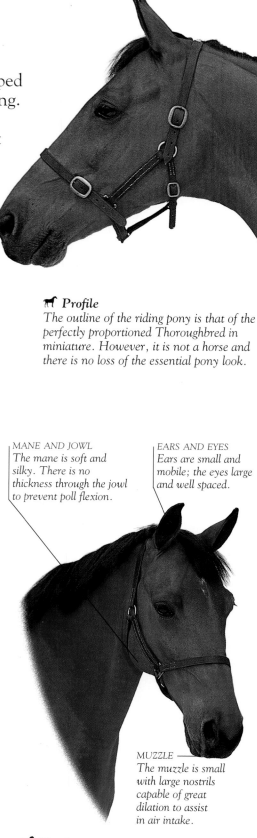

🐎 **Profile**
The outline of the riding pony is that of the perfectly proportioned Thoroughbred in miniature. However, it is not a horse and there is no loss of the essential pony look.

MANE AND JOWL
The mane is soft and silky. There is no thickness through the jowl to prevent poll flexion.

EARS AND EYES
Ears are small and mobile; the eyes large and well spaced.

MUZZLE
The muzzle is small with large nostrils capable of great dilation to assist in air intake.

🐎 **Head**
The skin covering the head is thin, the veins easily seen. The impression is of great refinement and intelligence, but the essential pony character is retained. A horse's head should never be seen on a riding pony .

NECK
The neck is fairly long, the graceful curve joining smoothly into the body at withers and shoulder. Too short a neck would restrict the action.

SHOULDERS
The shoulder exemplifies that of the supreme riding animal. The shoulder blade is long and well sloped, and the humerus short.

KNEES
Above the knee, the muscles are big and long; below it the cannons are short. The knee itself is flat and large to allow for the passage of the tendons.

HOOVES
Riding pony hooves are of the best. They are equal in size, open, well formed and hard. There is no feather at the heel.

♞ Presence
Presence is an essential attribute of the riding pony. It is the personality and the star quality that demands attention and says uncompromisingly, "Look at me."

• QUARTERS
Quarters are well muscled but not heavy or excessively rounded. They run into similarly muscled gaskins.

• TAIL
The tail is well set, high on the quarter. A low-set tail denotes a conformational defect.

♞ Color
The pony in this illustration is palomino. Riding ponies can be any color: black, brown, bay (as main picture), gray, palomino and even shades of roan. White markings are permissible but skewbalds and piebalds are not.

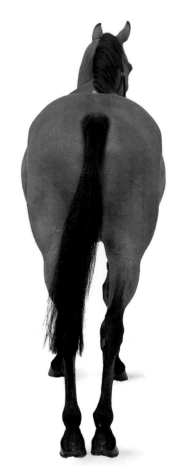

BODY •
The withers in the riding pony are clearly defined, the back of medium length, the trunk well ribbed, and the girth deep. In a good example, the body is as near to perfection as can be imagined.

HOCK •
The hock is big, free from any lumpiness and not puffy. It is low to the ground, the point in line with the chestnut on the inside of the foreleg.

HIND LEG •
The hind leg is inclined to speed. That is, there is length from hip to the point of the hock for maximum propulsion.

♞ Rear view
The view from behind presents a picture of symmetry. The action is straight and true, with the hind hooves following exactly in the track made by the fore shoes.

Preventive care
"No foot, no 'oss" is one of the essential equestrian truths. Horse shoes were in general use in Europe from the Romano-Gallic period and from the outset the farrier, the master of fire, was held in particular respect.

A handsome turnout
This first-class cob of excellent conformation is a good all-around utility horse, which will also take its turn in the hunting field. The turnout of both the cob and its rider is neat and workmanlike.

You and Your Horse

The acquisition of a horse, like marriage, is a matter not to be "taken in hand unadvisedly…".

Owning a horse and looking after it yourself is one of life's more satisfying experiences, allowing, as it does, for the development of a special relationship that would be impossible in a riding school situation, for instance. Horses, however, are entirely dependent upon the human agency throughout their lives and their ownership brings responsibilities and demands great commitment. Before you buy a horse, honestly assess your abilities as a rider and your ability to provide basic facilities – a paddock, a stable and sufficient money to keep the animal fed, trimmed and shod, and to allow for veterinary expenses and insurance. The system of horse-keeping you employ – whether the horse will be kept stabled or in pasture – depends very much on the time that is available to you, and that too is a matter you need to consider carefully.

~ STABLE AND RIDING EQUIPMENT ~

Given that you can afford a horse, it is necessary to have a set of stable tools and a wheelbarrow to clean out the stall, as well as the essential tack and stable items of riding equipment, such as buckets, a manger and a haynet. Nor can one do without a halter and a lead rope, a saddle, mounted with leathers, stirrups and a girth, and a bridle. For riding clothes, at a pinch, you can make do with jeans, sturdy ankle boots and a rainproof jacket, but a hard safety hat with proper fastenings is essential.

Regular grooming (above)
Cleanliness, it is said, is next to Godliness, and for the sake of the horse's health, it is necessary to make sure that its skin and the coat are kept clean by regular grooming.

The horse-owner's tools (above) *"A workman is only as good as his tools." A basic requirement of the horse-owner is a complete set of good-quality grooming tools.*

Learning through play (right)
Foals learn their first lessons while running with their dams. If they are to develop fully, they need room to run and play and the company of other young animals.

A balanced diet (above)
Regular feeding of a balanced diet of feed in the quantity relevant to the size of the horse and the work expected of it, is an integral part of horse management.

Buying a Horse

IT IS ADVISABLE to take certain precautions when contemplating horse ownership. Before you set out to buy a horse, you should first make an honest assessment of your riding ability, examine the facilities you have for keeping a horse and think about the purpose for which the animal is to be used.

Law of Purchase

Buying a horse is not much different from the purchase of any other commodity. So far as the law is concerned, the principle in most countries is *caveat emptor*, let the buyer beware! However, the law is designed to give buyers some protection. Sellers must tell the truth when a specific question is asked, it is unethical to sell a horse that is not suitable for the purpose for which it was offered for sale.

A problem, of course, is that a horse is a living creature and subject to the unpredictabilities of that state. It may be that a horse, which performs perfectly well with one person, will not do so with another. Very good horsemen and women can manage most horses and so have a wider choice when seeking a purchase. Conversely, novice riders are more limited because of their inexperience.

Cost

For most people, cost is an important consideration when buying a horse. There are several factors that affect price:
1. Conformation and appearance;
2. Performance ability and/or record;
3. Weight-carrying capacity if that is a matter of concern;
4. Age and manners.

The soundness of the horse is not an issue, since no one in his right mind knowingly buys an unsound horse. As far as age is concerned, in general terms, an unbroken 2 or 3 year old will be cheaper than a 4 or 5 year old who has been schooled. From that age, all else being equal, the horse increases in value up to the age of 10. Thereafter, the price levels off until around 12–15 years, when the value of the animal begins to drop, the

🐎 Pony sales
Young, unbroken pony stock can be bought at sales throughout the country. However, it requires experience and some skill to make a satisfactory purchase in this way.

speed of the decline increasing as the years pass. Manners may be stretched to include temperament and whether the animal meets the demands made on a horse of today. For instance, is it safe in traffic under ordinary conditions and is it easy to box, shoe and clip?

VETERINARY INSPECTION

Before parting with cash, it is always advisable to have an intended purchase examined by your own veterinarian who will provide a certificate detailing specific points, and noting any blemishes. The veterinarian will examine the horse thoroughly, checking its wind, limbs, sight, etc., and will state whether, in his opinion, the horse is sound in those areas. Having taken this precaution, you can feel safe in your new horse. The certificate, however, does not constitute a guarantee in those respects nor, of course, in regard to its performance and possible behavior.

CHECKING THE ACTION
The horse should be trotted on a hard surface, such as concrete, so that the veterinarian can observe any irregularities in its action. Lameness is quickly made apparent on a hard surface. It is not so easily detected on soft ground where the horse sinks into the surface.

EYE EXAMINATION
Thorough examination of the eyes for incipient cataracts and other visual deficiencies is essential. Faulty eyesight not only lowers the performance potential of the horse, but may also be the cause of persistent shying.

HOOVES EXAMINATION
The veterinarian will pay particular attention to the hooves, examining each one carefully for any sign of disease. Lameness in the horse usually occurs in the lower limbs as a result of diseases in the hoof or of malformation, but if diagnosed early, can sometimes be corrected.

If you aspire to purchase a well-bred horse of handsome appearance and impeccable conformation, who has won eventing, dressage, and show jumping, and is furthermore just 7 years old, perfectly mannered and able to carry 200lb (91kg) easily during a day's hunting, expect a correspondingly hefty price tag.

Where to Buy

Many horses are bought at public sales, and at those conducted by reputable auctioneers; buyers are protected by the "conditions of sale," which should be studied carefully. Whether such sales are the best places for the novice to buy is, perhaps, unlikely. It may not be possible to examine the horse and ride it as thoroughly as might be desirable.

As another option, you can buy from a dealer. He will certainly allow you to ride the horse and to watch while it is ridden, with ample time to observe the animal being handled and to ask questions. A well-established dealer is a businessman and will want to satisfy the customer, so it is unlikely that he would attempt to sell a horse that he knows is unsuitable.

Finally, you can buy privately. It should not be taken for granted that buying privately is the most satisfactory way of acquiring a horse, however many horses are bought and sold in this manner.

How to Buy

Having made an appointment to see a horse for sale, it is important that you should arrange to go with a friend. If your

Aging the horse
An experienced horseman can tell the age of a horse by examining the teeth. It also gives him an opportunity to see whether the mouth has suffered damage from the bitting arrangement.

The test ride
A buyer should always try to ride his intended purchase. Ten minutes in the saddle, on the flat and even over one or two small fences, reveals much about the animal and the standard of training. It is prudent, however, to have the horse ridden by the seller, or his employee, before mounting yourself.

friend is knowledgeable about horses, so much the better, but his prime function is to be a witness to the sale, in the event that any dispute concerning the sale arises.

At the start, tell the seller the purpose for which the horse is required. It is not unreasonable to ask him to provide a form of guarantee (either verbally or in writing) that the horse, to the best of his knowledge, is sound, quiet to ride in all respects, free from stable vices and suitable for your stated requirements. Although the seller does not have to give such an assurance, if he declines you might put your own interpretation on the refusal and look for another horse.

Ask specific questions about the horse's performance, travelling, shoeing and so on. The blanket question, "Has the horse any vices or problems I should know about?" is certainly the final one to ask.

If you are still interested, the horse should be trotted-out so that the action can be observed and you can gain an overall impression. When the horse is tacked-up, take note of the bitting arrangements. Before you mount, the horse should be ridden by the seller to see how it performs with someone it knows.

If you are keen to buy after riding the horse yourself, do so "subject to a veterinary certificate" and have your own veterinarian carry out the inspection. It should be noted that the veterinarian's certificate is not a guarantee of soundness – it is simply an opinion expressed by a suitably qualified person.

GETTING YOUR HORSE HOME
Having bought the horse, it has to be taken to its new home and settled in to an initially strange environment. It is important that the horse finds this first contact with its new owners a pleasurable one, and it is worth taking trouble to ensure that every care is exercised so that the chances of the horse becoming upset are reduced.

PREPARATION
Prepare the stall in advance for your horse's arrival. Lay the bed and prepare some feed or a haynet. Even if the horse travels only a short distance, it is advisable for it to wear protective travelling boots and a tail bandage, lest it knock the lower limbs or rub its tail against the trailer. Common-sense precautions help to insure an uneventful transfer.

LOADING
Allow ample time for the loading process. Since the horse may be somewhat suspicious of a strange trailer, you must be ready to reassure it while still acting firmly, and with confidence.

STABLING
Once you reach home, put the horse in its stall, and allow it some time to settle down before giving it feed. Your contact with the new horse, grooming it and checking its blanket will help to reassure and settle your new horse.

Stable Management

Horses are stabled so that they may be made fit for particular purposes, like hunting, or one of the competitive disciplines such as show jumping or steeplechasing. Any of those pursuits demand a high standard of fitness and presentation, requirements that are facilitated by the horse being kept in an indoor, or stable, situation.

Pasture

A horse that lives outdoors and is unclipped may only be worked at slow paces during the winter because of its low-energy feed. During the summer, a competition horse cannot be kept fit unless it is stabled and its grass intake is thus restricted. If allowed to graze on lush grass, the horse will become fat and soft. If worked in this condition, it would run the risk of damage to limbs and organs.

Successful Stabling

The essence of effective stable management is keeping horses healthy and happy in an unnatural environment. To achieve this, these procedures must be followed:
1. The horse must be fed regular, small meals that provide vitamins, minerals, proteins and bulk in relation to the restrictions of the digestive system and the amount of energy expended. Bear in mind that the horse has a small stomach in relation to its size (see Diet pp.206–07).
2. The horse has to be kept clean and the muscles developed and toned by regular grooming (see Grooming pp.202–03).
3. The horse must be provided with a living environment that allows it to feel comfortable and relaxed.

Stable Design

The design and position of the stable must be a prime consideration. The stable must be dry, warm and well ventilated

🐎 Stalls
These Percherons are stabled in individual stalls and are tied onto a sliding rope, which allows them to lie down. This stabling method is often employed where there are numbers of horses to accommodate, and has the advantage of providing the horses with company.

without being drafty. Furthermore, provision has to be made for effective drainage and, if at all possible, the stable should be sited facing toward the sun so that it receives the benefit of what sunshine may be available throughout the year. The inmate should be able to see its fellow horses and take an interest in what is going on in the yard.

There is no doubt that a box stall, in which the horse is at liberty to move about, is the best form of horse accommodation. It should not measure less than 12ft x 10ft (3.6m x 3m) and if it is somewhat larger, that is all to the good.

🐎 Yard equipment
Basic equipment for managing the stable and keeping the yard clean and tidy are a wheelbarrow, shovel, tined fork, muck sheet or skip, and a stout yard broom. The possession of a full complement of tools, kept in good condition, reduces the labor involved and allows the work to be completed more easily and more quickly. Stout wellington boots or short rubber boots are sensible footwear for yard staff.

BROOM

FOUR-TINED FORK

SHOVEL

WHEELBARROW

STRAW

SHAVINGS

MUCK MAT

MUCK SHEET

HOSE PIPE

RAKE

PITCHFORK

SHORT RUBBER BOOTS

WELLINGTON BOOTS

SHAVINGS RAKE

Bedding

The bed is the most important factor in keeping a horse stabled. The bed contributes to the warmth and comfort of the stall and therefore to the welfare of its occupant. Maintaining it is one of the more demanding of the stable chores that must be performed regularly.

A bed can be made from wheat straw, shavings or even, these days, from shredded paper. It has to be deep enough to induce the horse to lie down safely, without sustaining injuries from contact with the hard floor. Another important object is to provide a warm, dry bed that is absorbent and deodorizing.

Mucking Out

Without doubt, the guiding principle of good horse management must be that "cleanliness is next to Godliness." In the context of the horse, who has no need for the consolations of religion, cleanliness is a paramount requirement and, all else being equal, leads to a comfortable and stress-free existence.

In some stables, it is the practice to clean the beds out every day. Any slightly damp bedding, as in the case of straw, can be put out to dry and then used again. The soiled bedding goes to the trash. The bed is then remade with fresh bedding after the floor has been thoroughly washed down and disinfected.

To save time and cut down on the expense, many people use a deep-litter method for making the horse's bed. This involves removing manure regularly and topping up the bed with clean, fresh straw or other bedding. The stall is completely cleaned out once a week, once a month or at longer intervals.

With the deep-litter method, it is important that the manure is picked up regularly throughout the day, whenever it is necessary to enter the stall, in fact. This practice prevents the horse from trodding the manure into the bed and thus creating more work.

In order to reduce the amount of labor and to make the job easier, the possession of a full set of tools is absolutely essential. The basic tools are a well-balanced wheelbarrow, a shovel, a pitchfork, and a four-tined fork, a muck skip and/or muck sheet (a stout piece of sacking will do) with which to collect manure.

Stable Fittings

In a box stall, labor can be reduced and the whole operation made significantly more convenient by the provision of certain fittings. Rings are necessary for tying-up and for hanging haynets. (It is less wasteful and far more satisfactory to feed hay from nets than loose on the ground.) A removable manger set in a corner of the box is a sensible way of

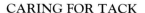

CARING FOR TACK

Saddles and bridles are stripped down every day after they have been used, and all the component parts are cleaned thoroughly and treated with saddle soap and a leather preparation.

feeding and it can be taken out for cleaning without trouble. The best way to provide a constant supply of fresh water is by installing self-filling water bowls. These are ideal from the horse's viewpoint, save hours of time for the groom or owner and insure that fresh water is always available. Otherwise water must be provided in a strong plastic bucket, which must be refilled constantly. Both bucket and water must be clean.

🐎 *Using a muck skip* (above)
To save labor and to keep the stable clean and sweet-smelling, pick up manure throughout the day, making use of a fork and the convenient muck mat or wheelbarrow.

🐎 *Sweeping the stable* (right)
A well-run stable is kept immaculate at all times, with frequent sweeping and the removal of loose straw or hay.

Basic Equipment

EARLY RIDING EQUIPMENT was mainly concerned with control. The first bits were just thongs tied around the lower jaw, but by 2300 B.C. bits of horn and bone were used, and metal snaffles were common in the Near East by 1400 B.C. The curb bit was invented by the Celts of Gaul 1,000 years later.

Saddles and Harness

The first saddle to be built on a wooden frame, or tree, was introduced by the Sarmations at the onset of the Christian era, but it was another 300 or 400 years before the stirrup was in general use.

LEATHER CARE •
Essentials include saddle soap and sponges to clean the leather, a soft cloth to polish it, and oil, which can be applied with a brush, for keeping it supple.

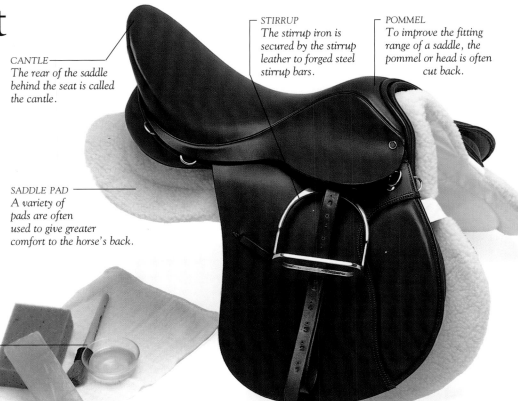

CANTLE
The rear of the saddle behind the seat is called the cantle.

SADDLE PAD
A variety of pads are often used to give greater comfort to the horse's back.

STIRRUP
The stirrup iron is secured by the stirrup leather to forged steel stirrup bars.

POMMEL
To improve the fitting range of a saddle, the pommel or head is often cut back.

BRIDLES

The snaffle is the simplest form of control. The eggbutt cheek piece prevents pinching of the lips. The double, or Weymouth, bridle, for educated riders and horses, employs both curb bit and snaffle.

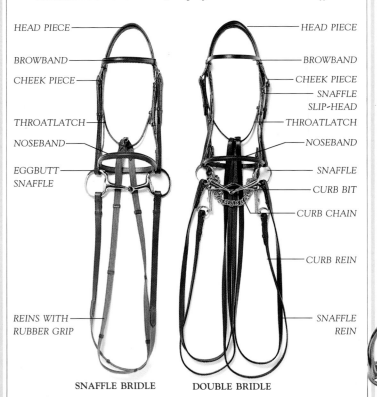

HEAD PIECE

BROWBAND

CHEEK PIECE

THROATLATCH

NOSEBAND

EGGBUTT SNAFFLE

REINS WITH RUBBER GRIP

HEAD PIECE

BROWBAND

CHEEK PIECE

SNAFFLE SLIP-HEAD

THROATLATCH

NOSEBAND

SNAFFLE

CURB BIT

CURB CHAIN

CURB REIN

SNAFFLE REIN

SNAFFLE BRIDLE   **DOUBLE BRIDLE**

🐎 Saddle

The principal types of saddle are: dressage, jumping, stock seat and the general-purpose, as here. Traditionally they are made of leather, which is supple, strong and long lasting. Today, saddles made of synthetic materials are also available. These are less expensive and easily maintained though not as durable. Both types of saddle are made on either laminated trees, usually inset with springs to give resilience, or plastic trees.

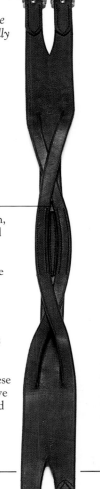

GIRTHS •
Girths can be made of leather, cotton, wool, web or nylon. Here, the shaped leather girth is a Balding pattern, designed so that it cannot pinch or chafe at the elbow. The other is made of cotton and is padded. For preference, steel buckles are used.

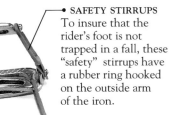

• **SAFETY STIRRUPS**
To insure that the rider's foot is not trapped in a fall, these "safety" stirrups have a rubber ring hooked on the outside arm of the iron.

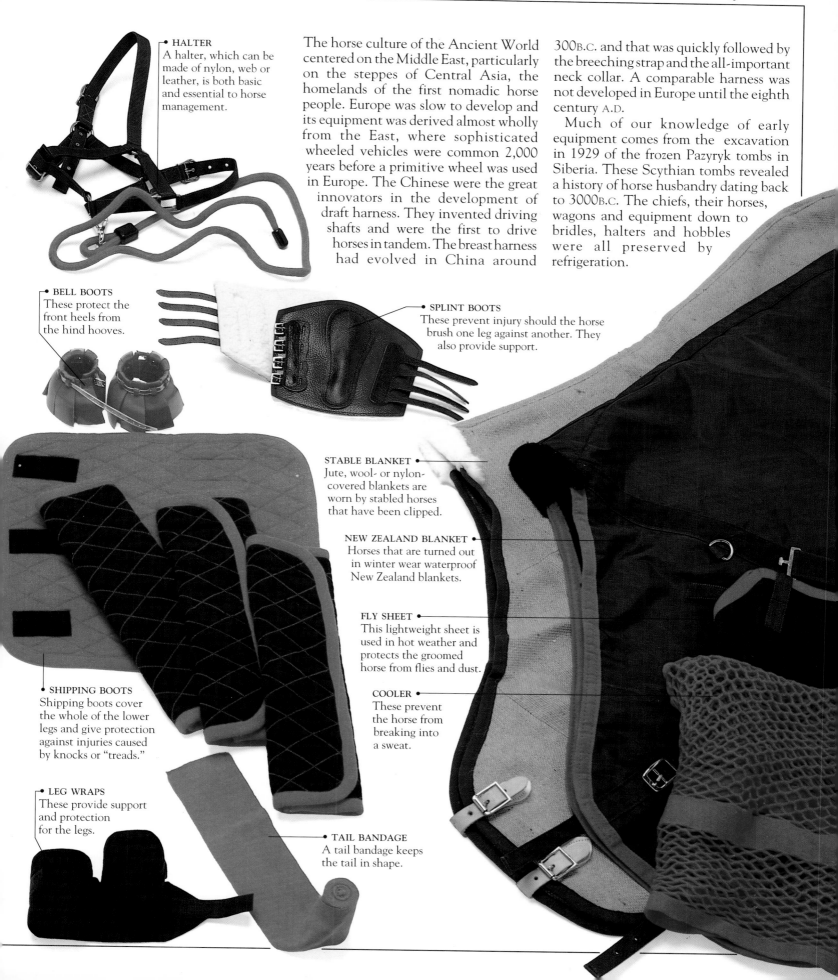

HALTER
A halter, which can be made of nylon, web or leather, is both basic and essential to horse management.

The horse culture of the Ancient World centered on the Middle East, particularly on the steppes of Central Asia, the homelands of the first nomadic horse people. Europe was slow to develop and its equipment was derived almost wholly from the East, where sophisticated wheeled vehicles were common 2,000 years before a primitive wheel was used in Europe. The Chinese were the great innovators in the development of draft harness. They invented driving shafts and were the first to drive horses in tandem. The breast harness had evolved in China around 300 B.C. and that was quickly followed by the breeching strap and the all-important neck collar. A comparable harness was not developed in Europe until the eighth century A.D.

Much of our knowledge of early equipment comes from the excavation in 1929 of the frozen Pazyryk tombs in Siberia. These Scythian tombs revealed a history of horse husbandry dating back to 3000 B.C. The chiefs, their horses, wagons and equipment down to bridles, halters and hobbles were all preserved by refrigeration.

BELL BOOTS
These protect the front heels from the hind hooves.

SPLINT BOOTS
These prevent injury should the horse brush one leg against another. They also provide support.

STABLE BLANKET
Jute, wool- or nylon-covered blankets are worn by stabled horses that have been clipped.

NEW ZEALAND BLANKET
Horses that are turned out in winter wear waterproof New Zealand blankets.

FLY SHEET
This lightweight sheet is used in hot weather and protects the groomed horse from flies and dust.

COOLER
These prevent the horse from breaking into a sweat.

SHIPPING BOOTS
Shipping boots cover the whole of the lower legs and give protection against injuries caused by knocks or "treads."

LEG WRAPS
These provide support and protection for the legs.

TAIL BANDAGE
A tail bandage keeps the tail in shape.

Clothes

RIDING CLOTHES are traditional in style and materials while being essentially practical. Modern riding gear makes increasing use of developments in synthetics and in manufacturing technology and recognizes a more casual and fashion-conscious approach.

The first riding clothes were worn by the horse people of the Asian Steppes in the centuries before the Christian era. They wore rough, wool tunics, and trousers, which they tucked into felt boots. On the other hand, the horsemen of classical Greece, who lived in a hotter climate and were, in any case, obsessed with the human form, rode naked and bareback.

Modern riding clothes follow precepts that were established over 200 years ago. They date back to the mid-seventeenth century when gentlemen began to wear well-fitting jackets, vests, breeches, and boots, which were stout enough to keep out the cold and wet.

A century later, the horsemen of the English hunting shires had perfected a form of apparel that was entirely practical but was distinguished by the elegance of the cut and the quality of the materials – a reflection, it has been said, of "a genius for well-bred understatement."

HAT
Safety in the saddle, especially on hard roads, is ensured by firmly secured, protective headgear.

RIBBON CROWN

TAB CHIN STRAP

JODHPUR BOOTS
These short, elastic-sided boots, made of leather, support the ankle and are worn with jodhpurs.

GARTER STRAP

JACKET
For casual riding, a showerproof and windproof quilted jacket or vest, which is both comfortable and warm, is a useful item of clothing.

JODHPURS
Jodhpurs, extending to the ankle, originated in the Indian state of Jodhpur, where they are still a commonplace garment. Modern, close-fitting jodhpurs are made from two-way stretch materials.

SWEATER
A warm sweater or a thick shirt is ideal if the weather is cold.

RIDING BOOTS
Long, leather or rubber boots are worn with breeches and help to maintain the position of the rider's leg.

BREECHES
Breeches are shorter than jodhpurs and are worn with riding boots. They are usually made of stretch material.

VELCRO FASTENERS

WAXED-COTTON JACKET
A comparatively new arrival on the equestrian scene is the ubiquitous waterproof and windproof, waxed-cotton jacket. Ideal for wet-weather casual riding, the coat has an extra generous cut that allows freedom of movement and keeps the saddle dry, too.

STRING GLOVES

WOOL GLOVES

LINING
Lining is reinforced at the lower edge with waterproof material. It keeps out both rain and sweat from the horse.

GLOVES
String or wool gloves, with reinforced palms and fingers, keep the hands warm and clean while giving a better grip on the rein. Riding gloves need to be one size larger than normal.

JUMPING WHIP
The jumping, or cross-country, whip has a broad flap, or keeper, that makes a cracking noise but does not cut.

SCHOOLING WHIP
Schooling, or dressage, whips are longer than jumping whips and can be used without taking the hand from the rein.

HACKING JACKET
Tweed jackets are considered correct for everyday wear. Ladies may wear navy or black coats for hunting or show classes.

TIE PIN

TIES AND STOCKS
Hunting ties or stocks are white. Those for hacking can be colored.

SHIRTS
A collar and tie is acceptable for showing. When a stock is worn, a collarless shirt is more convenient.

Grooming

GROOMING IS PRIMARILY carried out for appearance's sake, however, it has other objectives as well. Grooming cleans the skin so that it can work to maximum effect. Grooming and strapping, when the horse is rhythmically thumped with a pad on the shoulders, quarters and neck, also encourage muscle development and tone, and promote circulation.

When to Groom

Stabled horses that are clipped, kept under artificial conditions, and fed quantities of heating food, create additional waste matter. Much of this waste is removed through an increased rate of breathing and through excrement, but much is also disposed of through the skin, the pores of which must be clean if the function is to be fulfilled.

In the case of the stabled horse, grooming is best carried out after morning exercise, when the horse is warm and its pores are open. Strapping, sometimes called wisping, builds up muscle – both on horse and human – but it is better done toward the end of the day in order to maintain the rate of circulation during the night.

Horses kept out at pasture should not be overly groomed since you remove the waterproofing layer of grease from the coat. It is sufficient to brush off the worst of the mud before going for a ride.

Method of Grooming

Grooming is best carried out from front to rear, starting high up on the horse's head behind the ears. Stand away from the horse – the secret of grooming lies in getting one's whole weight behind the brush, which cannot be done when too close to the horse. The body brush can be used for cleaning the head but great care must be taken not to bang the bony projections with its hard edge. After every few strokes, clean the brush on the curry

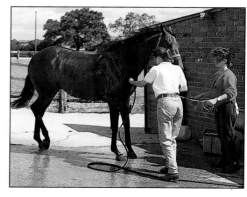

Washing your horse
There is disagreement on the advisability of washing horses, but most show animals are washed. Choose a warm day and dry the horse well afterwards, and it will cause no harm.

comb, which is held in the opposite hand. The stiff dandy brush is used for cleaning muddy legs, which usually, but not always, are left unclipped as a protection against the cold and the odd thorn. It is far too stiff and harsh to be used on the horse's body.

THE GROOMING ROUTINE

First, pick out the hooves. Next, brush the body from front to rear; brush the legs; brush out mane and tail and "lay" them with a damp brush; sponge nose, eyes and dock. Finish off by rubbing over with a dampened cloth or chamois leather.

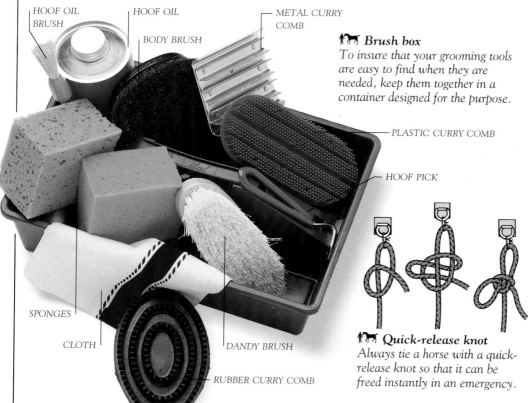

HOOF OIL BRUSH

HOOF OIL

BODY BRUSH

METAL CURRY COMB

SWEAT SCRAPER

THICK-TOOTH COMB

FINE-TOOTH COMB

Brush box
To insure that your grooming tools are easy to find when they are needed, keep them together in a container designed for the purpose.

PLASTIC CURRY COMB

HOOF PICK

SPONGES

CLOTH

DANDY BRUSH

RUBBER CURRY COMB

Quick-release knot
Always tie a horse with a quick-release knot so that it can be freed instantly in an emergency.

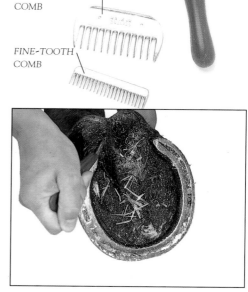

1 Carefully clean out each hoof from heel to toe by using the hoof pick, directing the point away from you. Catch any dirt you remove in a mat, which should be strategically placed for that purpose, rather than allowing it to fall on the floor or into the bed.

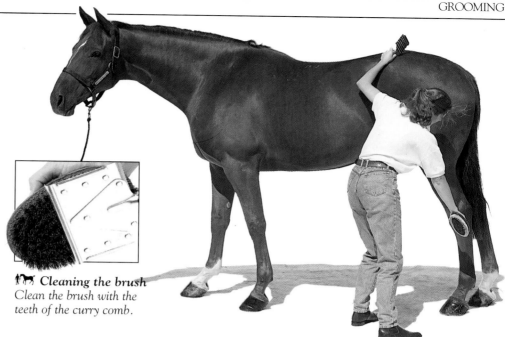

2 Clean the horse briskly, from front to rear, using firm strokes of the brush, always keeping your free hand in contact with the horse. Your hand will reassure it and when placed on the neck will act as a deterrent against a quick nip. Be very careful not to hit the bony projections of the head with the brush, and never bang the brush down in the area of the loins where it might cause damage to the kidneys. Some horses are very ticklish between the hind legs and on the belly. In these cases it is far better to dispense with the brush and simply use the hand alone. Next brush the legs. Wash your brushes regularly to remove sweat and grease from the bristles, and then dry them thoroughly.

Cleaning the brush
Clean the brush with the teeth of the curry comb.

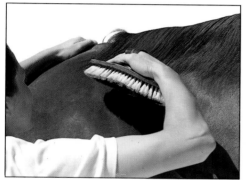

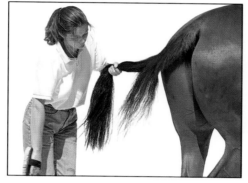

3 Once the mane has been carefully combed and brushed out, "lay" it with a dampened brush. This keeps the hair in place, adding to the final appearance. The tail can be similarly treated. Thin excess hair from the mane by carefully pulling it out from the underside.

4 Using a soft brush that will not break or damage the hairs, brush the tail out. Brush the strands out separately while holding up the tail in your other hand. When necessary, tails are thinned by pulling out the surplus hair a little at a time, taking care not to hurt the horse.

5 After dampening the tail, a bandage can be put on to keep the hair in place and to encourage the retention of the shape. Tail bandages are left on for no more than an hour or two, and are not put on so tightly as to interfere with the circulation or damage the hair follicles.

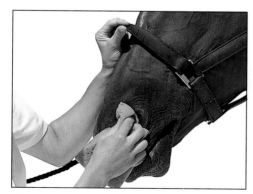

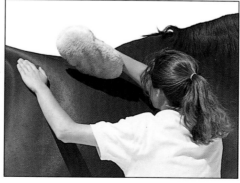

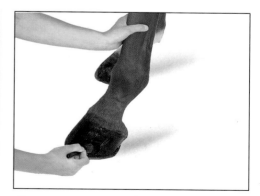

6 As a regular part of daily grooming, clean the nose out with a damp sponge. The same applies to the eyes. A separate sponge (preferably of a different color to distinguish it) is used to clean out the dock, and the sheath of geldings. Wash the sponges after use.

7 A final polish is given by smoothing a dampened cloth or a chamois leather over the whole of the horse. This puts a "bloom" on the coat. A piece of jute sacking, a rough string cloth, or a buffer may also be used and they will produce perfectly good results.

8 Frequent wetting of the hooves removes oil secreted by the coronary band. Help nature and add to appearances by regularly oiling the hooves. Hold the leg as you apply oil to prevent the horse from kicking. Never use boot polish as it acts as a seal and stops oil absorption.

Shoeing

THE INVENTION of the nailed horse shoe is attributed to the Celts of Gaul, the foremost ironworkers of the ancient world. The Celts were established in Britain by 450 B.C., and it is possible that they were shoeing horses before the Roman invasion.

The Need for Shoes

Shoeing was unnecessary for horses in the Middle East because of the dry conditions, which encouraged the formation of exceptionally strong, hard horn. In the wet conditions of Europe, however, hooves became soft and easily broken, leaving horses footsore and lame. The road systems created by the Romans and the damp atmosphere also contributed to excessive wear of the hooves.

The object of shoeing the hoof has not changed. The shoe protects the hoof of the working horse from being worn away more quickly than it could be replaced by natural growth, and it also improves the gripping property of the hoof.

The farrier's job is to shoe the hoof in such a way as to preserve its natural function and the horse's natural action. He also seeks to remedy conformational defects resulting in faulty movement, and to counter the effect of disease. Corrective shoeing ensures that the horse remains sound, its working life is extended and its performance is improved.

The horn grows between $1/4$ and $3/4$in (0.5 and 2cm) per month, therefore, the shoes need to be removed every four weeks so that the excess growth can be removed. A new set of shoes should be fitted if the old ones are unserviceable.

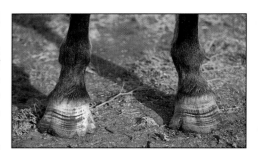

🐎 A pair of neglected hooves
These hooves have been neglected. The hooves have become overgrown and have spread and become malformed, while the horn has split.

Fitting Shoes

Before the farrier can fit each horse shoe, the hoof has to be prepared. This entails removing any surplus growth from the hoof until the surface is level. Hooves that turn in or out can be corrected by removing the overgrowth that usually causes these common faults.

THE SHOEING PROCEDURE

1 The nail ends, or clenches, are cut off and the shoe is eased from the hoof from the heels. It is then pulled off backward from the toe.

2 The hoof is cleaned and trimmed with the curved drawing knife, which has its point turned over for safety. The blunt edge is used for cleaning the hoof.

3 The surplus growth on the hoof wall is removed with the hoof cutters, preparatory to the hoof being rasped level and the shoe being fitted.

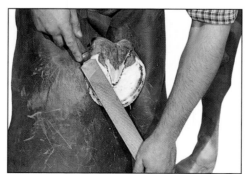

4 The surface of the hoof is made level by rasping the underside. This is an essential stage in preparing the hoof for fitting of the shoe.

5 The farrier, wearing the traditional, divided, leather apron, shapes the hoof by carefully rasping the rim, avoiding unnecessary contact with the wall.

The shoe is fixed to the hoof either by hot- or cold-shoeing. Hot-shoeing involves heating the shoe until it is red-hot. It is then placed on the hoof for a few seconds, burning a brown rim where it touches. The object is to check the fit and to ensure the whole shoe is in perfect contact. If the brown rim is incomplete, the hoof must be rasped again until the surface is level. A well-made shoe follows the rim of the hoof wall and is neither too wide, too long nor too short. Hot-shoeing allows the farrier to make adjustments to the shape of the shoe more easily and it should ensure a perfect fit. Cold-shoeing is when the completed shoe is nailed to the prepared hoof without first being heated, and it is not thought to be as satisfactory. Once the fit has been perfected, the shoe is nailed to the hoof wall. The number of nails used should be as few as possible to avoid weakening the hoof. Generally, six nails per shoe is considered ideal, but as many as eight may be used, if necessary.

TYPES OF SHOE

FULLERED SHOE
A fullered shoe has its center hollowed out.

HALF SHOE
Half front shoe with stamped nail holes.

"TIP" SHOE
These may be worn by horses at pasture.

FEATHER-EDGE SHOE
Shoes worn on the hind feet to prevent clipping.

SHOE PADS
Shoe with a complete pad to protect the sole.

HOOF CUSHION
Shoe fitted with hoof cushion to provide grip.

🐎 *Picking up hooves*
The farrier shows the correct way to pick up a hoof.

6 The farrier shapes the furnace-heated shoe on the rounded "beak" of the anvil. The shoe is held with the shoe-tongs and shaped using a heavy hammer.

7 Nail holes are punched in the shoe with a stamp that is shaped to the exact size of the nail head. The hammer used at the forge is a called a sledge.

8 Holding the hot shoe with a long punch (a pritchel), the farrier places it on the hoof for a few seconds to check the fitting and that the contact is level.

9 The nails are driven home while the hoof is held between the farrier's knees. The nail-ends are "wrung" off in the hammer claw and turned to form clenches.

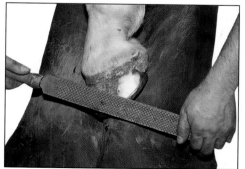

10 The rim of the hoof is tidied with a rasp and the farrier also rasps just under the clenches so as to be able to hammer them over flat.

11 The finished hoof. The nails are driven home flush with the shoe, the toe-clip is central and the clenches follow the line of the coronary band.

Diet

IN THEIR NATURAL state, horses do not use energy unnecessarily. They move slowly from one feeding ground to the next and, as long as the area is large enough, they can exist solely on grasses and herbs. When the weather is cold and feed less plentiful, they naturally lose weight; and when the opposite climatic conditions prevail, they just as naturally put on weight.

Energy Expenditure

Energy expenditure is very different for the domestic horse, who is expected to work under saddle or in harness, often at speed and over distance. As a result, he

expends great amounts of energy and, if he is not to lose condition dramatically, he must be fed foods other than those that are natural to him. These foods must be fed in balance and it may also be necessary to include vitamin and mineral supplements to maintain peak condition.

Feeding Objectives

The elementary feeding objectives are:
1. To maintain health at a level that encourages resistance to disease and reduces the severity of any illness, so allowing for a more rapid recovery.
2. To produce, in conjunction with exercise and grooming, a physical condition compatible with the work that the horse is required to do.
3. To feed so as to avoid mental stress at whatever the level of fitness. A diet that is too rich or one that is too high in protein can cause stress and result in behavioral problems.

Principles of Feeding

The principles involved in feeding are:
1. Intake of food energy must equal energy output. Too much overloads the system, resulting in digestive and circulatory problems, and too little causes loss of energy and condition.

2. Feed little and often. A total of 4lb (1.8kg) per concentrate feed is the limit.
3. After feeding, allow one hour for digestion before working.
4. Observe the ratio between bulk and concentrate. Bulk, which is primarily made up of hay, must form between $1/2$ and $2/3$ of the diet for the proper function of the digestive system.
5. Water must always be available to allow food to be fully utilized.

FEEDING SUGAR BEET

If sugar beet is fed dry to the horse, it swells in the stomach and could have fatal results. Therefore both pulp and nuts must be soaked for a minimum of twelve hours before feeding. Sugar beet has a high fiber and sugar content but its protein quality is poor.

FEED SCOOP

COMMERCIAL GRAIN MIX
A commercial grain mix is a balanced feed of oats, barley maize, and other ingredients.

BRAN
Bran is a product of wheat, after flour has been extracted. A daily feed of 2lb (0.9kg) is sufficient.

OATS
The principal source of energy, oats contain fats, starches and a good percentage of protein (11%).

CORN
High in energy but lacking protein and somewhat indigestible, corn can be mixed with other grains.

CHAFF
Chaff is either hay that has been cut in a chaff-cutter, or a mixture of hay and oat straw.

HAY CUBES
Hay cubes are a general feed. They vary in protein according to the purpose required.

BARLEY
Barley is less heating than oats and, when boiled, it is good for putting on condition.

LINSEED
Linseed is high in protein (26%) and an excellent conditioner. Always boil seed before feeding.

MINERALS
Minerals occur in plants or can be fed as a supplement. They help control constant body changes.

GARLIC POWDER
Garlic is a well-proven, natural remedy without side effects. It is a useful food supplement.

LIMESTONE FLOUR
Feeding 2oz (57g) limestone flour daily will correct any adverse calcium/phosphorus ratio.

Roots and fruit
Roots and fruit provide variety in the diet. They are succulent and contain valuable minerals and vitamins. Carrots must be sliced lengthways to prevent the horse from choking.

MOLASSES
Molasses and molassine meal provide easily assimilated energy.

COD LIVER OIL
Cod liver oil is a conditioner and good for the coat.

SALT LICK
A salt lick provides sodium chloride, not found much in plant growth.

FEED BOWL

FEED CHART
There are a few basic rules to follow when feeding your horse. Depending on the type of work your horse is doing, calculate the proportions of bulk food (hay) to concentrated food (Bulk : Concentrate).
Light work =3:1 Moderate work =2:1 Heavy work =1.5:2

QUANTITIES
These vary according to the individual. As a rough guide based on height:

Height (hh)	Under 12	12–13	13–14	14–15	15–16	over 16
Daily feed lb (kg)	14–16 (6.3–7.2)	16–18 (7.2–8)	20–22 (9–10)	22–24 (10–11)	24–26 (11–12)	26–28 (12–12.5)

Calculate intake more accurately using the weight of your horse in average working condition. The total intake is between 2–2$\frac{1}{2}$% of the body weight. Estimate weight by the following formula (using inches):

$$\frac{Girth^2 \times Length}{300} = \text{Weight in lbs}$$

Girth is the measurement around the largest part of the barrel. Length is from the point of the shoulder upwards to the point of the buttock.

WHEN TO FEED
Feeding little and often is ideal. A hunter on 12lb (5.4kg) concentrate food daily is given, preferably, four feeds of 3lb (1.3kg). The bulk of the hay, say 8lb (3.6kg), is given at night. The other 4lb (1.8kg) is fed in two small nets during the day.

Hay and water
Water is as essential to life as solid food, while hay is the equine staff of life. It is the principal source of fibrous roughage, has a high level of digestible protein and 6–7 per cent mineral content.

HAYNET

WATER BUCKET

Health

THE APPEARANCE of a healthy horse is unmistakable and, conversely, so is the appearance of an unhealthy one. The state of health is apparent through the skin, muscle tone and eye expression as well as the manure. It can be further ascertained by the animal's temperature, pulse and respiration.

Maintaining Health

There are several principles to follow to keep your horse in good condition. A primary factor is a regular and sufficient diet incorporating, in proper proportion, the constituents of a balanced food intake and corresponding to the type of work that is required of the horse (see pp.206–07). In addition, a domestic horse should have access to shelter against the worst of the weather, a system of parasite control and the animal should be protected against a variety of diseases through vaccines. The teeth and hooves should be attended regularly. Finally, the animal should be constantly supervised.

POISONOUS PLANTS
Pastures and fields can contain a surprising variety of plants that are poisonous to horses and which, if eaten in quantity, can cause severe illness and even death. Pastures should be inspected and all such plants eliminated before horses are grazed there.

RAGWORT (above)
Whether in growth or dry in hay, rag-wort is deadly.

BRACKEN (above)
Bracken is poisonous when green and remains so if cut in that state.

DEADLY NIGHTSHADE
This plant is poisonous, but animals do not often eat it.

ACORNS
If eaten in large quantities, acorns are fatal.

YEW
Yew poison-ing is lethal.

State of Health

In health, the eye is big and the membranes under the lids and those of the nostril are an even pink in color. Redness denotes inflammation, white suggests debility, yellow is symptomatic of liver disorders and bright purple is indicative of blood aeration problems. The coat of a healthy horse lies flat and has a glossy sheen. A dry, staring coat can mean malnutrition and/or a heavy parasite infestation. If the hair can be pulled easily from the mane, other symptoms of ill-health will be found.

The skin should be clean and loose. Tightness may be due to the onset of disease, a parasite infestation or malnutrition. Lice may be found on horses in

Unhealthy horse (above)
This horse is in poor condition. There is a pronounced loss of flesh on the neck and general signs of malnutrition. The coat is stary and it is probable that the animal is heavily infested by parasites.

Healthy horse (left)
A healthy horse on good, well-managed grazing, which is properly fenced and watered. Good grass is in itself usually a natural, balanced diet for equines, but in the winter they need supplementary feeding to maintain condition.

REGULAR HEALTH CHECKS

A calendar should be kept in every stable on which are entered dates relative to shoeing, worming, vaccination, tooth rasping, etc. This will provide a complete record for each horse. However, regular observation of the horse constitutes an even more important health check. Stabled animals should be observed night and morning, and horses at grass inspected at least once a day.

RASPING TEETH
Horses' teeth become sharp with age and use, and may cut the cheeks and tongue, causing discomfort and discouraging mastication. They need to be floated every six months.

DEWORMING
Domestic horses harbor parasites; the red worm is the most dangerous. Effective against all known parasites, deworming doses are usually effective if given at six-weekly intervals.

PREVENTIVE VACCINES
All equines should be injected against tetanus and a variety of diseases including equine influenza, the incidence of which has increased rapidly over the past decade.

poor condition and will cause skin to tighten. A lice-ridden horse rubs continually and its coat appears blotched.

The limbs should be cool and free from swelling. Puffiness indicates sprains, poor circulation, parasitic irritation or a possible heart condition.

Manure varies in color and texture according to the state of health, although loose bowel movements are a normal occurrence when horses are on new grass. The droppings should be well formed, slightly moist and without any strong smell. The presence of mucus is the result of a digestive disorder. Strongly smelling, yellow droppings may be connected with a liver condition and/or indicate the presence of red worms.

The urine should be nearly colorless. If thick and highly colored, there may be kidney trouble. Bloody urine points to an inflammatory condition of that organ. Excessive urine flow can mean diabetes, and an obvious dribble accompanies bladder inflammation.

The horse in bad condition can be recognized by the poor covering of flesh over the pelvis. The bone structure can be seen clearly, the flanks are hollow, there is a deep cavity under the tail and no muscle between the hind legs. There are grooves in the quarters either side of the tail. The backbone is visible and the base of the neck lacks muscle on both sides, feeling narrow and slack. The neck itself is soft and without flesh.

Temperature and Pulse

The normal temperature of the horse is 100–101.5°F (37.8–38.5°C). Above this, one may suspect some general infection. However, horses vary in their temperature and the normal, healthy temperature of your horse should be taken and noted for future comparison. The temperature is taken by inserting a clinical thermometer in the rectum. Temperatures vary through the day, so it is necessary to take two or three readings at different times.

A normal pulse rate is 32–44 beats per minute. An increase when at rest usually signifies some form of fever. The horse is in distress if the pulse rate reaches 50 beats a minute at rest. The pulse can be felt on the inner surface of the lower jaw, just behind the elbow and behind the eye. Obtain the pulse rate by counting the number of beats in 20 seconds on a stop-watch and then multiply by three. Respiration is normally 8 to 15 breaths a minute when the horse is at rest. A faster rate while at rest indicates pain and a probable rise in temperature. Check the respiration by standing behind the horse and counting how often the flanks rise and fall in 60 seconds, or use a stop-watch in the manner suggested for pulse rate measurement. Each rise and fall is equal to one breath.

Inspecting wild horses
Wild Camargue Horses are brought in annually for inspection. In general, feral horses do not suffer from the ailments that affect the domestic horse. If they live in a large enough area they do not appear to carry heavy parasitic burdens, nor contract the various viruses that plague their domesticated brethren.

Pregnancy and Birth

MARES USUALLY REACH PUBERTY between 15 and 24 months but, occasionally, it may be later. It is possible to breed from 2 and 3 year olds, but 4 is more acceptable.

Coming into Season

From early spring though autumn, mares come into season (a condition referred to as "heat" or being in estrus) at regular intervals between 18 and 21 days. Each heat lasts five to seven days. During heat, a mare will accept a stallion. There are a number of unmistakable signs that indicate a mare is in season, although they do not all occur simultaneously. Mares may appear irritable and unsettled, and will seek the company of other horses more than usual. The tail is swished fairly constantly and the clitoris (the small, sensitive organ lying within the lips of the vulva) is protruded. Urine is passed frequently in small quantities and mucus is present around the lips of the vagina.

It is possible to establish the phase of the mare's cycle by internal examination, but the most certain way of finding out whether she is ready to be mated is by trying her with a stallion – a practice known as "teasing." At stud farms, it is usual to have the mare brought to one side of a padded partition and the stallion to the other. The partition prevents either animal from being injured. If the mare is ready, she will adopt the mating posture and hold her tail to one side. If she is not, she will bare her teeth at the stallion and attempt to bite or kick him.

Pregnancy and Birth

The average gestation period of the brood mare is 11 months and a few days. Obviously there are variations but, as a rule, a colt foal is carried longer than a filly. The term for colts is approximately 334 days and for fillies 332 1/2, but there is a possible variant of 9 1/2 days either way.

When full term is reached, highly bred horses, like the Thoroughbred, require

🐎 Mating
Mating, when the semen enters the vagina and uterus, eventually reaching the Fallopian tubes, occurs two to five days before the end of estrus.

more attention than the self-reliant pony breeds. It is usual for highly bred mares to foal in a foaling stall with attendants keeping watch on closed-circuit television. Pony stock are nearly always allowed to foal outside and problems rarely occur. The pony mares give birth quickly, as they would under feral conditions where a protracted birth might attract the unwelcome attention of predators.

FOAL DEVELOPMENT IN THE WOMB

TWO MONTHS (right) At two months, the length of the embryo is approximately 3–3 3/4in (7–10cm) from poll to dock. The limbs are distinctly formed and the sex is recognizable.

FOUR MONTHS (left) The foal now weighs about 2lb (1kg) and measures between 8–9in (20–23cm). The first traces of hair occur around the lips. The hooves have formed.

SIX MONTHS (right) Hair over the body is much more apparent. External sex organs are formed. The length has increased to about 22in (56cm) and the weight may be upwards of 12 1/2lb (5.5kg).

Signs of Foaling
The foal's presence is apparent from the fifth month of pregnancy and the foal's movements can be seen from the sixth month. As the pregnancy approaches its completion, the mare's belly drops. Signs of foaling are the udder enlarging and wax appearing on the teats.

ELEVEN MONTHS (right) The foal is ready to pass through the pelvic arch. It now weighs 85–107lb (38.5–48.5kg) and measures upwards of 43in (109cm). Its teeth show through the gums.

TEN MONTHS (right) Weight increases to 64–74lb (29–33.5kg); length to 34–37in (85–92cm). Coat and long hairs are fully grown and foal is ready to turn for birth.

EIGHT MONTHS (left) The foal assumes an upright position. Both mane and hair along spine grow. Weight increases to 36–42lb (16–19kg); length 27–29in (68–73cm).

LABOR AND BIRTH

Labor has three phases: involuntary uterine contractions as the fetus is positioned for expulsion, and the cervical and associated structures relax; voluntary expulsive effort when the foal enters the pelvis, passes through the cervix and is born; and the expulsion of fetal membranes, the afterbirth.
Before and during contractions, the mare is restless, lying down and getting up again. During labor, contractions become more frequent until they occur every few minutes. This stage lasts up to six hours until the water bag ruptures and allantoic fluid is emitted from the vagina.

1 After the waters break, the mare lies down and strains as the labor pangs increase in strength. She will often grunt loudly and will sweat noticeably as the birth sequence approaches its climax.

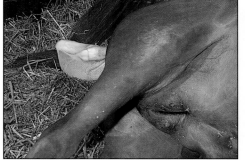  

2 In a normal presentation the front hooves of the foal are the first to appear between the distended lips of the vulva. They are covered in transparent membranes, the caul, which burst as the birth progresses.

3 The head lies on the extended forelegs and appears after the hooves. Once the shoulders appear, the heaviest part has been delivered and the rest follows swiftly. As this happens, the membranes over the nose break and breathing starts.

4 The foal kicks free from the mare, at which point the umbilical cord may be broken off. Nature's "blood valve" will close, precluding the exit of blood from the foal while allowing an inward flow from the placenta.

5 Within a short time of birth, the mare will have got to her feet, breaking the umbilical cord if it has not already been severed. Within half an hour or so, the mare will lick the foal. By doing so, she warms her newborn offspring.

THE AFTERBIRTH

The afterbirth is expelled up to four hours after foaling. If it has not appeared after that time, veterinary attention is necessary. If any afterbirth is retained within the mare, septicemia can occur.

6 After half an hour, the foal will muzzle the mare. The colostrum, the first milk the foal receives, is essential to its well-being. It acts as an antibiotic and ensures the passing of the meconium from the system in the first bowel movement.

Foal Development

A NEW FOAL will be on its feet and suckling its dam within half an hour of its birth, and its development is correspondingly rapid when it is viewed in human terms. Foals born inside can be turned out with the mare on the second day, so long as the weather conditions are not harsh. If it is cold and wet, the mare and foal must be brought in at night.

Early Days

The foal's relationship with human beings begins almost as soon as it is born. In some instances, it is necessary to clear the mucus and membranes from around the nostrils at the time of birth, and during the first 24 hours of life it will need to be injected against joint-ill and tetanus. Initially, the mare may act defensively

🐴 **Two weeks old**
At two weeks, the young foal will already have become accustomed to the presence of humans.

🐴 **At rest**
Young foals need a great deal of rest and therefore spend a lot of time lying down.

toward her foal, placing herself between the attendant human and her helpless youngster. A good-tempered, kindly mare will soon get over this understandable apprehension, and if she demonstrates her confidence in humans the foal will quickly follow suit.

Handling

It is best to begin handling the foal in the stable rather than outside, and to this end the mare should be brought in for a short period each day. At this stage, the foal will naturally follow its dam without outside encouragement.

When the foal is no more than three days old, it should be possible to handle it with the help of someone holding the mare. The mare is placed alongside the stable wall and the foal needs no persuasion to come up along the near-side of his mother. The trainer or owner can then place the right arm around the foal's rump and the left around the chest. In a few days, the young animal will consent to stand quietly within the embracing arms so long as it is allowed to be close to its dam, his flank touching her side to give him confidence.

The next step should be to teach the foal to lead in hand and that, too, begins within the confines of the stall. The mare is led quietly around and the foal will instinctively seek to follow her. It can be encouraged to do so by being pushed gently forward with the right arm, while

🐴 **Six weeks old**
(above) At six weeks, foals have become increasingly self-reliant as they have become stronger. When they reach this age they may share their dam's feed but they still need a regular supply of her milk (right).

the left arm is held ready to restrain any violent forward plunge the foal might take.

Within a few days after birth, the foal can be fitted with a soft leather halter and by then should submit happily to being led around by the attendant, so long as it is not too far from its dam. The slip is first put on in the stable, the foal being gently pushed into it from behind, rather than risking a battle and possible injury by trying to pull the slip over the foal's nose. In a day or so, a soft halter can be placed around the foal's head and, in a short while, it will be possible to lead it in this fashion both to and from the paddock and stable. The foal can be reassured by the attendant scratching its chest, withers and quarters in simulation of its dam's affectionate "love-nibbles" which she gives him at those places.

🐎 *Ready, set, go*
Foals are on their feet within half an hour of birth and in an incredibly short space of time are able to keep up with their dams – a necessary accomplishment in the wild.

From the second week of its life, it is advisable to make the foal used to being touched and stroked by humans. Its hooves can be picked up for a second or so as well. This exercise will prepare the young animal for the time when the farrier will first trim its hooves – when he is about three months.

At three or four months, the foal learns to load into a trailer with its mother. The technique for trouble-free loading is to load the mare first. The foal, anxious not to be separated from its mother, then will follow quickly into the trailer.

Feeding and Care

If the grazing is good and the mare has been fed well, her milk and the grass will be ample food for the foal up to the age of two months. Toward the end of that time, the foal should be sharing its dam's grain. As a guide, a foal requires 1lb (0.5kg) of grain per day for every month of its age up to five to six months. In addition to oats, boiled linseed and barley, the feed could also include powdered milk, 2oz (60g) rising to 8oz (227g) per day, and cod-liver oil to promote bone growth. In winter, the foal needs an ample supply of soft, meadow hay, which will not overtax its immature teeth nor its digestion. Apart from nutrition, a foal's other basic needs are plenty of sleep (rather like a young baby), as well as the company of other horses and plenty of space to romp in.

It is usual for colt foals, other than those intended for use as stallions, to be gelded before weaning takes place. Gelding can be carried out later but yearling colts can become unacceptably boisterous if left entire. Deworming is an essential measure to be taken before weaning. (Courses of anti-tetanus injections are administered after.)

Weaning

The weaning of foals from their dams usually takes place between 4½ and 6 months, when the milk hairs have darkened and the foal is able to feed on its own. In practical terms, this is an unavoidable step. However, weaning can cause stress to both mare and foal

🐎 *Two to six months old*
(left) Foals lose their furry, milk hairs any time after two months. (above) By the time he is five to six months old, the foal is strong enough to be weaned from its dam. Handle them both sympathetically during this stressful time.

and, therefore, the owner must help to minimize distress to the animals by handling them sympathetically.

Foals can be prepared for the final separation by being kept away from the dam for short periods. The mare can be exercised, for instance, while the foal remains in the stall with a companion and with food available. The eventual, full separation must be total for at least four weeks, the mare being kept off the premises if possible while the foal is kept in a deeply bedded and very secure stall. After a week the foal can be turned out for short periods in the paddock so long as the mare can be neither seen nor heard.

Good feeding for young stock is essential to good health, as is the freedom that allows them to develop naturally. By the time the foal is a yearling, it should be having not less than 7lb (3kg) concentrate feed a day, plus salt, an appropriate mineral supplement, cod-liver oil and so on. Hay should be fed ad lib and ample supplies of clean, fresh water must be constantly available.

🐎 *At six months*
Foals, after weaning, are healthier if turned out at least during the day in the winter.

🐎 *A year*
Yearlings, when shown, are expected to be turned out immaculately, like this one.

Walking the dogs
This couple on horseback take the dogs for a walk, seventeenth-century style, with the lady riding pillion. The pillion, still used in Spain today, was an early forerunner of the lady's side-saddle.

The Horse and Man

"All our history is his industry. We are his heirs, he our inheritance." To the Horse by Ronald Duncan.

I t is wonderful and humbling to contemplate how great are the ways in which horses are used for our benefit.

~ WORKING HORSES ~

Although in the majority of western countries horses are no longer employed in agriculture, there are European countries where the horse is still integral to the rural economy and, in some of the Soviet Republics, horses are kept in herds on the steppes to provide meat, milk and hides in a way of life that has not altered in its essentials for thousands of years. The majestic heavy breeds are more popular than ever and are still to be seen in great numbers at agricultural shows. The great brewing houses are their staunchest supporters. They often maintain stables, using heavy horses for short-haul urban deliveries.

~ HORSES FOR RECREATION ~

The armies of most countries maintain a mounted body for ceremonial purposes, and in some countries horses and mules are still used operationally, as in China, India and in some Soviet Republics. Police forces all over the world also have mounted branches for patrolling city streets and parks and for crowd control. Today, our association with the horse largely concerns sporting and recreational pursuits and a whole industry has grown up in horse-related holidays that are available all over the world, from China to the Rocky Mountains.

Hunting kit
All sports have their uniform. Best known of the clothes worn for riding is probably the traditional red coat of the hunting field, worn with white breeches and top boots.

Popular riding (left)
Western riding is part of the American tradition and continues to be popular all over the United States. It is a much favored seat for pleasure and trail riding but many horsemen and women enjoy riding in the "English" seat as well.

Partners in work (left)
Horses play a large part in recreation but many of them are man's essential partners in work. This Camargue Horse, wearing the prototype western saddle, is used to round-up and move the black cattle of the Rhone delta.

Work

O N JULY 20TH, 1969, Neil Armstrong landed the lunar module Eagle on the surface of the moon, and thus completed the mission of the American Apollo II spacecraft. When Armstrong left Eagle to be the first to set foot on an alien planet, he observed that it was a small step for man, but a giant step for mankind.

Horse Power

It is extremely improbable that, in the resulting euphoria, anyone on our planet paused to reflect that the mission in space accomplished by Apollo II was made possible by the exertions of an animal that had served mankind for something over 6,000 years. Yet it is an incontrovertible fact that up to no more than 50 years before Apollo II made lift-off, the economy of the world was underpinned by horse power.

Mobility

Horse power bestowed mobility on the human race. It was the essential lynchpin in the creation and destruction

Working in a rural community
There are still many parts of the world where the horse is essential to the rural economy. Here, on the South Pacific island of Tonga, the horse takes the place of both bicycle and car, and is able to carry a man in addition to the shopping or farm produce. Without a horse the hard life would be more difficult.

of many kingdoms and empires, and it was a vital element in the creation and maintenance of our civilizations.

Man's first association with the horse, a species long established in recognizable form on the Earth when man was no more than an unidentifiable lemuroid, was that between hunter and hunted: the horse providing a convenient larder on the hoof. After it was domesticated, the horse rapidly became man's partner in the development of civilization.

War and Communication

From the earliest times, horses pulled loads and carried packs, but most particularly they were used for the purpose of warfare and, of course, for communication. The empires of the Hittites, the Assyrians, and the Persians were won by huge bodies of chariot-borne troops – the equivalent of the modern armored divisions.

At Kadesh in 1286B.C., the Hittites used 3,500 chariots in their battle to defeat Rameses I of Egypt. At Waterloo in 1815, the British and French cavalry numbered upwards of 30,000. A century later, in the First World War, well over 1.5 million horses were employed as cavalry and to service the opposing armies. They endured the most terrible conditions; the British alone had horse casualties amounting to 500,000. In the Second

Working in leisure
The gypsy caravan was once common enough in Britain. Today, such carts are likely to be part of the tourist industry. In Ireland and Wales particularly, there are plenty of opportunities to take a horsedrawn holiday.

World War, despite mechanization, horses were still used in vast numbers. The Russian army alone had a strength of 1.2 million horses.

For the greater part of our history, the world's network of communication has depended upon the horse. The Persians, who wrested supremacy from the Assyrians in the sixth century B.C., operated a remarkably efficient postal system. They were able to complete a journey of 1,500 miles (2,415km) in 7 to 14 days, using relays of horses. Eighteen hundred years later, Genghis Khan operated the Yam, the forerunner, perhaps, of America's Pony Express. Relays of messengers galloped along the caravan tracks crossing the Mongol Empire, each riding about 150 miles (242km) a day.

Pony Express

The Pony Express was formed by William H. Russell. It was inaugurated in 1860, before the coming of the telegraph, to carry the mail along the route between St. Joseph, Missouri and Sacramento, California. Much of the route was through

Working in transport
(below) This pony, one of many used in agricultural and draft work in the Philippines, draws his heavy load through the rush-hour traffic of the Quirino Boulevard, Vigan, with complete equanimity.

Working in forestry (right)
In many parts of the world, horses play an important part in forestry. Not only are they environmentally friendly, but they can haul felled trees far more efficiently and economically than a tractor.

hostile Indian territory. The distance of 1,966 miles (3,164km) was covered by 400 ponies in 10 days.

Post and Passengers

In Britain, the mail was carried by post-boys on horseback and mailcart until the introduction of the mail coach in 1784. The system was pioneered by John Palmer, the Postmaster General. The first journey took place on August 2nd, and ran between Bath and London. It was accomplished in 15 hours, and ran on time.

Soon, passenger coaches were being operated to the same standards, all running to a timetable at an average 10mph (16kph) on good roads. The Royal Mail coaches, however, were faster, covering their routes at 12mph (19kph).

Railways and Canals

The coming of the railways put an end to the era of the mail and road coaches but, along with the Industrial Revolution, they actually encouraged far greater use of horses. Horses were used for haulage and distribution from the rail centers; for every sort of transport within the burgeoning cities and towns; for shunting rolling stock; and for heavy work in the goods yards. Indeed, the railway companies were the largest employers of horses for well over a century. In 1890, London had a horse population of

300,000; and in 1928, the London Midland and Scottish Railway still owned 9,681 horses. The last horsedrawn railway passenger service was the Fintona branch line in Northern Ireland – it continued in operation until 1957!

Horses were used in pack transport well into the nineteenth century. Thousands of ponies worked in the mines, and the

Working in the police force
Police horses are employed in most major British cities as well as other countries around the world. They undergo rigorous "nuisance" training before doing regular duties involving street patrols and crowd control. They must have the characteristics of being steady in traffic and reliable in crowd situations.

important canal network employed large numbers of "boaters," towing loads of between 50 and 60 tons (60–70,000kg). Today there are still one or two horses working on the canals.

Agriculture

It was comparitively recently that horses were used in the cultivation of the land. In the Middle East and Asia, oxen and donkeys were used more effectively, and in Europe the ox, which was cheaper to keep if slower than the horse, served the needs of agriculture well into the eighteenth century. In the end, the horse, quicker and better able to cope with increasingly sophisticated farm machinery, won the battle of agricultural motive power. Although the golden age of horsepower farming was short-lived, in its day, the agricultural horse was the glory of farming throughout Europe and America.

In the 1860s, the American horse population was about 7 million; by 1914 it was 25 million. Millions of acres were cultivated and harvested by huge machines, drawn by teams of up to 42 horses. The horses had, indeed, helped to create the "bread basket" of the world.

Now, when the tractor, the car and the airplane have taken over the world, horses are still at work in the service of man. Today, the horse is largely used to satisfy the need for leisure and recreation.

Driving

THE USE OF HORSES for pulling chariots probably preceded their use for riding. In the valleys of the Tigris, Indus and Euphrates, and in Syria and Egypt chariots were used by successive warlike empires in the 2,000 years before the Christian era. These flat, open lands were ideal for wheeled vehicles. Two or four horses, harnessed to a light chariot, provided swift transport for two or three people.

Chariot Racing

For 1,500 years, chariot racing was the national sport of Ancient Greece. The first Olympic chariot races were included in the twenty-fifth Olympiad in 408B.C.. Chariot racing was a popular spectator sport in the Roman circus. There were the four chariot groups – green, red, blue and white – each supported by a political faction that provided a safety valve for the potentially rebellious populace.

Harness

The harness used for horse vehicles was originally based on the ox yoke, which was employed for centuries before the

Pony carts
It became fashionable in the nineteenth century for ladies to drive their own ponycarts. Here, a Liverpool-style pony gig is drawn by a Shetland. The Shetland is still used in harness.

general establishment of wheeled vehicles. Horses were also hitched to a central pole in a similar fashion to oxen.

The Chinese made the most significant improvements in both harness and vehicles. By 1300B.C. they were using sophisticated wheeled vehicles, which they drove on carefully constructed roadways of specific widths. They invented the single horse vehicle, which was drawn by means of lateral shafts, and they were also the first (largely on account of the width of the roadway) to drive horses in tandem – one behind the other.

Breast Harness

The Chinese also invented the breast harness, indistinguishable from that in use today, in 250B.C.. Then came the breeching strap, which allowed the horse to hold or brake the load. Finally, they developed the neck collar, acclaimed as one of the world's greatest inventions.

The collar allowed maximum tractive force to be applied to a load. When it finally reached Europe in the eighth and ninth centuries, the collar ensured the ultimate use of heavy horses in agriculture.

Hungarian Coaches

The evolution of driving and coaching in Europe was made possible principally because of improvements that were made by the Hungarians, who to this day figure prominently in driving sports. The Hungarians produced prototype road coaches in the late fifteenth century. These coaches were built at a village called Kocs in the Komorne, and the word coach (*kocsi*) derives from it. The Hungarian coach was distinguished by having the front wheels smaller than the rear wheels, thus allowing the fore-carriage to turn on a very full lock. It was a light coach with a much lower center of gravity than that of its predecessors. This

Horse-driving trials *(above)*
A team of Welsh Cob crosses tackles the water hazard during the marathon section of a horse driving trial. Numerous natural and artificial obstacles, all demanding great driving skills, are included in the course.

Boxcart *(left)*
This unusual boxcart is a vehicle used by the American religious sect, the Amish. The Amish maintain a severely simple lifestyle in which the motorcar still has no part.

🐎 *A driving class*
A lady whip drives a high-stepping pair to an elegant phaeton in this artist's impression of the show held at Newport, Rhode Island, in 1901. At the turn of the century, show jumping was virtually unknown and the principal feature of the horse show was the driving classes. Horse shows were an important event in the social calendar and had a special, garden party atmosphere.

increased its stability and allowed it to be driven at greater speeds. The Hungarians also improved suspension. First, they developed a body supported on leather slings, like a hammock. Then, they invented multileaved elliptical springs, which improved performance and passenger comfort. Over time, reliable axle boxes evolved and the quality of the harness improved enormously, being made stronger, lighter and more flexible.

Driving Wagers

In Europe, carriage driving was at its peak during the seventeenth and eighteenth centuries, although English gentlemen were still making wagers on the speed and endurance of their horses under harness well into the nineteenth century. Toward the end of the seventeenth century, Captain John Gibbs won £500 (a very large sum 300 years ago) when he drove a four-in-hand to a light chaise up and down the steepest part of the Devil's Dyke at Newmarket.

Another famous Newmarket wager took place in 1750 between the Earls of March and Eglintowne, and Theobald Taafe and Andrew Sproule. The wager, for £1,000, called for a chaise carrying one passenger to be driven by a postillion-controlled four-horse team over 19 miles

(30.4km), in under an hour. The winners were the lords, whose Thoroughbred team was, in fact, running away for the first four miles (6.4km). They completed the distance in 53.27 minutes.

Driving Clubs

The Regency bucks of the seventeenth and eighteenth centuries, led by the Prince of Wales, the Prince Regent, took to driving enthusiastically and it became a fashionable, if hair-raising, pastime. This passion for driving gave rise to the formation of driving clubs. The influential Coaching Club was formed under the presidency of the eighth Duke of Beaufort in 1871, and survives and flourishes to this day. The Duke put a "subscription" coach on the London to Brighton road in 1866, and subscribers paid for the privilege of driving it on different days. Mr. Alfred Vanderbilt brought two coaches – the Viking and Venture – with 25 full teams of horses from America between 1908 and 1914, and ran them regularly between London and Brighton.

Driving as a Sport

Driving continued to exert its appeal after the Second World War, although traffic was making the roads increasingly

unsuitable for horsedrawn vehicles. Private driving classes were arranged at shows, driving meets were organized, and the art of driving, once a utilitarian skill, began to take on a competitive image.

In Europe, competitive driving of a very high standard was well established. It became a sport recognized worldwide, largely due to Prince Philip. As President of the *Fédération Equestre Internationale* (FEI), he watched the driving events at Aachen in 1968, and it was at his instigation that the first international driving event took place in 1970.

Driving Trials

Horse driving trials for singles, pairs and teams are based on the ridden three-day event format with one extra phase: the spit-and-polish section called "Presentation." This is followed by a dressage phase. Competition B is the marathon, which is the equivalent of the speed and endurance test in eventing. A full marathon covers 17 miles (27km) and includes numerous obstacles. The final phase is the obstacle driving, a competition which, like eventing's show jumping, tests the fitness of the horses after the exertions of the marathon on the previous day.

Classical Equitation

CLASSICAL EQUITATION has its roots in the school riding that developed in the baroque riding halls of Europe during the Renaissance. The interest in classical learning in the Renaissance led to the rediscovery of the works of the Greek general, Xenophon (c.430–355B.C.), which discussed riding as a science and as an art. The Renaissance horsemen owed much to this Master, though they also improved and extended a system of horsemanship that already existed.

Medieval Riding

The medieval knights were more at home with the sword than the pen. They left little record of the manner in which they trained their horses, but that they were competent and sometimes accomplished horsemen cannot be disputed.

To be effective, or even to survive, "in press of battle" called for an obedient and handy horse that could be ridden with one hand, while the other carried the sword, lance or mace. There cannot be much doubt that the medieval warhorse was trained in movements designed to discourage the close proximity of foot soldiers intent upon unhorsing the knight. Those movements formed the basis of what are termed the "airs, or schools, above the ground," the rears, leaps and kicks that are still practiced at the Spanish Riding School at Vienna, Austria and the Cadre Noir at Saumur, France.

It is unlikely that the "airs" performed at these two establishments bear much resemblance to those made on the battle-fields of the Middle Ages. Instead, they are probably supreme refinements of a

"Black Mass"
The impressive quadrille of the Cadre Noir, in which French traditional classical equitation is preserved, is often called the "Black Mass".

medieval ideal that may have little basis in reality. Nonetheless, the parade paces of *piaffe* and *passage* (the advanced movements included in Grand Prix competitions) were known and practiced by Xenophon, and so was the *levade* – the half-rear on strongly engaged hind legs. The Roman (Byzantine) circus practiced these movements, as well as some recognizable airs above the ground.

These airs mark the division between dressage, the sport, and *Haute Ecole* equitation. The principal remaining movements of classicism not included in dressage competitions are the dramatic Spanish Walk and the *pas d'école*. Translated as "passage at walk," *pas d'école* is the prerogative of the commandant of the Cadre Noir.

The Airs

There were seven airs in the classical equitation of seventeenth century Europe. Today the classical leaps performed at the Spanish School have been distilled to three essentials – *levade*, *courbette* and *capriole*. The leaps performed at the Cadre Noir vary a little in detail and incorporate *croupade*, when the horse kicks high behind while balancing on the forefeet.

In *levade* the forehand is elevated on deeply bent hind legs, the hocks being

AIDS
Apart from the rod, the "helps" (aids) were the voice, tongue, bridle, calves, stirrups and spurs.

SEAT
Eighteenth-century riders employed a straight-legged seat, using a streamlined version of the medieval saddle.

Halt on the single rein
An exemplary halt brought about by the engagement of hocks and quarters beneath the body. Pressure on the bit is minimal in the extreme.

REIN
The apotheosis of classical horsemanship was the looping rein, which preserved lightness in the mouth.

ROD
The rod, or wand, one of the seven "helps", was used on the shoulder in turns, circles and pirouettes.

lowered to 8–10in (20–25cm) above the ground. *Levade* provides the base for the subsequent *courbette*, when the horse bounds forward on the hind legs while maintaining the bent foreleg position, and also for the soaring *capriole* (the leap of the goat). In this ultimate air, the horse leaps from all four legs simultaneously, striking out with the hind legs while the body is virtually suspended horizontally.

Neapolitan School

Naples was the center of the Renaissance revival up to, and beyond, the eighteenth century. A riding academy was founded here in 1134 and, in 1532, Federico Grisone opened the world's most famous school. After Xenophon, Grisone is considered the first of the classical Masters. His book *Gli Ordini di Cavalcare*, (The Rules of Riding) was published in 1550.

The Neapolitan School gave way to the enlightened systems exemplified by the later French Masters, some of them pupils of Grisone's disciple, Giovanni Pignatelli. Standing head and shoulders above them all is François Robichon de la Guérinière (1688–1751). He regarded the airs as the high point in the classical art and the manifestation of collection (i.e. the concentration of the horse's forces brought about by engagement of the quarters, flexion of the hind leg joints and the shortening of the base). He remains the inspiration for the classical schools at Vienna and Saumur.

Spanish Riding School

The Spanish Riding School in Vienna was founded in 1572 as an adjunct to the Court for the education of the nobility in the equestrian arts. Josef Emanual Fischer von Erlach designed its present home, the Winter Riding Hall, between 1729 and 1735. The Spanish Riding School acquired its title because it used only horses brought from Spain. A stud was founded in 1580 by Archduke Charles II at Lipizza, near Trieste, and in time the white stallions bred there acquired the name Lipizzaner. The descendants of the five principal lines of those early imports still perform in the Winter Riding Hall.

French School

The French tradition is preserved by the black-uniformed Cadre Noir, which became the instructors' corps for the school at Saumur. Unlike the Spanish School, it was in a state of continual development,

🐎 *Nuno Oliveira*
The late Maestro Nuno Oliveira was the greatest twentieth-century exponent of the Classical Art. Here, he rides his Andalusian in the spectacular Spanish Walk, a movement not called for in modern dressage competitions.

producing innovative horsemen whose collective talent has never been exceeded. Its base was classic, but it was combined with other forms of competitive sport. This philosophy was made possible by the largely Thoroughbred or Anglo-Arab horses favored by the French school – horses with greater scope and speed than the "stuffier" Lipizzaners of Vienna.

🐎 **Woodcut of Federico Grisone** (*above*)
Grisone founded the famous school of Naples in 1532. It had a vital influence on the evolution of academic horsemanship. Grisone's book, Gli Ordini di Cavalcare, *became the equestrian best-seller of all time.*

🐎 **Execution of the capriole** (*right*)
In the picture by Baron d'Eisenberg, a Spanish horse executes the soaring capriole, *"leap of the goat," in exemplary fashion while his rider displays an enviable, classical nonchalance. (The horse was not at all easy to train and was, therefore, named Difficult!)*

Western Riding

THE HORSE WAS RE-INTRODUCED to North America in the sixteenth century by the Spanish conquistadores, who also brought their equipment and all their horse-lore. The Spanish influence survives in the skills of the western horsemen, overlaid by the practical requirements of cattle ranching that was the reality of the western school of horsemanship.

On the trail (above)
This is a cowboy of reality. His dress and equipment are strictly utilitarian, as are the horses that carry him and his few possessions.

Barrel-racing (below)
The skills of horse and rider are fully tested in this race around barrels at high speeds.

Clothing

The equipment of the cowboy evolved in order to meet the needs imposed by an empty country, one that was beset with every hardship, and in which a man on foot stood little chance of survival.

The cowboy's broad-brimmed hat, the Stetson, fulfilled a variety of purposes. It served as a protection for the head against the sun, and in winter it could be tied down to cover the ears. It could also be used to scoop up water or waved to shoo a steer during herding.

Levi Strauss, a New York tailor, perfected cowboy trousers. He bought denim, a hardwearing material, and used it to make low-hipped, narrow-legged trousers. Today we know them as jeans.

The cowboy tucked his jeans into soft but very strong, leather boots with high, forward-sloping heels, which he could dig into the ground when holding onto a roped calf. The cowboy was especially particular about his boots, which he might have to wear for days on end, and he usually had them made to measure. His spurs jangled when he rode around the cattle and warned them of his presence.

The rest of his wardrobe consisted of a flannel shirt with a loose vest of cloth or buckskin and a cotton bandana. The ubiquitous bandana served as a bandage, a face mask, and as a filter for drinking

Rough territory
The cactus and thorny shrubs of the mesquite country made stout leather chaps essential equipment. The chaps also kept him warm in winter and improved his grip on the saddle.

water. Some cowboys also wore cuffed leather gloves to protect their hands against the bitter western winters and to protect them when a steer pulled hard against the rope.

Chaps and Lariats

Dress varied according to the terrain. In the mesquite country of Texas, which was full of thorny brush, a pair of chaps (*chaparajos*) were essential. These leggings were made of heavy leather with fringed

🐎 **Roping a steer** *(right)*
A good roping horse was an indispensable partner in cattle ranching. Once the steer was roped, the horse braced against the impact and kept the rope taut even when the rider had dismounted. Such horses were both intelligent and highly trained.

🐎 **Cowboy outfit** *(below)*
Allowing for some ornamentation, the cowboy's dress was extremely practical. The Stetson served a variety of purposes and the chaps were just as essential.

outer seams. In California, where the range was more open, the chaps were made of sheepskin or even fur, and included more ornamentation – silver-plated studs, spurs and so on. There were also differences in the lariat (riata or lasso) and the way in which they were used. The Texan favored a 30–40ft (9–12m) lariat made of manila rope, while the Californian threw his "big loop" with a 60–65ft (18–20m), rawhide rope.

Saddles and Bridles

Saddles varied widely in design and were often made to measure. They all were derived from the conquistadores' saddle. Additions and refinements were made as necessary or in accordance with individual preference. Basically, the western saddle was a working platform, which afforded optimum comfort during long days on the cattle trails. It was heavy – 30 to 90lb (13 to 40kg) – and was equipped to carry not only the cowboy but also his gear and, of course, it had a horn to which the lariat could be tied.

Most cowboys used a simple curb bit after the horse had been broken in, the hackamore acting on the nose. Open reins were used and cow ponies were trained to stand when the rider dismounted and dropped the reins.

Western Horses

Many of the horses used in the early days were Mustangs (see pp.74–5) of original Spanish stock. They were small but tough, balanced and wiry. Breaking was carried out by bronco-busters and was rough and ready, but the horses had to be able to work with cattle and they acquired skills beyond the comprehension and ability of most European horsemen.

Geldings were preferred to the less-reliable mares. The elite of the *remuda*

🐎 **Cutting cattle**
A cutting horse can separate one animal from a group. Highly trained and working instinctively, in the same way that a sheepdog moves sheep, it needs no more than minimal indications to anticipate the calf's movements.

(the herd of broken horses kept on a ranch) was the cutting horse, which was able to take a designated beast out of the herd. Good roping horses were also prized. They placed their rider in the best position to throw his lariat with no more than minimal signals. Then they braced themselves against the struggling animal, always keeping the rope taut even when the rider dismounted. These horses worked almost instinctively and were schooled to unbelievably high standards.

Rodeos

The cowboy and his special skills are no longer needed in the modern cattle business, but they still survive in the popular rodeos that run competitions of skill based on events that were once commonplace in the lives of cowboys. Typical of these competitions are calf and steer roping, cutting competitions, wagon-racing, bull-dogging, bronco-busting and barrel-racing.

The rodeo began as an informal contest between cowboys on round-ups and developed into the main feature of public fairs. The first rodeo to charge admission was that held at Prescott, Arizona, in 1888. Today, most of the rodeo riders are professionals, and they move around the circuit from one event to another, like show jumpers. Rodeos held all over the western United States and in Canada attract large and enthusiastic audiences, and in those areas conventionalized western dress is still worn widely.

Hunting

FROM THE BEGINNING of time, hunting, whether for food or pleasure, has been elemental to the human condition. The arts of Assyria and Egypt show warriors hunting lions and wild oxen. Genghis Khan and Tamerlane staged the "Great Hunt" to train their warriors, and the hunting field was considered a good training ground for cavalry officers.

Hunting the Fox

In Britain, organized hunting has been practiced since the Norman Conquest, its roots belonging to *la vénerie française*, when the traditional quarry was the stag and the bear, and later the hare. It was only toward the end of the seventeenth century that the English began to hunt the fox. Initially it was a slow business, with hounds being bred for their tongue and scenting prowess rather than for speed, and there was little opportunity to jump. However, by the end of the eighteenth century much had changed. Land was being enclosed with fences;

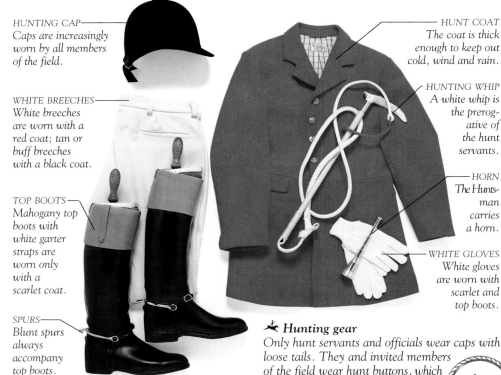

HUNTING CAP
Caps are increasingly worn by all members of the field.

WHITE BREECHES
White breeches are worn with a red coat; tan or buff breeches with a black coat.

TOP BOOTS
Mahogany top boots with white garter straps are worn only with a scarlet coat.

SPURS
Blunt spurs always accompany top boots.

HUNT COAT
The coat is thick enough to keep out cold, wind and rain.

HUNTING WHIP
A white whip is the prerogative of the hunt servants.

HORN
The Huntsman carries a horn.

WHITE GLOVES
White gloves are worn with scarlet and top boots.

🐎 Hunting gear
Only hunt servants and officials wear caps with loose tails. They and invited members of the field wear hunt buttons, which are always worn with scarlet.

and hounds, as well as horses, were bred more and more for speed, particularly in respect of the latter as the influence of the Thoroughbred was increasingly felt.

The golden age of fox-hunting is generally regarded as the period between 1820 and 1890. The great estates were then still intact. There were no cars or motorways carved through the countryside, no fumes to confuse the scent and artificial fertilizers were still unknown.

The Modern Sport

Somehow, hunting survived the two World Wars and, today, it is the sport of thousands of men and women. Nowhere is hunting carried out more extensively than in Britain. Indeed, to some degree, it still remains the bastion of British equestrianism, as it gives excellent experience of cross-country riding and it is a powerful factor in the production of good competition horses.

The Pony Club bases its branches on the hunt counties and each hunt runs an

🐎 "An invisible thread"
Only the Huntsman carries and blows the horn. He uses it in a number of accepted calls to communicate with his hounds, his whippers-in and the field. Otherwise, it is said that a good Huntsman is joined with his hounds by "an invisible thread," each trusting the other.

annual point-to-point race that acts as an encouragement to the sport of professional racing.

In America point-to-point is less developed, but hunting is popular and much on the British pattern. Early colonists in Virginia, Maryland and Pennsylvania established the sport at about the same time that it was taking its modern form in Britain. Thomas, sixth Lord Fairfax, was the first to own a pack of hounds in Virginia in 1747, and George Washington was an early American Master.

The red English fox was imported into America, but the indigenous gray fox provides the sport for many packs. In the West the quarry is sometimes the coyote.

Organization

The organization of American hunting is much the same as that of Britain and Ireland where the governing body is the Masters of Foxhounds Association. There is the Master (or Joint Masters) who arranges and controls activities and employs the hunt servants to care for the hounds. The hunt servants are the Huntsman (or Kennel-huntsman if the Master hunts hounds) and his assistants (the whippers-in). Masters, hunt servants and invited hunt members wear scarlet coats with hunt buttons. Lady members wear navy or black coats.

Dressage

THE WORD DRESSAGE comes from the French verb *dresser*, which in the horse context means training ("dressing") the riding or driving horse. The meaning is now extended to cover the sport of dressage, a highly organized discipline. A dressage test, the first phase in the horse trials event, is designed to show that while the horse is at peak fitness it remains obedient and submissive to the rider.

Classical Riding

Dressage has its origins in the progressive systems of training described by the Greek soldier, historian and agriculturalist, Xenophon (c.430–355 B.C.), who wrote about riding as a science and an art. Nearly 1,000 years later, his writings were the inspiration for the horsemen of the Renaissance, who practiced what we now term "classical" riding.

Classicism reached its zenith in the eighteenth century in the work of François Robichon de la Guérinière (1688–1751), who has been called the father of classical

Objectives of dressage
"By virtue of a lively impulsion and the suppleness of his joints, free from the paralyzing effect of resistance, the horse obeys willingly and without hesitation." FEI rules.

riding. His book *Ecole de la Cavalerie* is the equestrian bible of the Spanish Riding School in Vienna (founded in 1572), where his teaching is preserved in all its purity. Guérinière perfected gymnastic exercises that strengthen and enhance the natural paces. He developed the ultimate suppling exercise – the shoulder-in (*l'épaule en dedans*) – as well as many of the school exercises practiced today.

Competitive Dressage

The forerunners of competitive dressage tests were those tests conducted for the best-trained charger at the nineteenth-century military schools in Europe. These individual tests were first included in the Olympic Games of 1912 and a team dressage competition was introduced in 1928 at the Amsterdam Olympic Games. The advanced movements of *passage* and *piaffe* were first included in Olympic tests in the 1932 Los Angeles Games, and canter pirouettes were first performed at the Olympic Games in Berlin in 1936. (The classical airs above the ground have no part in competitive dressage.)

Dressage Tests and Competitions

Dressage tests at lower grades are conducted in a 130ft x 65ft (40m x 20m) arena, while international competitions and those at medium level use an arena measuring 196ft x 65ft (60m x 20m). In addition to the four international competitions – Prix St. Georges, Intermediare One, Intermediare Two and the Grand Prix – there is the increasingly popular *Kur*, or freestyle test. This is often ridden to music and restores some of the art to the sport. Each section comprising a test is marked on a scale signifying a standard: 10 excellent, 9 very good, 8 good, 7 fairly good, 6 satisfactory, 5 sufficient, 4 insufficient, 3 fairly bad, 2 bad, 1 very bad, 0 not performed.

Development of physique (above)
"The harmonious development of the physique and ability of the horse" which will result in the horse being "calm, supple, loose, flexible… confident, attentive and keen…." Taken from the FEI rule book.

Change of lead (left)
Britain's leading dressage rider, Jennie Loriston-Clark, demonstrates how to perform the change of lead at the canter. The change of lead at every stride is one of the more difficult movements called for in advanced dressage.

Show Jumping

UNTIL THE END of the nineteenth century, jumping was not a feature of the equestrian world. The first jumping competitions were tests for hunters. The Royal Dublin Society staged a high and wide "leaping" competition on Leinster Lawn, Dublin, in 1865, and that is the first record of an organized competition. A year later, a jumping class (*concours hippique*) was included at the Paris Show, but this was a cross-country event.

Olympic Games

In 1900, in Paris, jumping competitions were held as part of the Olympic Games. There were three competitions: a timed "prize jumping," won by Haegeman of Belgium; a long jump won by his compatriot van Langendonk; and a high jump won by Gardières of France, who cleared 6ft $^{13}/_{16}$in (1.84m).

Additional impetus was given to the sport by the inauguration of the International Horse Show at Olympia, London in 1907. It was a splendid extravaganza that was to become the backbone of the sport in the years between the World Wars, and was to stage the first Nations Cup competition.

Development of Rules

The rules took some time to develop and, at first, were very complex. Britain and America used slats, or slip fillets, in their national rules until after the Second World War. The slats rested on the top of the fence and penalties were given if they were dislodged. The system was further complicated by a distinction between knockdowns made with either fore or hind legs. The time taken to complete the course was not considered important, and judging was imprecise.

However, after the Second World War the rules were formulated on an international basis. Time became an integral factor and added much to the excitement of a competition. The clarity of the new rules allowed a greater degree of participation on the part of the onlooker, making it easy to follow the competition.

Today, courses are built with accuracy and artistry to test the ability of both horse and rider. Some of the principal factors involved are: the size and type of the fences built, the number of strides in combination fences, and the time allowed to complete the course.

Principal Events

The principal international shows, judged under the rules of the *Fédération Equestre Internationale* (FEI) are the Olympic Games, held every four years; the World Championships held in the even years between the Olympic Games; and the World Cup, a series of indoor competitions run in regional leagues and culminating in a final. There are also European and American championships and the Nations Cup competitions, which are staged each year by participating nations. The President's Cup is awarded to the country that scores the most points in the year's Nations Cup competitions.

FAULTS TABLE
The following method is common to national and international rules

1st disobedience	3 Faults
2nd disobedience	4 Faults
3rd disobedience	Elimination
Knockdown	4 Faults
Fall of horse or rider	8 Faults
Exceeding time allowed	$^1/_4$ Fault for a second or part of a second
Exceeding time in a timed jump-off	1 Fault for a second or part of a second
Exceeding time limit	Elimination

The forward seat
It was the Italian, Captain Federico Caprilli (1868–1907) chief instructor at the Pinerolo cavalry school, who first recognized the need for the rider to sit forward at fences. Caprilli's "forward seat" is the basis for the modern jumping position demonstrated in this picture.

Eventing

LIKE SO MUCH of our equestrian heritage, eventing, or horse-trials, have their origins in the military practice of using competitions to test the endurance, speed and obedience of the horse, as well as the ability of the rider. In French, eventing is "concours complet" – the complete test – and it was France that held the *Championat du Cheval d'Armes* in Paris in 1902. This competition comprised a dressage test, a steeplechase, a 30-mile (48km) race over roads and tracks and, finally, a jumping test.

Three-Day Event

The first Olympic three-day event was restricted to military riders. It was held at the Stockholm Games in 1912 and was won by the host nation.

Civilians were allowed to compete after the Second World War, and from that point the sport developed dramatically. The greatest factor in the encouragement of eventing as a sport was the establishment of the Badminton Horse Trials on the Duke of Beaufort's estate in Gloucestershire in 1949.

Horse trials are based on a qualifying progression, beginning with novice one-

Rest period (above)
The 10-minute compulsory break before the cross-country course is an opportunity to check details and make the horse comfortable.

Eventing kit (right)
The event rider's equipment includes the very important body protector, a necessary precaution in a sport where falls are inevitable.

SWEATER Usually in the rider's chosen colors.

BODY PROTECTOR Saves injuries to the upper body.

HELMET Crash helmets must be worn by eventers.

day events and culminating in the full three-day event, horses being graded according to performance records.

Phases

In the three-day event, the dressage phase takes place first. The second day is the speed and endurance phase, which covers about 16 miles (25km) and is central to the competition. This phase begins with a section of roads and tracks that leads to the steeplechase course. Following the steeplechase, there are more roads and tracks before the cross-country course.

The steeplechase is 2 miles (3.2km), and the cross-country is 4½ miles (7.2km) and 32 fences. Many of the fences are combinations so, in fact, the horse makes well over 32 jumps. The whole adds up to about 1½ hours of effort. On the final day there is a veterinary inspection and a show jumping test, to prove the horse is "fit for further service."

Roads and tracks (above)
A competitor on the roads and tracks section. The total length of the roads and tracks test in a three-day event is 9½ miles (15.2km) and attracts large numbers of spectators.

Water combination (left)
The complicated combination of fences involving jumping in and out of the water is always one of the most spectacular and exciting obstacles of the entire cross-country course.

Racing

IF ONLY BECAUSE MANKIND is very competitive, it is certain that the matching of one horse against another began early in the history of equine domestication. In the Ancient World, chariot racing preceded ridden races by centuries, and was always more popular. The first recorded, ridden race was at the Greek Olympiad in 624B.C.

Sport of Kings

Modern racing, particularly on the flat or over fences, and harness racing, to some degree, owes its existence to the Thoroughbred: the "superhorse" that was developed in Britain during the seventeenth and eighteenth centuries. Racing in Britain has traditionally enjoyed Royal patronage, hence its title

the "Sport of Kings." James I was an enthusiast who put the town of Newmarket on the map as the headquarters of racing. After the Restoration, Charles II continued developing the sport at Newmarket and, with the encouragement of Queen Anne, the Ascot racecourse, the most fashionable of British courses, was laid out in 1711. The Jockey Club, racing's governing body, was founded in about 1752; *An Introduction to the Stud Book* appeared in 1791 and the first volume of the *General Stud Book* was published in 1808.

Britain operates the Pattern racing system, which is a series of races set over appropriate distances to provide proper tests for the best horses of all ages, including Group One championships.

The Classics

Group One includes the Classics for 3 year olds. These are the Derby and the Oaks, held at Epsom; the 2,000 Guineas, and the corresponding race for fillies,

🐎 *Training racers* (above)
Early mornings on the gallops are a feature of training centers, like those at Newmarket, where Thoroughbreds are prepared for racing.

🐎 *The field* (below)
The field over one of the fences at Cheltenham. The Cheltenham meetings stage the most prestigious races in the calendar, including the Gold Cup and the Champion Chase.

Red Mile

The Red Mile Raceway in Lexington, Kentucky is a major center of American harness racing. Many of the best Standardbreds are reared in the Blue Grass country and trained here.

the 1,000 Guineas, both run at Newmarket; and the Doncaster St. Leger. The Derby (first run in 1780), the 2,000 Guineas (1809) and the St. Leger (1776) constitute the coveted European "Triple Crown." This is the ultimate accolade of the Turf and has only been won by twelve horses since its inauguration in 1853.

Racing Worldwide

Racing all over the world follows the British pattern. The most influential racing nations in Europe, other than Britain and Eire, are France and Italy. In Italy, Federico Tesio's Dormello Stud has bred many successful race horses, including Donatello II, Nearco and Ribot. Racing thrives in both Australia and New Zealand, but the greatest influence is exerted by the multimillion dollar industry in the United States.

The first American racetrack was laid out on Long Island in 1664 by Richard Nicolls, the first governor of New York. It was near the site of the present Belmont Park. Today, the center of the American

Thoroughbred is the 2,500 square miles (4,022sq km) of Blue Grass country in Kentucky. The Kentucky Derby, run at Churchill Downs in Louisville, was founded in 1875. The American Triple Crown consists of this race, the Preakness Stakes and the Belmont Stakes.

Steeplechasing

Steeplechasing takes place on a small scale in Europe and America, but its home is in Britain and Ireland where it is enormously popular. The first recorded match, and the one that gave the sport its name, took place in Ireland when Messrs. O'Callaghan and Blake raced their hunters over the 4¹/₂ miles (7.2km) separating Buttevant Church from St. Leger Church – from steeple to steeple.

The most famous of the English steeplechases is the Grand National, which has been held in April at Aintree since 1837. There are 30 fences on the course, and it is unique among jumping races. Nonetheless, Cheltenham is generally regarded as the center of steeplechasing, and its Gold Cup is recognized as the jewel in the crown of British steeplechasing.

The big race in continental Europe is Czechoslovakia's *Gran Pardubice*. This is similar to a cross-country race and

incorporates numerous natural hazards. America's best known jumping race is the Maryland Hunt Cup, which is run in open country over post and rail fences.

Harness Racing

America is the world's leading harness-racing nation. Upward of 30 million spectators attend the floodlit evening meetings at raceways like Meadowlands in New Jersey, Roosevelt on Long Island and the Red Mile at Lexington.

Most harness races are for pacers, with the legs moving in lateral rather than diagonal pairs, but there are also races for conventional trotters. Races are usually set over one mile (1.6km), and times of 1.54 minutes or less are not unusual.

Messenger

The British connection with harness racing extends no further than the export of the Thoroughbred Messenger to Philadelphia in 1788. He never raced in harness but is at the base of the American Standardbred, the breed on which the sport is largely founded.

In many European countries and certainly in Russia, harness racing is more popular than Thoroughbred racing. In New Zealand and Australia, it is almost a national pastime.

Polo

POLO, played almost entirely at the gallop, is the fastest game in the world. A form of polo was played in Persia and China about 2,500 years ago by both men and women. It was called *changar,* meaning mallet in Persian, but the word polo is from the Tibetan word for a ball, *pulu.* British soldiers and civilians serving in India during the nineteenth century were responsible for bringing polo to the West. The British played on 12.2hh ponies in the state of Manipur, between Assam and Burma, where it was the national game.

Hockey on Horseback

The first recorded game in Britain took place in 1869 when officers of the 10th Hussars at Aldershot played what was described as "hockey on horseback." Polo was introduced to America in 1878 by the newspaper tycoon James Gordon Bennett Jr. He was inspired by a visit he had paid to Hurlingham (later the headquarters of British polo) two years previously.

The Americans quickly established a formidable supremacy with their superbly drilled and mounted teams. The Anglo-American Westchester Trophy was first played in 1886 with teams reduced to four players a side. The Americans did not win this trophy until 1909, but thereafter they proved unbeatable.

Leaders in the Field

Polo was first played in Argentina in 1877 and by the 1930s Argentina had become the world's leading polo nation. Argentinian-bred ponies – often Criollo/Thoroughbred crosses – were and still are the best in the world.

Rules

Polo "ponies" may be of any height. The teams comprise four players and there are usually two mounted umpires. A polo field measures 300yd x 200yd (275m x 180m). It is marked with a center line and penalty lines at 30yd, 40yd, and 60yd (27m, 36m, 55m) from each back line. The object is to score goals by hitting the willow ball through goalposts 10ft (3m) high and 24ft (7.3m) apart, while traveling, usually at full speed. When a goal is scored, the teams change ends.

Players are handicapped according to ability. High goal polo is when the total team handicap is around 19 goals; a medium goal game is between 15 and 18

🐎 *Fast and physical*
Polo is fast and highly physical. Safety rules are strict but it is permissible to ride an opponent off the ball. However, a foul is incurred for crossing another player's right of way.

goals. A match is divided into chukkas of seven-and-a-half minutes duration. There are five or six chukkas in a high-goal match, four at smaller events. The ponies are changed after each chukka and no pony plays more than two chukkas in a match. Penalties are given for such faults as crossing a player's line dangerously and bumping. However, it is permitted to ride an opponent off the ball or to hook his stick.

GLOVES
Gloves give grip.

STICK
The stick is made of bamboo.

HELMET
The helmet may have a face guard.

BOOTS
Brown boots are obligatory.

KNEE GUARDS
These are a sensible, protective precaution.

BALL
The ball is made of willow.

🐎 *Polo clothing* (left)
Clothing has changed very little since the game's inception. The head of the stick has been improved, helmets are now worn universally and few players would not wear knee guards.

🐎 *Early polo* (above)
This is an early game of American polo, before the number of players was reduced to only four a side and before helmets were generally worn. There are umpires keeping watch on the left and right.

Long Distance

D ISTANCE RIDING can be divided in general terms between competitive trail rides and endurance events. The endurance events are races, the winner being the first horse past the post that also passes the stringent veterinary checks, a feature of the modern sport. Endurance rides may cover between 25 and 100 miles (40 and 160km) in one day; or there are divided rides in which the 100 miles (160km) is covered in two days.

Competitive trail events are ridden over a set distance at a stated speed, such as 30 miles (48km) at a speed of 7–8mph (11–13kph). Veterinary checks are included as in the endurance rides.

Cavalry Tests

The first one-man one-horse rides, the forerunners of the modern sport, were held in the 1890s and early 1900s as cavalry tests, particularly by the mounted forces of Germany and the Austro-Hungarian Empire. They were designed to improve riding and fitness standards, but often turned out to be events in which horses were ridden to death. The organizers of the 1903 Paris-Deauville ride attempted to put matters right by imposing speed restrictions. However, the sport has its true foundations in the supervised rides that were first held by the American cavalry.

Endurance Rides

America remains the world leader in endurance riding. The Americans base the sport on the innovative Vermont 100-Mile, held in 1936. This three-day ride adhered to the strict regulations formulated for the cavalry tests.

Over 500 rides are held in the US each year, including the famous 100-Mile Western States Ride, known as the Tevis Cup Ride. This is probably the toughest endurance test of horse and rider of them all. First held in 1955, the course runs from Tahoe City, Nevada, to Auburn, California, over the steep Sierra Nevadas.

Despite the formidable terrain and the awesome 9,500 ft (2,850m) climb through the snowbound Squaw Pass leading to the El Dorado Canyon, where temperatures can reach 100°F (38°C), the distance is usually covered by the leaders in 11 to 12 hours.

The Australian equivalent of the Tevis Cup Ride is the Tom Quilty Ride. This is held annually over the same distance. The event is very demanding and places

⚞ Foot work
Endurance riders often find it helpful to run on foot over some parts of the course. This is a sensible practice that helps to ease aching and stiffening muscles and gives the horse a rest by relieving him of the weight on his back.

⚞ Fitness and management
Long distance riding calls for great fitness in both the horse and the rider, combined with the exercise of high level management skills.

just as great a premium on fitness and skillful horse-management, factors that are an integral part of the sport.

Arabian Horses

In Britain, the sport was pioneered by the Arab Horse Society, which held endurance rides between the World Wars. Arabian horses, part- and purebred, still dominate the distance riding event all over the world. The Society still stages an annual marathon over the classic $26^{1}/4$ miles (42km) which, although it includes a walk section, is a race with competitors often riding a finish to the line.

The British Open Endurance Riding Championship is the 100-mile Summer Solstice Ride held by the Endurance Horse and Pony Society. The other British society that organizes distance rides is the Long Distance Riding Group – part of the British Horse Society. This group runs two 100-mile rides and the well-known Golden Horseshoe final, over 100 miles (160km) of rugged Exmoor country. The Golden Horseshoe final is not a race. Gold medals are awarded to all who pass the veterinary checks and complete the course at not less than 8mph (13kph).

Sidesaddle

THE SIDESADDLE is often referred to as the "Queen of Saddles" although, more accurately, it might be called the "Saddle of Queens," for its introduction to the equestrian scene owes almost everything to royal horsewomen.

Anne of Bohemia

The sidesaddle originated some 600 years ago in the courts of mainland Europe. It was brought to England by Anne of Bohemia, the wife of Richard II.

Until the end of the fourteenth century, English women seem to have ridden astride; and more active female riders continued to do so into the sixteenth century and after. It was only later that women began to hunt in a sidesaddle.

Anne's saddle was based on a pack saddle to which was fitted, usually on the nearside, a wooden foot rest, called a *planchette*. The rider sat at a right angle to the horse, with her feet on the platform. For additional security, the saddle had a horn or pommel at the front which she

Jumping sidesaddle
The modern saddle, which provides a particularly secure, firm seat, allows the sidesaddle rider to jump fences on equal terms with those riding astride. This was not possible until the invention of the "leaping head" by Jules Pellier in 1830.

could hold in the right hand. Riding in such a saddle, a woman was not much more than a passenger and the horse was often led by a groom. A more practical variation of the *planchette* saddle allowed the woman to ride pillion behind a man, for it was virtually impossible for her to handle the reins and maintain her seat.

Catherine de Medici

The next important modification to the design was brought about by another Queen, Catherine de Medici. By about 1580, this able horsewoman was riding in a saddle fitted with a second horn placed on the nearside below the first one. This allowed the rider to hook her right leg over the additional pommel, wedging it between the two and sitting to face the front. Clearly, this arrangement contributed to a more secure seat.

Catherine's saddle persisted almost unaltered for some 200 years but it presented obvious problems, and was very difficult to keep in place on the horse. This last failing was largely overcome by the introduction of a balance strap in the early seventeenth century. The strap was fitted to the rear of the saddle on the offside and came down to join the line of the girth. It went a long way toward reducing the incidence of sore backs.

Pellier

The invention that revolutionized sidesaddle riding and entirely altered the concept of cross-country riding was made in 1830 by an otherwise obscure Parisian riding master, Jules Charles Pellier. He produced the "leaping head:" initially a third pommel placed below the other two. The leaping head was screwed into the saddle tree and curved outwards over the rider's left thigh. The top pommel was soon discarded. In the new saddle, the rider was able to sit in a secure position. She could now jump fences – a feat that was difficult and unsafe when using the two upright pommels.

Elizabeth of Austria

The new saddle gave impetus to the increasing number of English ladies who followed hounds in the latter part of the nineteenth century. They were given encouragement by the example of yet another royal horsewoman, Elizabeth, Empress of Austria. She visited England

"Queen of Saddles"
There is no more graceful sight in the show ring than a lady riding in the "Queen of Saddles." Today, there are numerous sidesaddle classes as well as a Ladies Sidesaddle Association two-day show.

and Ireland on "sporting tours" between 1876 and 1882, and earned herself a reputation as a fearless horsewoman.

Under the influence of a coterie of horsewomen as brilliant as the Empress of Austria, the design of the saddle changed. In time, the dipped seat was replaced by the level one, which allowed the rider to sit on her right thigh with her shoulders facing the front. Previously she had had to twist uncomfortably at the waist to face forward.

About the same time as the leaping head appeared, the old and unsafe slipper iron disappeared. It was replaced by numerous ingenious safety stirrups until, ultimately, a quick-release leather based on the stirrup bar provided a solution.

Decline and Revival

Sidesaddles were common in the hunting field well into the 1920s, when sweeping habits and petticoats had long been supplanted by breeches and the neat sidesaddle skirt. In some circles it was still considered unladylike to ride astride. After the Second World War, expense and the shortage of grooms contributed to a decline in sidesaddle riding.

Its revival in Britain in the 1970s was largely due to the formation of the Ladies Sidesaddle Association, which now has upward of 2,000 members. Sidesaddles are now being made again. Their construction is a job for the skilled expert and their fitting is no less so.

The Horse and the Law

THE LAWS CONCERNING horses vary from country to country and cover all sorts of contingencies, from buying and selling to the humane treatment of feral horses.

Stables and Care

In Britain a variety of laws govern stables, the horses that work at them, the riders who train at them and the instructors who teach at them. The British Riding Establishment Acts impose statutory obligations that require establishments to meet certain minimum standards of care and supervision. In the United States, however, no similar federal laws exist. As a result, standards in the US vary widely. The few laws that do exist are legislated by individual states.

The majority of laws that regard horses in the US are concerned with the humane treatment of horses, although these, too, are few and far between, and may be turned over by judges who do not consider the humane treatment of horses an important legal topic. Humane organiza-

tions, most notably the American Horse Protection Association, act as watchdogs and fight for stronger laws.

Buying a Horse

When buying or selling a horse, the rule is *caveat emptor*, "let the buyer beware." In the US it is a violation to sell a horse in need of veterinary care. However, the definition of care varies and violations are difficult to prosecute. Malice is the usual standard for prosecution in cases in which a buyer or seller misrepresents himself. Legal recourse is also possible if a contract between the buyer and seller has been broken. Unfortunately, very few buyers use contracts.

The Loss of Trails

Great Britain is a nation of riders, and its laws protect the rights of equestrians. An opposite influence holds sway in the United States, and, as a result, riding trails are shut down almost daily. Many recent legal cases regarding the rights of trail riders in the US have helped to preserve trails and equestrian interests.

⚘ *Riding trails*
The American riding trail is rapidly vanishing, some due to urban sprawl though many others are barred because of legal or environmental concerns. Equestrians are forming coalitions to protect and extend the rights of trail users.

The litigious nature of American society has made the potential liability of riders, horse owners and property holders a key element in the issue of providing trails for riders. Safe riding habits, therefore, are of paramount importance to riders, not only to preserve their health, but the very trails they wish to use.

ROAD SAFETY

Riding in traffic on modern roads is a hazardous pastime that many riders wish to avoid. Unfortunately, it cannot always be avoided. The Horsemanship Safety Association organizes road safety tests for young people and trainers. Paramount is the ability to control a horse so as to be able to follow the rules of the road, but great attention is also paid to safety equipment.

PROTECTING THE HEAD

The most vulnerable part of the rider is the head, and most accidents involve head injuries. Helmets have been designed and manufactured to a high safety specification. Such headgear, secured by a harness, is compulsory for Pony Club members, show jumpers, event riders and race jockeys. All safety groups are currently lobbying to make the wearing of safety helmets by children under 14 years of age compulsory when they are riding on roadways.

SAFETY EQUIPMENT

The brightly colored, fluorescent tabards and cross-belts, which allow riders to be seen easily by motorists, are a most valuable

"SAM BROWNE"-STYLE BELT

STIRRUP FLASHLIGHT

LEG OR ARM REFLECTORS

ROAD SAFETY EQUIPMENT
Road safety equipment focuses on two principal areas. First, protective headgear and clothing help to mitigate physical injury. Secondly, those reflective items such as the fluorescent strips, cross-belts and flashlights ensure that the rider's presence on the road is obvious to motorists.

form of safety equipment. It has been shown that motorists respond significantly when they see riders who are dressed in this protective clothing. Their attention is secured by the bright, warning colors and their automatic reaction is to slow down and give horse and rider a wide berth.

Speed is a critical factor in most road accidents and if the car driver can be persuaded to take his foot off the accelerator there will be a commensurate rise in the safety level. For riding across country and for racing, a body protector (a sort of flak jacket) is often worn as a safeguard against back injuries. This garment is now used increasingly by those people who have to ride on the roads.

PROTECTION FOR THE HORSE

Fluorescent clothing is not confined to the rider alone. Strips are available to encircle the horse's legs like a set of boots and they can also be put around the tail. This kind of protection is even more necessary when riding your horse in the dusky conditions of evening or winter. In those circumstances, the wearing of a stirrup flashlight is a further and wise precaution.

Glossary

*Words in **bold** within an entry have their own entry in the glossary.*

A

ACTION the movement of the skeletal frame in respect of locomotion.

AIDS the signals made by the rider or driver to communicate his wishes to the horse. The natural riding aids are legs, hands, body weight and voice.

B

BACK OF THE KNEE a conformational fault in which the forelegs curve backward.

BETWEEN HAND AND LEG a phrase indicating that the horse moves forward because of the rider's leg to take up contact with the hand (the bit). The horse is then framed between hand and leg.

BLOOD WEED a lightly built Thoroughbred Horse without substance or bone.

BONE the measurement taken around the cannon below the knee. Upon the bone measurement depends the ability to carry weight.

BOSOMY an over wide chest.

BOTH LEGS OUT OF THE SAME HOLE the asymmetrical appearance of front legs, that result from too narrow a chest.

BOW HOCKS outward-turned hock joints.

HOTBLOOD
Either an Arabian or Thoroughbred. The Shagya is mostly Arabian, topped up with Thoroughbred.

COLDBLOOD
A generic name for heavy, European horse breeds descended from the prehistoric Forest Horse.

B (continued)

BOXY HOOVES hooves that are "boxed" in like like those of a donkey's, that is, upright with the heels closed instead of open, which prevents the **frog** from reaching the ground and acting as an anti-concussive and non-slip device.

BREED an equine group whose members have been selectively bred for consistent characteristics over a period of time and with pedigrees recorded in a stud book.

BRUSHING the hoof or shoe striking the inside of the opposite leg at or near the fetlock; usually caused by poor conformation or action.

C

CARRIAGE HORSE a relatively light, elegant horse suitable for private or hackney carriage use.

CART HORSE a heavy, coldblood draft horse.

CAVALRY REMOUNT a horse used for service in an army unit.

CLOSE-COUPLED short connections between component parts.

COACH HORSE a powerful, strongly built horse able to draw heavy coaches.

COARSENESS AROUND THE JOWL accumulation of flesh at the jowl, which restricts the flexion of the head.

C (continued)

COLDBLOOD a generic name for heavy, European horse breeds descended from the prehistoric Forest Horse. See also **warmblood**.

COLT uncastrated male horse less than 4 years old.

COMMON BONE bone of inferior quality, coarse-grained, lacking density and with a large, central core.

COMMON a horse of coarse appearance, usually the progeny of cold-blooded, non-pedigree or generic stock.

COMMON-BRED a horse bred from mixed, non-pedigree parents.

CONFORMATION the way a horse is "put together," with particular regard to its proportions.

COW HOCKS hocks that turn inward in the manner of a cow; the opposite conformational fault to **bow hocks**.

CROSSBREEDING mating of unrelated horses; introducing outside blood to a breed.

CROSSING OVER a faulty action in which the hooves are placed in front of each other.

D

DEEP GOING wet ground made heavy by rain, in which the horse's hooves sink deeply.

DISHED PROFILE a concave head profile, typical of Arabian horses.

DISHING the action of the foreleg when the toe is thrown outward in a circular movement.

DOCK to amputate the tail for the sake of appearance. Illegal in Great Britain.

DONKEY HOOVES see **boxy hooves**.

DOUBLE MUSCLING pronounced muscling at the croup, often evident in heavy breeds.

E

EWE NECK one that is concave along the upper edge with a consequent, protruding muscular development on the under side.

F

FILLY female horse under 4 years old.

FEI abbreviation for *Fédération Equestre Internationale* (International Equestrian Federation), the governing body of international equestrian sport.

FOREHAND the part of the horse in front of the rider – head, neck, shoulders, withers and forelegs.

FOREHAND

FROG rubbery, triangular pad of horn between the bars on the underside of the hoof; it acts as a shock absorber.

G

GASKIN second thigh.
GELDING castrated male horse.

H

HAND unit of measurement to describe a horse's height. One hand is 4in (10cm).
HARD HORSE an enduring horse that is not susceptible to unsoundness or illness.
HAUTE **E**COLE the classical art of advanced equitation.
HEAVY HORSE any large draft horse, such as the Shire, Suffolk Punch and Percheron.
HINDQUARTERS the part of a horse's body from the rear of the flank to the beginning of the tail, and downward to the top of the second thigh.
HOLLOW BACK a concave shape, between wither and loin; a "sway back," the opposite conformational fault to a **roach back**.
HOT a horse that becomes unduly excited is said to "hot up."
HOTBLOOD either an Arabian or Thoroughbred.

L

LIGHT HORSE any horse, other than a heavy horse or pony, that is suitable for riding.
LIGHT OF BONE insufficient measurement of bone to support the body weight and that of the rider without strain.

M

MARE female horse 4 or more years old.

N

NICK the division and re-setting of muscles under the tail to give an artificially high carriage.

P

PARIETAL BONES the bones on top of the horse's skull.
PEDIGREE the details of ancestry recorded in a breed stud book.
PIGEON TOES a conformational fault in which the hooves point inward.
POINTS external features of a horse, comprising its **conformation**.

Q

QUALITY the element of refinement in the appearance of breeds and types. Usually due to Arabian or Thoroughbred influence.
QUARTERS see **hindquarters**.

R

RIDING HORSE a horse suitable for riding, which has conformation leading to a comfortable riding action (as opposed to draft or carriage).
ROACH BACK a convex curvature of the horse's spine between wither and loin; the opposite conformational fault to a **hollow back**.
ROACHING removing the horse's mane for appearance, as in the cob to show off its muscular neck, and for practical reasons as in the polo pony to ensure that the stick does not get caught in the mane.
ROMAN PROFILE or Roman nose associated with primitive, coldblood heavy horse breeds and "common" ancestry; a convex profile.

S

SCLERA the white outer membrane of the horse's eyeball.
SECOND THIGH the lower thigh; the area between the upper thigh and the hock joint.
SHORT OF A RIB a conformational fault of slack loins, caused by too wide a space between the point of the hip and the last rib.
SICKLE HOCKS a conformational fault; seen from the side, the hocks are too angled at the joint, causing weakness of the hind legs.
SLAB SIDED a horse with flat ribs.
SPLIT UP BEHIND a conformational fault caused by weakness of the second thighs; seen from behind, the thighs divide too high, just beneath the dock.
STALLION uncastrated male horse 4 or more years old.
STAMP OF HORSE type of horse.
STUD BOOK a book kept by

a breed society in which the pedigrees of purebred stock are recorded.
SUBSTANCE the physical quality of a horse's body, in terms of its build and general musculature.
SWAN NECK a conformational fault in which the upper neck curves upward so that the head joins the neck in a nearly vertical line, which makes it difficult to control the horse and also reduces the potential for free movement.

T

TACK equipment used for riding and driving.
THROAT LATCH the leather strap, part of the headpiece, that passes around the horse's throat.
TIED IN BELOW THE KNEE legs that are much narrower just below the knee than further down toward the fetlock joint; a conformational fault that indicates a horse that is **light of bone**.
TYPE horses that fulfil a particular purpose, such as a cob, hunter and hack, but do not belong to a specific breed.

W

WARMBLOOD in general terms, half-bred or part-bred horses, the result of Thoroughbred or Arabian crosses with other blood. See also **coldblood**.
WELL-SPRUNG RIBS long, rounded ribs that give ample room for the full operation of the lungs and provide a comfortable seat for the rider.
WHIP the driver of a carriage.

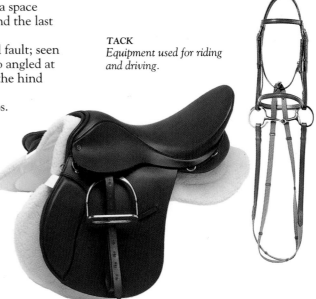

TACK
Equipment used for riding and driving.

Index

Entries in **bold** indicate featured breeds. Page numbers in *italic* indicate illustrations.

Acknowledgments

Dorling Kindersley would like to thank Janos Marffy, Sandra Pond and Will Giles for illustrations; Dr. James Bee of the Royal Veterinary College, London for his advice on the foal development sequence; Robert Oliver for the use of his stable yard; Giles Hine for help with the horses; Graham Young the blacksmith; M. Mauget and M. Porte in France: Gaetano Manti in Italy; Pat Renwick and the Shetland pageant; The Kentucky Horse Park, Lexington, USA; Steven Cluett, Tracey Hambleton, Gill Sherman, Diana Weeks and Kevin Williams for additional design assistance; Paul Dewhurst for shadow artwork; Sharon Lunn for silhouette diagrams; Irene Lyford for the index; Emma Matthews for keying-in and Jenny Speller for picture research.
Props were provided by Baileys Feed Suppliers; Scatts of Basingstoke; Old Basing Saddlery of Old Basing; Ian McNeills of Medstead; Mr. Compton of Calcutt & Sons, Sutton Scotney.
And, of course, thanks to all the horses and ponies we photographed and their owners who were so patient (these are all acknowledged in the picture credits below). Thanks also to those we were, unfortunately, unable to include in this book.
Bob Langrish would like to thank Sally Waters, Janet Lorch, Dr. Mikhail Alexeev, Colin Wares, Dinny Lund, Evegeny Lepetukhin.

Picture Credits

Apart from the studio photographs on pp.196–7, 198–201, 206–7, 214–15, 224–7, 230–33, 235, which are by Tim Ridley, all photographs are by Bob Langrish unless otherwise stated.
Animal Photography includes photographs by Sally Anne Thompson and R. Wilbie.

key: *b* bottom, *c* center, *l* left, *r* right, *t* top

p.1 **Haflinger** – *Nomad* (see pp.128–9)

pp.2–3 l **Clydesdale** – *Blue Print* (see pp.168–9); *r* **Miniature Shetland Ponies** – (see pp.156–7)

p.5 **Lusitano** – *Montemere-O-Nova* (*Romano*) (see pp.40–41); Bewick Woodcuts

p.6 tl, tc Peter Newark; *br* Mary Evans

p.7 t Mary Evans; *cr* **Irish Medium Draft** – *Quist* and *Rajah*, West Midlands Mounted Police, Birmingham, UK (Ridden by PC Michael Barratt and PC Roger Green); *cl* Mary Evans; *b* Auscape

p.8 l **Avelignese** – *Noaner* (see pp.128–9); *r* **Arabian** – *Muskhari Silver* (see pp.14–15); *tl* Mary Evans

p.9 t Bewick Woodcuts; *cr* **Appaloosa** – *Move Over Nugget*, Mr. & Mrs. George, Patchendon Stud, UK

p.10 b American Museum of Natural History

p.11 t American Museum of Natural History; *bl* Mary Evans; *br* Ardea

p.12 t Ronald Sheridan; *bl* C. M. Dixon; *b* Bruce Coleman

p.13 t C. M. Dixon; *bl, br* Ronald Sheridan

pp.14–15 **Arabian** – *Muskhari Silver* Janet and Anne Connolly, Silver Fox Arabians, UK; *bl* C. M. Dixon

p.17 bl Ardea

p.18 bl Animal Photography

p.22 t **American Saddlebred** – *Kinda Kostly* (see pp.66–7); *b* Only Horses

p.24 tl **Avelignese** – *Noaner* (see pp. 128–9); *br* Only Horses

p.25 t Only Horses; *br* **Avelignese** – *Noaner* (see pp.128–9)

p.26 t Mary Evans; *bl* **Thoroughbred** – *Lyphento* (see pp.34–5); *br* **Shagya Arabian** – *Artaxerxes* (see pp.38–9)

p.27 t Bewick Woodcuts; *cr* **Falabella** foals (see pp.138–9); *b* Only Horses

pp.28–9 **Arabian** – *Persimmon* Pat and Joanna Maxwell, Lodge Farm Arabian Stud, UK; *tr* Mary Evans

pp.30–31 **Barb** – *Taw's Little Buck* Kentucky Horse Park, USA; *tl* Peter Newark; *bl* Bruce Coleman; *cr* Ardea

pp.32–3 **Andalusian** – *Campanero XXIV* Nigel Oliver, Singleborough Stud, UK; *bl* **Andalusian** – *Adonis-Rex* Welshpool Andalusian Stud, UK *tr* Kit Houghton

pp.34–5 **Thoroughbred** – *Lyphento* Conkwell Grange Stud, UK; *tr, br* Peter Newark

pp.36–7 **Anglo-Arabian** – *Restif* Haras National de Compiègne, France; *tr* Mary Evans

pp.38–9 **Shagya Arabian** – *Artaxerxes* Jeanette Bauch & Jens Brinksten, Denmark; *br* Only Horses

pp.40–41 **Lusitano** – *Montemere-O-Nova* (*Romano*) Nan Thurman, Turville Valley Stud, UK; *br* **Hispano-Arabian** – *Ultima*, Mr. and Mrs. Davies; *bc* Johnny Watson

pp.42–3 **Akhal-Teke** – *Fafakir-Bola* Moscow Agricultural Academy, USSR; *bl* Animal Photography; *t* Peter Newark

pp.44–5 **Lipizzaner** – *Siglavy Szella* John Goddard Fenwick & Lyn Moran, Ausdan Stud, UK; *bl* Animal Photography; *br* Only Horses

pp.46–7 **Budonny** – *Barin* Moscow Agricultural Academy, USSR; *bl* **Tersk** Moscow Race Track, USSR; *tr* Animal Photography

pp.48–9 **Kabardin** – *Daufuz* Korache Stud, USSR; *tl* Mary Evans

pp.50–51 **Don** – *Bageg* Moscow Agricultural Academy, USSR; *bl* **Karabakh** Moscow Race Track, USSR; *tr, bc* Mary Evans

pp.52–3 **Morgan** – *Fox Creek's Dynasty* Darwin Olsen, Kentucky Horse Park, USA; *tl* Bewick Woodcuts

pp.54–5 **Quarter Horse** – *Doc's Maharajah* Harold Bush, Kentucky Horse Park, USA; *t* Peter Newark; *bl* Ardea

pp.56–7 **Hackney** (horse) – *Whiteavon Step High*, (pony) – *Sunbeam Superstar* both owned by David Vyse; *tl* Bewick Woodcuts

pp.58–9 **French Trotter** – *Pur Historien* Haras National de Compiègne, France; *tr* Peter Newark; *bc* Woodcut

pp.60–61 **Orlov Trotter** Moscow Hippodrome, USSR; *tl* Mary Evans; *bl* Animal Photography

pp.62–3 **Standardbred** – *Rambling Willie* Farrington Stables and the Estate of Paul Siebert, Kentucky Horse Park, USA; *tl* Bewick Woodcuts

pp.64–5 **Friesian** – *Sjouke* Sonia Gray, Tattondale Carriages, UK; *trl* Mary Evans; *trr* Animal Photography

pp.66–7 **American Saddlebred** – *Kinda Kostly*, Kentucky Horse Park, USA

pp.68–9 **Missouri Fox Trotter** – *Easy Street* Ruth Massey, Kentucky Horse Park, USA; *bl* **Cayuse Indian Pony** – *Teton* Kentucky Horse Park, USA

pp.70–71 **Tennessee Walking Horse** – *Delight's Moondust* Andrew and Jane Shaw, Kentucky Horse Park, USA; *bl* Animal Photography

pp.72–3 **Peruvian Paso** – *Sol de Salana* James Foster, Kentucky Horse Park, USA

pp.74–5 **Mustang** – *Patrick* Kentucky Horse Park, USA; *tl* Peter Newark

pp.76–7 **Irish Draft** – *Miss. Mill*, *bl* (foal) – *Gort Mill* Mr. R. J. Lampard

pp.78–9 **Norman Cob** – *Ibis* Haras National de Saint Lô, France; *bl* Mary Evans; *tr* Mary Evans/Bruce Castle Museum

pp.80–81 **Cleveland Bay** – *Oaten Mainbrace* Mr. and Mrs. Dimmock

pp.82–3 **Gelderlander** – *Spooks* Peter Munt, Ascot Driving Stables, UK; *trr* Mary Evans

239

pp.84–5 **Dutch Warmblood** – *Edison*
Mrs. Dejonge; *tl* Mary Evans

pp.86–7 **Frederiksborg** – *Zarif*
Langløkkegard
Harry Nielsen, Denmark;
bl Mary Evans; *tr* Animal Photography

pp.88–9 **Selle Français** – *Prince D'elle*
Haras National de Saint Lô, France

pp.90–91 **Danish Warmblood** – *Rambo*
Jorgen Olsen, Denmark;
bl Einer Anderssons Pressbild

pp.92–3 **Trakehner** – *Muschamp Mauersee*
Janet Lorch, Muschamp Stud, UK;
br Animal Photography

pp.94–5 **Hanoverian** – *Défilante*
Barry Mawdsley, European Horse
Enterprises, UK

pp.96–7 **Holsteiner** – *Lenard*
Sue Watson, Trenawin Stud, UK;
tr Mary Evans

pp.98–9 **Maremanna** – *Barone*
Mr. Attilio Tavazzani, Centro Ippico di
Castelverde, Italy;
br Kit Houghton

pp.100–101 **Murgese** – *Obscuro*
Istituto Incremento Ippico di Crema, Italy;
tr Istituto Geografico de Agostini

pp.102–03 **Oldenburg** – *Renoir*
(Modekönig)
Louise Tomkins;
tr Animal Photography

pp.104–05 **Camargue** – *Redounet*
Mr. Contreras, Les Saintes Maries de la
Mer, France

pp.106–07 **Rocky Mountain Horse** –
Mocha Monday
Rea Swan, Hope Springs Farm, Kentucky
Horse Park, USA

pp.108–09 **Furioso** – *Furioso IV*
A. G. Kishumseigi, Hungary;
tl Mary Evans

pp.110–11 **Nonius** – *Pampas*
bl foal both owned by A. G. Kishumseigi,
Hungary

pp.112–13 **Knabstruper** – *Føniks*
Poul Elmerkjær, Denmark;
br Animal Photography

pp.114–15 **Pinto** – *Hit Man*
Boyd Cantrell, Kentucky Horse Park,
USA;
bc Peter Newark

pp.116–17 **Palomino** – *Wychwood*
Dynascha
Mrs. G. Harwood, Wychwood Stud, UK;
tr Ardea

pp.118–19 **Australian Stock Horse**
(photographed by Hawkesbury
Photographics) – *Scrumlo Victory*
Mrs. R. Waller, Ophir Stud, Australia;
bl, tc Mary Evans; *tr* Auscape

pp.120–21 **Appaloosa** (photographed
by Stephen Oliver) – *Golden Nugget*
Sally Chaplin;
tr Bewick Woodcuts

pp.122–3 **Bashkir Curly** – *Mel's Lucky Boy*
Dan Stewart Family, Kentucky Horse Park,
USA

pp.124–5 **Landais** – *Hippolyte*
tr **Pottock** – *Thouarec III*
both at Haras National de Pau, France

pp.126–7 **Ariègeois** – *Radium*
Haras National de Tarbes, France;
bl Only Horses

pp.128–9 **Haflinger** – *Nomad*
Miss. Helen Blair, Silvretta Haflinger
Stud, UK;
bl **Avelignese** – *Noaner*, Istituto Incremento
Ippico di Crema, Italy;
tr Animal Photography

pp.130–31 **Italian Heavy Draft** – *Nobile*
bl **Bardigiano** – *Pippo*
both at Istituto Incremento Ippico di
Crema, Italy

pp.132–3 **Norwegian Fjord** – *Ausdan Svejk*
John Goddard Fenwick and Lyn Moran,
Ausdan Stud, UK;
bl Einar Anderssons Pressbild; *br* Animal
Photography

pp.134–5 **Icelandic Horse** – *Leiknir*
Kentucky Horse Park, USA;
bl, tr Animal Photography

pp.136–7 **Caspian** – *Hopstone Shabdiz*
Mrs. Scott, Henden Caspian Stud, UK;
tr Woodcuts

pp.138–9 **Falabella** – *Pegasus of Kilverstone*;
bl foals – *l Cleopatra of Kilverstone*;
r Bernardo of Kilverstone all owned by Lady
Fisher, Kilverstone Wildlife Park, UK;
trl Ardea

pp.140–41 **Exmoor Pony** – *Murrayton*
Delphinus
June Freeman, Murrayton Stud, UK

pp.142–3 **Dartmoor Pony** – *Allendale*
Vampire
Miss. M. Houlden, Haven Stud, UK

pp.144–5 **Welsh Mountain Pony** – *Bengad*
Dark Mullein
Mrs. C. Bowyer, Symondsbury Stud, UK;
bl, tr Animal Photography

pp.146–7 **Welsh Pony** – *Twyford Signal*
Mr. and Mrs. L. E. Bigley, Llanarth Stud,
UK; *tr* Bruce Coleman

pp.148–9 **Welsh Cob** – *Treflys Jacko*
Mr. and Mrs. L. E. Bigley (see pp.146–7);
tr **Welsh Pony of Cob Type** – *Llygedyn Solo*
Kitty Williams, Glebedale Stud, UK

pp.150–51 **Dales Pony** – *Warrenlane Duke*
Mr. Dickson, Millbeck Pony Stud, UK;
tr Mary Evans

pp.152–3 **Fell Pony** – *Waverhead William*
Mr. and Mrs. S. Errington

pp.154–5 **Highland Pony** – *Fruich of Dykes*
Countess of Swinton;
bl Animal Photography

pp.156–7 **Shetland Pony** – *Chatsworth*
Belle, Mrs. Hampton, Briar Stud, UK;
bl Mary Evans; *tr* **Miniature Shetland**
Ponies – *Parlington Pepsi*, (foal) *Parlington*
Dulcie, Mrs. B. & D. Johnston, Parlington
Stud, UK; *br* **Miniature Shetland Pony** –
Orion of Brindister, Christopher Stevens,
Catchpool Pony Stud, UK

pp.158–9 **Connemara Pony** – *Spinway*
Bright Morning
Miss. S. Hodgkins, Spinway Stud, UK;
tr Kit Houghton

pp.160–61 **New Forest Pony** – *Bowerwood*
Aquila
Mrs. Rae Turner, Bowerwood Stud, UK;
tl Bewick Woodcuts; *br* Animal
Photography

pp.162–3 **American Shetland** – *Little*
Trouble
Marvin McCabe, Kentucky Horse Park,
USA
bl Woodcut; *br* Kit Houghton

pp.164–5 **Shire** – *Duke*
Jim Lockwood, Courage Shire Horse
Centre, UK;
bc Mary Evans

pp.166–7 **Suffolk Punch** –
Laurel Keepsake II
P. Adams and Sons;
tl Bewick Woodcuts

pp.168–9 **Clydesdale** – *Blue Print*
Mervyn and Pauline Ramage, Mount Farm
Clydesdale Horses, UK

pp.170–71 **Percheron** – *Tango*
Haras National de Saint Lô, France;
tl Mary Evans; *br* Kit Houghton

pp.172–3 **Ardennais** – *Ramses du Vallon*
Haras National de Pau, France;
bl Kit Houghton

pp.174–5 **Breton** – *Ulysses*
Haras National de Tarbes, France;
bl Kit Houghton

pp.176–7 **Jutland** – *Tempo*
Jørgen Neilsen, Denmark;
tr Animal Photography

pp.178–9 **Boulonnais** –
Urus
Haras National de Compiègne,
France;
tr Einar Anderssons Pressbild

pp.180–81 **Belgian Draft** –
Roy
Kentucky Horse Park, USA;
bl Animal Photography

pp.182–3 **Hunter** – *Hobo*
Robert Oliver;
bl, tc Mary Evans

pp.186–7 **Hack** – *Rye Tangle*
Robert Oliver

pp.188–9 **Cob** – *Super Ted*
Robert Oliver

pp.190–91 **Riding Pony** – *Brutt*
Robert Oliver;
tr Animal Photography

pp.192–3 l **Cob** – *Silvester* and *r* **Hunter** –
Ovation both owned by Robert Oliver

pp.195 **Cob** – *Silvester*
Robert Oliver

pp.202–3 tr **Hunter** – *Ovation*
Robert Oliver;
bl studio photography by Stephen Oliver

pp 208–9 tl, tll Harry Smith

p.210–11 tl in foaling series Bruce Coleman;
others Jane Burton

pp.212–13 small picture series from left
to right 1st, 4th, 8th, 9th Jane Burton;
2nd, 3rd, 5th, 6th Bruce Coleman

pp.214–15 **Pinto** – *Hit Man* (see pp.
114–15); *tl* Mary Evans; *br* Animal
Photography;

pp.216–17 tl Animal Photography;
bl, tr, trr Bruce Coleman

pp.218–19 tl **Shetland Pony** – *Lockinge*
Edward
Abigail Hampton, Briar Stud, UK;
tr Mary Evans

pp.220–21 bl Mary Evans; *tl* Kit Houghton;
tr Johnny Watson; *bc* Peter Newark; *br*
Baron d'Eisenburg Painting Collection, Earl
of Pembroke, Wilton House, Salisbury, UK

pp.222–3 cl, tr Peter Newark; *bl, br* Animal
Photography

pp.230–31 blr Peter Newark

pp.234–5 tl Bewick Woodcuts; *bl* (above)
Shagya Arabian – *Artaxerxes* (see pp.138–
9); (below) **Suffolk Punch** – *Laurel*
Keepsake II (see pp.166–7); *t* **Welsh Pony of**
Cob Type – *Llygedyn Solo* (see pp.148–9)

pp.236 and 39 Bewick Woodcuts